MAINE

HOMEGROWN

MATT JENNINGS

HOME GROWN

with Jessica Battilana
Photographs by Huge Galdones

ARTISAN | NEW YORK

Library of Congress Cataloging-in-Publication Data is on file.

ISBN 978-1-57965-674-4

Cover icons by Grady McFerrin
Lettering art by Raphael Geroni
Illustrations on pp. 76, 138, 204, 272 by Grady McFerrin
All other interior illustrations and map by AntarWorks LLC

Artisan books are available at special discounts when purchased in bulk for premiums
and sales promotions as well as for fund-raising or educational use. Special editions or
book excerpts also can be created to specification. For details, contact the Special Sales
Director at the address below, or send an e-mail to specialmarkets@workman.com.

Published by Artisan
A division of Workman Publishing Co., Inc.
225 Varick Street
New York, NY 10014-4381
artisanbooks.com

Artisan is a registered trademark of Workman Publishing Co., Inc.

Published simultaneously in Canada by Thomas Allen & Son, Limited

Printed in China
First printing, October 2017

10 9 8 7 6 5 4 3 2 1

WITHDRAWN

For Kate, Sawyer, and Coleman.
You are my sun, moon, and stars.

This is wild country, flavored by the sea
and colored by the salt and sun.

—Captain John Smith

CONTENTS

FOREWORD BY ANDREW ZIMMERN

I met Matt and Kate Jennings in the fall of 2012. I had arrived in Rhode Island to film an episode of *Bizarre Foods*, and our first day of primary shooting was to take place at lunchtime at Farmstead, the intimate food shop, bar, and eatery the couple had opened several years earlier. Within those walls, Matt was cooking with a brilliant personal style that I had been following from the sidelines, knowing that one day I would have to tell his story. Farmstead had a reputation as one of America's best small restaurants, but it was more than that. At Farmstead, they made their own, well, *everything.* Matt sourced impeccable sustainable ingredients from premium purveyors and turned them into the restaurant's stunningly delicious food, the kind of smart, craveable cooking that is his calling card. He cured his own meats and made some of his own cheeses. Kate prepared all the breads, sweets, pastries, jams and jellies, and other provisions. And I came to learn that Kate was the heart of the restaurant. She was her husband's muse, his inspiration, his bellwether. Her presence was a rock—his rock. And that's why the book you hold in your hands is so precious. More on that later.

So I walk into the restaurant, and you have to realize that, Farmstead always had a line out the door; the place was packed. I spot Matt, a larger-than-life presence (although he's not so literally large anymore), taping white butcher paper over the charcuterie, salumi, and cheese displays at the front of the food shop that opened into the dining room. "This is bullshit," he says, pushing past me before turning back to give me a trademark Jennings bear hug, and I can see that he's red-faced with frustration. Kate introduces herself to me, smiling a gorgeous smile that does more than just light up a room;

it lets you know that everything is all right in the space around her. It's a lantern of serenity in the face of daily restaurant calamity. She shakes her head, following her husband into the kitchen. I have no clue what to do. I've just met two people I have been wanting to work with for years, and clearly something is wrong—horribly, horribly wrong. As our team sweeps in with cameras and cases, light bags and sound gear, a dozen storytellers getting ready for war, Matt emerges from the kitchen, Red Sox cap at a jaunty angle, cracks a huge smile, and tells me that the health inspector, who has given the restaurant nothing but perfect scores since opening day, has now decided to embargo the sale of cured meats and cheeses pending further testing and inspection. For no reason.

My mind switches gears, and I put on my executive producer hat. As a restaurant lifer, I know what's coming next: we will have to come back in a few days when Matt has straightened out this matter and can focus on us. But I am wrong. I didn't know Matt Jennings. After apologizing to a few customers who were in the middle of purchasing some fennel-and-red-wine-infused dry sausage, he shrugs off the turn of events that would have brought most chefs to their knees in panic and offers up an alternative plan—to go to a local market to film background content and shoot in the restaurant later—then shoves a hot cup of coffee in my hand as we stream back out onto the street. He spends the next two days working night and day with us, laughing and teaching, cooking and holding forth on all that is great about Rhode Island's food community, and in general treating us like we are the only thing in the world that matters.

Within a few days, all was back to normal at

the shop; matters were resolved with the health department, and I knew that I had gained a close friend who to this day will drop anything he's doing if I need a laugh, someone to listen, or occasionally a large shoulder to cry on. Matt Jennings is that kind of guy.

For Matt, the higher calling wasn't me, or the show, or resolving his momentary setback. For him, it was all about keeping his word and making sure that we got what we needed to showcase everything that makes New England's food culture so remarkable. It's never about him. Over the years, I can't remember ever encountering a chef with less pretension, less ego than Matt. And as you can see in this book, he has every reason to go down the other road. Despite his immense skill set, which dwarfs that of most culinarians, it's his humanity that is his greatest asset.

Why does that matter? Why lead with that story and that testimonial? Why should you care about the man when you came for the book, something to cook out of, to learn from, to take inspiration from? Well, it's simple, really. Allow me to let you in on a big secret: Life isn't about food. It's about people. Life is about relationships. And if someone is the master of that insight, if they act according to that principle and they happen to be one of the country's best chefs/restaurateurs, then their food will reflect that philosophy. It will nurture; it won't show off. Matt's food comes from the best place possible: his love of people.

There isn't a recipe for life. You simply live the best one you can. And as a culinarian, you demonstrate your love of people by honoring where your feet are planted. You bring joy by sharing food, you stand up for your sense of place, you elevate your provisioners—farmers, fishermen, growers—and, most important, your family. Which brings me back to Matt's wife, Kate.

This book *will* teach you how to cook; it reflects the best of modern New England cookery, and the recipes are superbly crafted. What it's not is a Farmstead book, or a Townsman book, although it is reflective of some of the food you can get at Matt's stellar eatery on the edges of Boston's Chinatown. When I read it for the first time and started cooking out of it—I made the Milk-Braised Chicken Legs and the Mussels with Red Curry Broth and Lemongrass, the Calabrian Chile Sausage and the Brown Bread; I made Matt's mom's clam chowder—I realized that this book really is homegrown in every sense of the word. It reflects Matt's upbringing in what for him is the only place in the world he wants to be, it celebrates the simplicity and delight of mealtime with his wife and their boys rather than the foods that require a restaurant kitchen and larder, and it is a testament to his love for his wife.

We all cook for someone, and most famous chefs think too much about the customer. If all you do is create with the customer in mind, then you are doomed to fail; in creating food for *everyone* to enjoy, you often fail to satisfy *anyone*. You wind up cooking from your head, not your heart. When you cook from a loving place, a place of responsibility for others and their happiness, you develop a personal style. And if you are skilled, then your food *will* delight your larger audience. I think Matt always cooks for Kate. I think he tosses everything through her like a prism, and it focuses his work around the most important audience of all: the people he loves most. This book wasn't born in a publisher's office and subjected to a public relations roundtable to measure its effectiveness. This book truly was grown at home. And because of that, *Homegrown* will make your kitchen a better place to cook in and a better place to eat in and will supply you with a lifetime of great recipes that your family will love. It's a book from the heart. An immense heart with more love for you than you realize . . . until you cook from it.

INTRODUCTION

I'm a New Englander. Maybe the deep-rooted love I have for this place took hold when I first walked down Yawkey Way to see Carl Yastrzemski play his last game at Fenway. Or maybe my formative years are to blame, when I lived with my mom in a second-floor apartment in the middle of a triple-decker home in Jamaica Plain, a neighborhood in Boston, watching the community activists march down Adelaide Street and, later that same afternoon, visiting the Dominican markets for fresh empanadas.

Of course, it could have been my time at culinary school in Vermont or mornings spent foraging in the woods for chicken mushrooms that sealed the deal and made me love this great region like no other. It might have been the annual visits to my aunt's house on Great Cranberry Island off the coast of Maine, the summertime clambakes featuring the season's first ears of Silver Queen corn and the last of local tomatoes in a salad with basil from the garden, bookended by a big pot of steamer clams on one end and grilled bluefish smothered with mayonnaise, dill, and gin—a favorite family recipe—on the other. Or maybe it was those summer evenings fishing for squid in the jet-black night off the end of a Nantucket pier, or winter evenings eating my mom's meat loaf by a roaring fire while the snow blew sideways outside.

It doesn't matter, really.

What matters is how connected I feel to New England. I have moved away and lived in other parts of the country—even the world—for stretches of time. Though I grew up in New England—in fact, probably *because* I grew up in New England—I have tried to leave it behind many times. I spent a few years in California, a couple more in the Northwest. I gave Italy a shot, cooking, eating, and drinking my way through Tuscany and Piedmont. But every time, I came back home. There is a magnetism to this place that I can't deny, no matter how hard my adolescent and twentysomething self may have wanted to try. Some of it has to do with our four seasons, which provide a pattern by which we live our lives (and, some contend, contribute to our character). A great deal of it has to do with the physical landscape of this great region, where coast, pasture, deep forest, and booming city are all within a few hours' drive of one another. And of course, there's just something about the place where you grew up, the physical backdrop to your first life experiences, that always makes it feel like home.

I returned to New England for the last time about a decade ago. I started building a life here. I married a woman who was raised in Vermont, and together we bought our first home. We opened an artisan specialty foods shop, then a restaurant, in Providence, Rhode Island, and had two sons, who, like me, will grow up visiting apple orchards in the fall and dipping their toes in the icy Atlantic on hot summer days. More recently, we moved our family from Providence to Boston, because I had an opportunity I couldn't resist: to open the restaurant of my dreams, Townsman, in the heart of the city. This time, I think I'm home for good.

Boston is forty miles from Plymouth Rock, the spot where the early colonists docked their boats in the New World. In elementary school, it was only a matter of time before you learned about the first Thanksgiving, before you donned a black construction-paper hat and acted out the Puritans' first feast in the annual school pageant.

In 1620, when the first Englishmen and women arrived in what is now Massachusetts, there was a sense that they'd reached a wild, vast, and unexplored wilderness; they would learn soon after disembarking from their boats (and raiding stocks of corn that the Native Americans had put up for the winter) that they were hardly alone in this place—at the time, the land that would one day be called Massachusetts was home to thirty thousand Native Americans from a dozen or more tribes.

We also know that the colonists, who arrived at Plymouth Rock in late autumn, would have been royally screwed if the native population hadn't come to their aid. It was too late to sow crops, and there was no cleared land for the colonists to do so even if the weather had been in their favor. And then there was the matter of what to plant—when the colonists put their first seeds in the ground the following spring, nearly everything they tried to grow, including wheat, failed. Lacking their familiar foodstuffs, they learned from the native population how to subsist on a diet heavy on corn and beans, how to cook cornmeal into a pudding (the likely origins of the Yankee specialty we now call Indian pudding), and how to bake a palatable bread using corn and rye (the ancestor of brown bread, page 202, which I serve to every guest at Townsman) instead of the wheat they were accustomed to. And thus our nation's first cuisine was born.

There's evidence that many of the dishes that compose the Yankee canon—from baked beans to Rhode Island cornmeal johnnycakes to pumpkin pie—were first introduced to European colonists by the native population. Though many of the native ingredients and recipes were first shunned by colonists, who considered them to be the foods of the "savages" after a freezing first winter during which half the colonist population died from disease and starvation, Indian corn and porridge made from it started to look pretty good.

The colonists also took advantage of the Atlantic's bountiful array of seafood, one of the many features of the region that brought them to the New World in the first place. Fish and shellfish were common in Europe at the time, but early colonists wrote letters home with news of tremendous quantities of cod (which, first dried and then reconstituted, was a staple of the European diet), shellfish of all kinds, and freshwater eels. Well into the late 1800s, however, shellfish was considered food for the lower class—lobster, now the embodiment of culinary luxury, was even fed to prisoners. Though the early settlers may have intended to make a living farming, as many of them had done in Europe, it was fishing that allowed the colonies to prosper. Between sending premium cod back to Europe and shipping lesser grades to feed slaves working the West Indian sugarcane fields (in exchange for both money and sugar), the colonists were able to make a decent living that allowed the settlements to flourish.

The ocean would continue to provide for generations to come; canneries (for oysters, clams, and lobsters) supported New Englanders throughout the 1800s, and later, the gustatory delights of the seaside would lure tourists to the New England coast for lobster rolls (page 106) and oysters (page 90), delicacies for settlers living in the Midwest. There may be fewer canneries today, and lobsters are certainly no longer considered trash, but the appeal of a pile of seafood enjoyed within sight of the ocean remains an enduring pleasure, for locals and tourists alike.

I know this firsthand, because I spent much of my youth working in the sweaty kitchens of the Cape and Islands, from fry shacks and clam huts to fine dining restaurants. My first job was as a stock boy in a small, family-owned grocery store on Nantucket Island. My stepfather's mother had a house on the island, so in the summer, as a break from the pavement and sweltering Boston summer, I would head out there in search of a summer job.

The owner of the grocery also owned the adjacent café. I'll never forget leaving my stock boy shift for the day and stopping by the back screen door of the café to watch the cooks setting up for dinner service. Amazing smells would permeate the air as they scurried around, chopping and sautéing and pulling things from the oven, the Grateful Dead blaring from the kitchen radio. The cooks laughed and shouted at one another, and they had a look: white, snap-front dishwasher shirts with the sleeves rolled up, bandannas wrapped around their long

hair, brightly colored socks pulled up to their knees—a few even had tattoos. At sixteen, I thought they were cool, like a band of kitchen pirates. I wanted to be one.

The next summer, I asked the owner if I could be a cook in the café. He looked at me sideways. "Really?" he said. "You know that's hard work, right?" I had no idea. But I didn't care. I wanted in. He allowed me to start in the kitchen, washing dishes and doing light prep. I would show up early in the mornings, scrape the dirty pans that had been left submerged in the sink from the night before, sweep and mop the floors, and ready myself for the lunch rush, when the cook in charge would demand his parsley cut finer, his butter clarified (not just melted— I quickly learned the difference), and his quart container of Coke refilled.

My high school summers eventually came to an end, and with them my job in the kitchen. I left for freshman year of college at Hampshire

College in Amherst, Massachusetts, but my time there was short-lived. Hampshire was cool, but a little too cool for me. Let's just say that I was lacking direction and more interested in three things that had little to do with school: music, drugs, and cooking.

I spent more time getting stoned and making pizzas at a local pizzeria than I did in class or working on assignments. Hampshire was a loose environment. There were no letter grades, no tests—students were supposed to develop interests and then, over the course of a couple of years, decide how they would incorporate this into their "Division," or thesis. Instead, I focused on my job at the pizzeria. I loved it. After a foundering year at Hampshire, I decided it was time for me to take some time to think about what I really wanted to be doing, so I withdrew from school, my lackluster grades reinforcing my decision.

I returned to Nantucket to work for the summer. This time I wanted to try to get a gig in a good restaurant kitchen and really learn how to cook. I was offered a job as a chef's assistant at a notable island restaurant. The chef, Rick, and I would do catered events in amazing homes for wealthy summer residents—cocktail party after cocktail party. In between the off-premise gigs, I would jump on the line to help out the cooks in the restaurant, slowly working my way up the ranks until I was master of the hot appetizer station. I was loving life. Going to the beach by day, cooking at night, and partying with the older cooks I had always idolized. They looked after me, and I had finally gained their respect. Life was good.

As that summer ended, I realized that I had a bunch of money in my newly established bank account. Most of my friends spent their summers doing odd jobs they hated, just to scrape together some pocket change for the rest of the year. But I actually loved my job. Cooking was fun, and getting paid for it was even better. But with winter fast approaching and the seasonal

job on the island coming to an end, I needed to figure out what I was going to do for work next.

My father had recently moved to Phoenix, so I decided to pack my stuff into my rusty Toyota pickup truck and drive west to Arizona, where I had a lead on a hotel job, thanks to a friend of my father's. I made arrangements to interview with a scary-sounding Austrian chef, Anton Brunbauer, the executive chef of the Hyatt Scottsdale at Gainey Ranch.

I picked up maps from AAA (remember that?), planned my route, and drove: through Ohio, Oklahoma, and Colorado and then down to Phoenix. I stayed in disgusting hotels on the side of the highway, burning through my hard-earned summer cash and a few hundred dollars I had borrowed from my parents. Once settled in Phoenix at my dad's house, I phoned Chef Brunbauer to set up the interview. I made my way over to Gainey Ranch to see what this place was all about. It was hot as hell in Phoenix in June, but the Hyatt Scottsdale was an oasis. Palm trees lined the perfectly manicured lawns and walkways. The sound of trickling fountains

filled my ears and birds darted overhead as I pulled into the massive employee parking lot. Everyone was dressed in these incredible uniforms: pressed, bright white, with their name tags neatly pinned to their chests.

I was directed to the chef's office, where I sat eagerly awaiting my first moment with him, my shirt tucked in, my tie straight, sporting a fresh haircut that my dad had demanded I get. Chef Brunbauer looked me up and down, smiled briefly, and invited me in. His office was a glass cube in the middle of the prep kitchen in the basement of the hotel. He smoked, and the office reeked of cigarettes. He looked like he hadn't slept in years. There were photos everywhere of him with celebrities and other chefs, some I didn't recognize, some I did. Was that Julia Child? "Yes," he said with surprise. "How do you know who she is?" "PBS," I replied, and he laughed. After talking for a while, he offered me a job as a prep cook. "Prep first. Everything else second. You won't be paid much."

That winter at the Hyatt was when I knew I was going to be a cook forever. I couldn't get enough. Running the waffle station at brunch, prepping fruit salad for one thousand people, it didn't matter—I loved it all. I was learning a lot; I had bought my first set of knives and was making some great friends. On my days off, I ate: my first sushi, my first dim sum, my first real tacos. By the time spring arrived in Phoenix, I started considering culinary school. "Think you're ready for school again?" my mom rightly asked when I told her I was considering it. I hesitated. I didn't know for certain, but I thought I might make a go of this cooking thing. She told me she would discuss it with my father and we could collectively make a decision.

Dad agreed it wouldn't be a bad exercise to at least consider some sort of formal education. I had narrowed my list of culinary schools down to a few, all in the Northeast, and drove the truck back to New England. When I returned, my mom and I toured the schools, checking out my short list of preferred places—Johnson & Wales, the Culinary Institute of America. Our last stop was New England Culinary Institute in Montpelier, Vermont. We cruised up 89 North, a highway that slices through the Green Mountain State, Neil Young singing from the tape deck, and talked about cooking and why I loved it so much.

The tour sold me, and I enrolled at New England Culinary Institute in the summer of 1995. It quickly became clear to me that some kids weren't going to make it—they showed up late, in rumpled chef coats, and bummed around, waiting for the next smoke break. But there was a small group of us who would stay up late reading *Food Arts* or watching reruns of *Great Chefs, Great Cities*, making notes in the margins of our volumes of *Larousse Gastronomique*.

My geek friends and I were offered opportunities that others weren't—foraging for mushrooms in the woods with our chef-instructors, visiting local farmers' markets, cooking in competitions, and butchering deer that had met their untimely demise on back roads in rural Vermont.

When I graduated, I moved home to Boston. I had heard about a young chef, Amanda Lydon, who had just opened her own restaurant, Truc, in the South End, and I applied to join her kitchen team. After an eventful year at Truc, during which time Amanda won a Best New Chef award from *Food & Wine* magazine, I decided it was time to get some more experience elsewhere. I caught wind of a new restaurant project by Stan Frankenthaler, the gregarious, beanie-wearing

chef from Cambridge. I was intrigued, and answered an ad for a part-time cook position at his restaurant Salamander in Copley Square.

On our days off, Chef Frankenthaler would take the cooks shopping in Boston's Chinatown. I was floored. There were mahogany-colored lacquered ducks hanging in windows, fruits and vegetables I had never seen before, tanks filled with spiny lobster and sea urchin. One day the sous-chef at Salamander, Michael, mentioned to me that he needed to pick up a certain variety of Chinese vinegar, and he couldn't find it anywhere. Another cook asked him if he had tried Formaggio Kitchen, the renowned specialty food shop in Cambridge. I accompanied Michael to Formaggio in search of the vinegar and was amazed by what I saw. It was a temple to artisan foods—esoteric condiments, a wall of artisan cheese, cured meats I'd never tried before, rare coffee. Quite simply, I fell in love.

One Sunday morning in the spring of 2000, I saw a "Cheese and Specialty Foods Manager" position at Formaggio advertised in the *Boston Globe*. This was my opportunity to immerse myself in a world of ingredients I'd previously had little exposure to, just as my time at Salamander had introduced me to the Asian pantry. I showed up to my interview at Formaggio ten minutes early, as I had been taught by my father.

The shop wasn't open yet, and I gently knocked on the front door. A tall, leggy blonde wearing cutoff jean shorts, a white V-neck T-shirt, clogs, and an apron let me in, showed me where to put my coat, and made me a cup of coffee while I waited to meet with the owner. I'm getting ahead of myself, but that blonde, Kathryn, would later become my wife.

I remember my interview with Ihsan Gurdal, Formaggio's owner. I was invigorated by his obvious passion for food and his commitment to sourcing the best products from the best producers in the world. I wanted the job, bad, and Ihsan hired me on the spot and told me to

come back the next week to begin my training, which he'd personally oversee.

Ihsan held up his end of the bargain, schooling me on cheese, teaching me the ins and outs of running a retail business. He sent me to Europe to source artisanal cheese and learn from others—a few weeks working with Dario Cecchini, the "mad butcher of Panzano," in Tuscany, a few more weeks at Neal's Yard Dairy in London, an eating tour of the South of France. I loved the work, but I began to love something else, too—Kate, the woman who had unlocked the door to the shop for me on my first day.

Kate was the assistant baker at the shop

and, lacking any formal training, was looking at culinary schools. By the time we had begun dating, she had set her sights on the advanced pastry program at the Culinary Institute of America. This unique, accelerated program was being offered at both the New York and the Napa Valley campuses. One night over dinner we made the decision, after lifetimes of living on the East Coast, to move to California. We had only been dating six months, but I knew I wanted to be with this woman. I needed a job, so I called Peg Smith, the co-owner of Cowgirl Creamery, an artisan cheese company in Point Reyes, just north of San Francisco. I tentatively accepted a position as Cowgirl Creamery's wholesale manager, and in the spring of 2001 Kate and I packed up a Penske rental truck with all our shared belongings—including our Lab-mastiff mix, Thurman—and hit the road.

Between my commitments for Cowgirl, I found unpaid work staging in the kitchens of the Bay Area. In my spare time, I'd explore the region: apprenticing with a local butcher, going diving for uni and abalone, visiting local wineries. At the completion of Kate's program, we were again at a crossroads. We had been offered the opportunity to stay in California, as Peg wanted me to open Cowgirl's newest retail location at the Ferry Plaza Market in downtown San Francisco. We could move to the city—a tempting opportunity after living in sleepy Napa Valley. Or we could move home.

In some ways, the East Coast had been an easy place to leave. The long winters and hot, humid summers, the buttoned-up reputation of its residents—Northern California was a sort of mecca by comparison, and we relished our time there. But we found ourselves missing all the things that we swore we'd never miss, including those brutal, dark, cold months (really!). And though the ingredients in California were spectacular and the long growing season a boon for any cook, I missed the cooking rhythms set by the four distinct seasons and the heightened sense of excitement that heralded the arrival of the year's first asparagus or corn, and the first snow flurries calling us to the kitchen to braise something rib-sticking. Children were still many years in our future, but Kate and I both knew that we would want those children to be raised in a familiar place.

As is so often the case, it took leaving a place to realize how much we loved it. California is justly celebrated as a food paradise, but I believe that New England is an equally rich region. We have a huge stretch of coastline and access to amazing seafood. There's still enough rural countryside to support farmers and ranchers, even right outside the city limits. We have four distinct seasons that dictate how and what we cook and force the residents of this region to be resilient and grateful.

We decided that if we were going to return home to New England, it would be for good and on our own terms. We would open a business, something small that focused on our passions—mine for artisan cheeses and charcuterie, and Kate's for baking and pastry. We sketched out our plans, anxious and excited.

My mother had recently retired to Little Compton, Rhode Island, a small seaside town about forty minutes south of Providence. We flew in for the weekend, explored Providence, and quickly decided to settle there and open our shop, which we'd decided to name Farmstead. After searching high and low for an affordable space in the city, my sights fell on the Cheeseshop of Providence. A forty-year-old business, the Cheeseshop was in dire need of new ownership—the lacquered wood panels of the small store, empty shelves and refrigerated cases, and outdated inventory were just begging for a makeover. So one day while shopping there, I made the shop owner, Donna, an offer. She took a long drag off her cigarette, squinted through her smoke, and said, "No. I'm saving this business for my grandchildren. But thank you."

She called me the next day and wanted to talk. She'd changed her mind. We took over the lease and were on our way to opening our specialty shop. Over the summer of 2003, we fancied up the old shop in DIY fashion. Tiles from Home Depot replaced the brown shag carpet. We built new shelving, purchased updated cases and equipment, and, the week

"I missed the cooking rhythms set by the four distinct seasons and the heightened sense of excitement that heralded the arrival of the year's first asparagus or corn, and the first snow flurries calling us to the kitchen to braise something rib-sticking."

before Thanksgiving, opened Farmstead in Wayland Square on Providence's East Side.

At first, the shop wasn't very well received. The aging clientele wanted their Huntsman cheese studded with cranberries, but it had been replaced with aged clothbound cheddar from the UK. They couldn't find their Nova lox and rye bread toasts. In its place were hand-sliced smoked salmon and biscuits made by Kate. But over time, a new clientele emerged. We got a little press in the local paper. Business picked up. Within the first year, we had paid back the money we had borrowed from our families and were in the black. Providence had welcomed us after all.

The little specialty shop grew. We hired our first employee, then another. And another after that. Soon our staff swelled to six and we contemplated taking over the space next door. I was hosting frequent cheese and charcuterie tasting classes paired with wine, and we needed a space to accommodate more seats. We decided to do it and planned on opening a small, casual wine bar where we could serve cheese plates and host events.

Kate and I had gotten married in 2005 and left for South Africa on a belated honeymoon in February of the following year, while a contractor we hired took command of the expansion. Upon our return, we realized we had more of a space than we had bargained for—in a rare situation, our dollar had stretched, and instead of a simple wine bar, our contractor had created an intimate bar *and* a forty-seat restaurant. All we needed was a chef. I decided it would be me.

The food in the bistro was based on the tenets of California cuisine, done New England–style— that is, fresh ingredients, sourced from growers I had personal relationships with, presented in an unpretentious way. I grew up eating many of the stalwart Yankee dishes that people associate with the East Coast, and those early experiences certainly shaped my cooking. Like so many cooks, when I began cooking professionally I used those seminal experiences as a springboard,

reimagining some of the iconic New England foods of my childhood.

In 2009, four years after opening the restaurant, I was named one of the Most Sustainable Chefs in America by the Mother Nature Network. A year later I was named one of *Food & Wine* magazine's "40 under 40 Big Food Thinkers Changing the Way Americans Eat," along with White House chef Sam Kass and Danny Bowien of Mission Chinese Food fame. Later that year, I received my first James Beard Award Nomination for Best Chef: Northeast. (I was nominated again in 2011, 2012, and 2014, making the finalist list three of those four times, an experience that gave me greater sympathy for Susan Lucci.)

Most chefs don't decide to close their successful restaurants and relocate themselves at the height of their careers. But in June 2014, we shuttered Farmstead. We wanted to return to Boston, to raise our two sons—born into the chaos of a restaurant—in a bigger city, closer to family. And we were presented with an opportunity we couldn't resist, to open a new hundred-seat restaurant on Boston's newly designed Greenway—the city's version of New York City's High Line—in a new apartment building at the nexus of four diverse neighborhoods—Downtown Crossing, the Leather District, the Financial District, and Chinatown, where I'd eaten Peking duck with Chef Frankenthaler so many years before.

There's a popular myth that the food of New England is plain at best, boring at worst. Boston's Puritan roots are a source of pride in Boston, but let's face it—the Puritans aren't known as the wildest bunch. Happily, the immigrant influx didn't begin and end with the English; the history of New England is a history of immigrants who fled persecution in Europe or the slave trade in the Caribbean, or who came to America for greater opportunities, like the first Chinese laborers, who came to

Massachusetts in 1870 to replace striking workers at a shoe factory in North Adams. The Chinese immigrants settled in a part of the city previously dominated by Syrian, Irish, and Italian immigrants, creating the first Chinatown in New England (and the only one in New England that still exists today, just blocks from my restaurant).

Between 1892 and 1954, 12 million immigrants passed through New York's Ellis Island and settled in communities throughout New England and beyond. These travelers shaped the food of New England, creating enclaves where the customs and foodways of their native lands were preserved; they brought with them ingredients and techniques, and opened restaurants that served the food they'd eaten back home. This is certainly true in Boston, where, in addition to Chinatown, there's the historically Italian North End neighborhood and, farther south, centered around the towns of Fall River and New Bedford, a large Portuguese community that settled in the region. More recently, immigrants from Latin America and Southeast Asia have settled in the region, further shaping our culture and cuisine. Though New England cuisine is our country's oldest, thanks to the constant influx of immigrants, it's ever-evolving. So when I say that I cook New England food, this is what I mean: a cuisine rooted in early American history, altered by immigrants from all corners of the globe, and further informed by my own travels around the world.

When I cook, the food I make celebrates this region: its ingredients, geography, and climate, its history and traditions. This book is my attempt to capture some of what I think makes this a special place to live and cook. I am not a staunch traditionalist, as you'll see, but the book includes my spins on some of the

region's most well-known and beloved recipes, including chowder, brown bread, baked beans, and lobster rolls. It also includes some recipes that showcase both my modern ways of using regional ingredients, like bluefish, local cheeses, and maple syrup, as well as ingredients from the global pantry we're now all fortunate enough to have easy access to.

I run a busy restaurant in the heart of downtown Boston, but this was never intended to be a Townsman cookbook. I know that the food we cook at home is different from the food we order in restaurants—it must be both simpler to make *and* worth the effort. And while not every recipe in this book is an easy weeknight meal, I've aimed to provide a mix of recipes, from ones that take a bit more time and energy, like the double-crusted Seafood Tourtière (page 123), to simpler favorites, like Farmstead Mac and Cheese (page 36), which had a cult following at the recipe's namesake. A few recipes call for special equipment or ingredients, but most can be made with stuff you can easily find at the grocery store. Most recipes will serve four to six people; the recipes that I've included in the Feasts are meant to serve a crowd.

New England's long coastline, dense forests, livestock-filled pastures, dairy barns, and abundant gardens and orchards are what I think of when I think of this place I call home. Even more than the four seasons, the New England landscape defines the food of this region. It was true when the Pilgrims first arrived nearly four hundred years ago, and it continues to be true today. So I've organized this book not by season but into chapters that celebrate this landscape: Dairy, Ocean, Farm, Garden and Orchard, and Forest. If you grew up in New England, my hope is that these recipes resonate with you, that they feel familiar. And if you've never set foot in this great region, I hope this gives you a glimpse—and a taste—of the place I'm proud to call home.

"When I cook, the food I make celebrates this region: its ingredients, geography, and climate, its history and traditions."

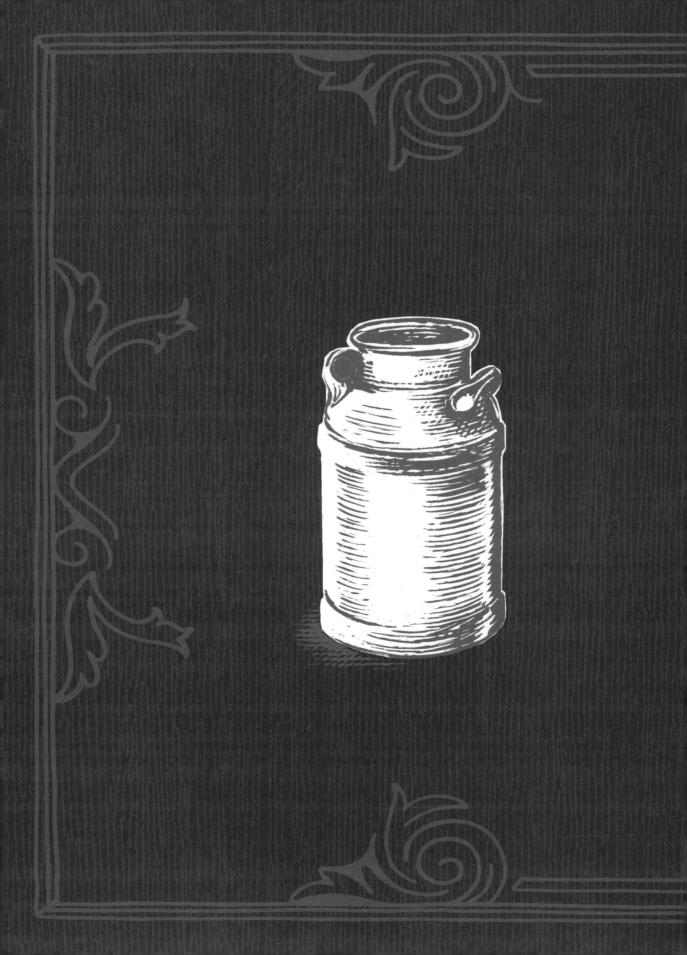

DAIRY

As humans, after all, we become that which we seek. Dairy farming makes men steady and reliable and temperate; deer hunting makes men quiet and fast and sensitive; lobster fishing makes men suspicious and wily and ruthless.

—Elizabeth Gilbert

Stop in any general store in any small New England town, spin the wire rack of postcards, and you'll find it: the one with a photo of a red-and-white dairy barn, the sort of iconic image that tourists have come to associate with the Northeast.

Beginning in the Colonial era, dairy farms were an integral part of the landscape and the economy of the region. The amount of farmland in New England peaked at around 16 million acres in the late 1800s, and large swaths of native forest were cleared to make room for grazing livestock. Until the late nineteenth century, the dairy operations were small, with anywhere from thirty to three hundred cows, and supplied a local clientele with fresh milk, cream, and butter.

Dairy farming is not an easy career. The animals need constant attention, milking twice a day even when it's ten below zero or a nor'easter has dropped a couple of feet of snow on the ground and the farmer has to dig a path to the barn. And the milk industry has not been kind to the small farmer; the price of milk drops year after year, and small farms have struggled to compete with mega-dairies. It's estimated that between 1970 and 2006, the number of dairy farms in the United States fell by 88 percent, and a large portion of those farms were located in New England.

Many small farms that have held on have done so by creating value-added products, like cheese, ice cream, and yogurt. In the last thirty years, there has been a spectacular (and delicious) increase in the number of artisan cheeses made by farmers in New England, cheeses that have changed the economic outlook for farmers while simultaneously supplying consumers and chefs with new ingredients, from Alpine-style cheese made in Vermont to Maine-made buffalo milk mozzarella.

Early in my career, I worked at Formaggio Kitchen, a seminal specialty food shop in Cambridge, Massachusetts, that ages and sells spectacular cheeses from around the world. This was around 2000, and at that time the shelves were stocked with local gems from seasoned cheesemakers, like the tangy blue cheese produced at Great Hill Creamery in Marion, Massachusetts, and wheels of goat cheese from Vermont's Lazy Lady Farm. I was working there at the right time, as a new generation of New England cheesemakers began trying their hand at making European-style cheeses from local milk—cow, sheep, and goat—with results that were often stunning. The farmers-cum-cheesemakers would swing by the shop with a wheel of cheese under their arm, inviting us to taste and offer our feedback.

Inspired by these exchanges with farmers and my time at Formaggio, my wife and I moved to Providence, Rhode Island, where we opened an award-winning cheese shop, Farmstead. In the ten years that Farmstead's retail shop and adjacent bistro were open, I stocked the cheese case with as many great local cheeses as I could find, and on the weekends I'd often pay visits to the farmers I'd gotten to know. The dairy barns buzzed with life again, with artisans mastering everything from hard grating cheeses made in the style of Parmigiano-Reggiano to cream-top yogurt, crème fraîche, and cultured butter.

Dairy products are mainstays in both my professional and personal kitchens, and the recipes here celebrate the versatility of these ingredients, from milk and cream to yogurt and eggs. The chapter includes recipes for both savory and sweet dishes, from lamb meatballs in yogurt sauce (page 43) to a coffee frappe (page 66) like the one I used to get at Brigham's, where a group of us neighborhood kids would gather in grass-stained uniforms after our Little League games. There's a recipe for a crowd-pleasing roasted wheel of cheese (page 29) and a collection of recipes for ice creams and toppings, so you can host an old-fashioned ice cream social on a hot summer day.

COW'S-MILK RICOTTA

Ricotta is a satisfying cheese to make at home, both because it's simple and because the homemade version is much better than most store-bought brands. Watching the liquid milk form into curds is a sort of magical process, and the resulting soft cheese has a variety of uses.

The more often you make ricotta at home, the better you'll become at it. Much of cheese-making is about "feel," relying less on written times and prescribed temperatures and more on experience, and if you make ricotta frequently you can tweak the method to suit your desired outcome, noting the difference between freshly drained curds and those that have sat overnight in the refrigerator. | MAKES ABOUT 2 CUPS

2 quarts whole cow's milk 1 cup heavy cream	½ teaspoon kosher salt 3 tablespoons fresh lemon juice	SPECIAL EQUIPMENT: Cheesecloth

Line a large sieve with a layer of heavy-duty fine-mesh cheesecloth and place it over a large bowl.

In a large heavy pot, slowly bring the milk, cream, and salt to a rolling boil over moderate heat, stirring occasionally to prevent scorching. Add the lemon juice, then reduce the heat to low and simmer, stirring continuously, until the mixture curdles, about 2 minutes.

With a slotted spoon, carefully scoop out the curds and transfer to the cheesecloth-lined sieve; discard the whey or save for another use—the protein-rich liquid can be added to homemade stock or a smoothie, or used in place of water or milk in any bread recipe. It's also an essential ingredient in the Whey-Brined Striped Bass (page 112).

Let drain for 1 hour. The cheese can be used right away, or transfer it to a bowl, cover, and refrigerate it; it will keep for 2 days, becoming thicker the longer it sits.

ONE CHEESE, SO MANY USES

Ricotta's milkiness makes it something of a chameleon ingredient; it has many uses, both sweet and savory. Here are some of my favorite ways to eat it.

- Scattered on salads or as a base for a creamy salad dressing
- Folded into whipped cream and eaten with fruit
- Pressed into a loaf pan, baked until firm, and crumbled over fresh tomatoes
- Folded into quick breads (use the whey, too!)
- Spooned over pasta
- Spread on a burger
- Smeared on toast with jelly
- Added to pancake batter

SWEET PEA AND RICOTTA PANCAKES

After a long New England winter, it's always a joy to cook the first green things of the season, and when sweet peas start flooding the markets in late spring, I stock up, using them in as many dishes as I can until their fleeting season is over.

Ricotta pancakes, in one form or another, have been in my repertoire since I first tried them in Tuscany, and you can vary the recipe depending on the season. In this springtime version, you'll make a puree of peas that gets folded into a batter that's enriched with full-fat ricotta. Serve the savory cakes with griddled asparagus, another of the season's best ingredients.

| MAKES 30 SILVER DOLLAR PANCAKES; SERVES 6 AS A FIRST COURSE OR LIGHT LUNCH

1 cup all-purpose flour, sifted	2 eggs, separated	Extra-virgin olive oil, for drizzling
1½ teaspoons baking powder	1½ tablespoons unsalted butter, melted and cooled, plus more for the griddle	Flaky salt, such as Maldon
1½ teaspoons baking soda		Freshly ground black pepper
½ teaspoon sugar		Honey, for drizzling (optional)
½ teaspoon kosher salt	2 ounces Gruyère, Pecorino Romano, or Parmigiano-Reggiano cheese, finely grated with a Microplane-style grater, plus more for garnish	
1 cup fresh or frozen peas (if frozen, thawed)		
1 cup buttermilk		
⅓ cup whole-milk ricotta, homemade (page 17) or store-bought	1 bunch asparagus, ends trimmed	

In a medium bowl, whisk together the flour, baking powder, baking soda, sugar, and kosher salt. Set aside.

If using fresh peas, bring a medium saucepan of salted water to a boil. Add the peas and cook until just tender, 2 to 3 minutes. Drain and rinse with cold water to stop the cooking.

Combine the peas and buttermilk in a blender or food processor and blend until smooth. Transfer to a large bowl. Add the ricotta, egg yolks, melted butter, and Gruyère and stir to combine. Mix in the dry ingredients until fully incorporated.

In the bowl of a stand mixer fitted with the whisk attachment, beat the egg whites on high speed until they hold stiff peaks. Very gently fold the egg whites into the batter.

Preheat the oven to 250°F.

Heat a large cast-iron skillet over high heat. When the pan is hot, add the asparagus and cook, turning with tongs, until just tender with blackened spots, about 7 minutes. Transfer to a plate and drizzle with olive oil. Season with flaky salt and black pepper and set aside.

Heat a griddle over medium heat and liberally grease with butter. When the butter stops foaming, spoon silver dollar–size rounds of the batter onto the griddle. Cook until golden brown on the bottom, about 2 minutes, then carefully flip and cook until golden brown on the second side, 2 minutes more. Transfer to the oven to keep warm while you cook the remaining pancakes.

Make a stack of four or five pancakes on each plate and serve some of the asparagus alongside; garnish the pancakes with Gruyère, drizzle with honey (if using), and serve.

MINTED PEA AND ARUGULA SOUP

Peas love arugula, and arugula loves peas. The sweetness of the peas is tempered by the peppery, bright flavor of arugula, and the addition of full-fat Greek yogurt gives this vibrant cold green soup a velvety richness.

I like fresh peas as much as the next guy, but you'll notice that this recipe calls for frozen peas. Don't laugh! Ask most professional chefs and they will tell you that you'll get better (and more brilliantly colored) results for purees and soups using frozen peas instead of fresh. Besides, who wants to shuck and blanch a couple of pounds of peas for a bowl of soup?

SERVES 4 TO 6 AS A FIRST COURSE

---

1 bunch arugula (7 ounces)	1 (16-ounce) bag frozen peas, plus ½ cup blanched fresh peas, for garnish (optional)	Kosher salt and freshly ground black pepper
1 bunch spinach (5 ounces)		½ cup crème fraîche (optional)
Leaves from 1 bunch mint	2½ cups whole milk	2 tablespoons heavy cream (optional)
1 tablespoon extra-virgin olive oil, plus more for drizzling	2 tablespoons cold unsalted butter	Chive blossoms, for garnish (optional)
½ cup minced yellow onion	1 cup full-fat Greek yogurt	
2 garlic cloves, thinly sliced	Zest of 1 lemon	

Bring a large pot of salted water to a boil. Fill a large bowl with ice and water; set it nearby.

When the water is boiling, add the arugula, spinach, and mint and cook just until wilted, about 30 seconds. Use a spider or slotted spoon to transfer the greens to the ice water bath. Reserve the blanching water. When cool enough to handle, remove the greens from the ice water bath and squeeze to remove the excess water. Transfer to a cutting board and coarsely chop.

In a large saucepan, heat the olive oil over medium-low heat. Add the onion and garlic. Cook, stirring occasionally, until soft and translucent, about 6 minutes. Add the blanched greens and mint, peas, milk, and butter and bring to a simmer.

Carefully transfer the soup to a blender and blend until smooth, adding some of the reserved blanching water if the soup looks too thick. Pass through a fine-mesh sieve into a clean bowl and discard the solids. Let cool to room temperature, then transfer to the refrigerator and refrigerate until cold, about 2 hours or overnight.

When completely cold, stir in the yogurt and lemon zest and season with salt and pepper. Serve the chilled soup right away, preferably in chilled bowls. If desired, whisk together the crème fraîche and cream to combine, then dot some on top of each bowl of soup. Drizzle with olive oil and garnish with blanched fresh peas and chive blossoms, if using.

EVIE'S PUB CHEESE

The South can keep their pimiento cheese: I've got my grandmother Evie's recipe for pub cheese, a concoction that has been part of every family gathering or holiday party for as long as I can remember. The cheese spread is a terrific snack, good for toting along to tailgates or potlucks. Serve the cheese with your favorite cracker; in my family, it's always Wheat Thins. | **MAKES 4 CUPS; SERVES 8 TO 10 AS A SNACK**

1½ pounds finely grated Colby cheese

1 cup mayonnaise, preferably Hellmann's

½ cup sour cream

½ cup cream cheese, at room temperature

½ small white onion, grated on a box grater

2 tablespoons finely minced red bell pepper

2 tablespoons minced cornichon pickles

2 tablespoons cornichon pickle juice

1 scallion, finely chopped

2 teaspoons onion powder

1½ teaspoons Worcestershire sauce

1 teaspoon sweet Spanish paprika

1 teaspoon Dijon mustard

1 teaspoon ground turmeric

1 teaspoon celery seed, crushed

1 garlic clove, minced

10 dashes of hot sauce

Kosher salt and freshly ground black pepper

Crackers, for serving

In a large bowl, combine the Colby cheese, mayonnaise, sour cream, cream cheese, onion, bell pepper, pickles and pickle juice, scallion, onion powder, Worcestershire, paprika, mustard, turmeric, celery seed, garlic, and hot sauce. Fold together with a rubber spatula until well mixed; season to taste with salt, black pepper, and hot sauce.

Serve the spread at room temperature with crackers alongside. The cheese can be made up to 4 days ahead and refrigerated; bring to room temperature before serving.

LITTLE GEM SALAD
WITH CHEDDAR VINAIGRETTE AND PISTACHIO GRANOLA

An interesting salad can totally steal the (dinner) show. Little Gem lettuce, a petite, romainelike variety, is delicate and crunchy. It's a great base for a salad loaded with rich ingredients, like the pistachios, cheddar, and dates used here. If you can't find that variety of lettuce, substitute Bibb, which is similar in flavor and texture.

Aged clothbound cheddar is nutty and a little funky. As cheddar ages, the lactic enzymes in the cheese actually break down and create sweet, musty flavors, which add another dimension to the salad.

The sweet-savory granola provides texture to the salad, but also those nuanced, toasty flavors that pair so well with the lettuce, sweet dates, and sharp cheese. This recipe makes more granola than you'll need for the salad. Store it in an airtight container for another salad or for snacking. | **SERVES 6**

FOR THE GRANOLA
1 cup old-fashioned rolled oats
½ cup raw pistachios
¼ cup raw pumpkin seeds
½ cup pure maple syrup
¼ cup extra-virgin olive oil
1 teaspoon kosher salt
½ teaspoon ground cinnamon
½ teaspoon ground cardamom

FOR THE DRESSING
2 tablespoons fresh lemon juice or white wine vinegar
2 teaspoons minced garlic
1½ teaspoons Dijon mustard
2 tablespoons extra-virgin olive oil
½ cup sour cream
2 tablespoons aioli (page 148) or mayonnaise
4 ounces aged white cheddar, half grated, the rest crumbled (about 1 cup)

2 scallions, thinly sliced
Kosher salt and freshly ground black pepper

3 heads Little Gem lettuce, quartered
8 pitted Medjool dates, coarsely chopped
1 cup fresh herb leaves (a mixture of parsley, tarragon, and chervil)

Preheat the oven to 300°F.

Make the granola: In a large bowl, stir together the oats, pistachios, pumpkin seeds, maple syrup, olive oil, salt, cinnamon, and cardamom. Spread the mixture on a rimmed baking sheet in an even layer and bake for 20 to 25 minutes, stirring every 10 minutes, until golden brown and crisp. Remove from the oven and let cool completely. The granola can be made up to a week ahead; let cool completely, then store in an airtight container.

CONTINUED

Make the dressing: In a medium bowl, whisk together the lemon juice, garlic, and mustard. Whisk in the olive oil, sour cream, and aioli until smooth, then switch to a spoon and stir in the grated cheddar and scallions. Season to taste with salt and pepper.

Place two quarters of lettuce on each plate. Spoon some of the dressing over, followed by some of the granola and crumbled cheddar. Garnish with the herb leaves and season with salt and pepper. Serve.

ON CHEDDAR

Cheddar cheese was a staple of my childhood, and cubes of it appeared on the tray of my high chair from a very early age. The cheese industry, and the cheddar industry in particular, helped build many New England communities. But the roots of cheddar are in fact British, having originated in the town of Cheddar, in Somerset in southwest England. These first cheddars were made with raw (unpasteurized) milk, often bound with cloth and aged in temperature-controlled caves for years before being sold.

Cheddar-making was brought to the New World by British colonists, and over the many ensuing years, it had turned into a bland, mild, industrially produced cheese that hardly resembled its roots (Kraft is considered the number one producer of cheddar in America, if that tells you something). But that has changed: New England artisans have expanded their cheese-making prowess and returned to making cheddar in a style that pays homage to our British ancestors' traditional methods of production. These new "British-style" cheddars rival the best of what I've tasted from Europe—they're robust in flavor, well aged until nutty and crumbly and, more often than not, made with raw milk.

To appreciate the difference between supermarket cheddar and its artisanal counterpart, conduct your own taste test. Buy a block of "regular" cheddar and then a second block of artisanal cheddar (which may also be labeled "cave-aged," "clothbound," or "farmstead," the latter meaning it is made only with the milk from one farm). First, you'll notice a huge difference in texture—the supermarket cheese is smooth and very creamy, while an aged cheddar is crumbly, breaking into craggy shards. Then there's the taste. A supermarket cheddar is likely to be sweet and mild and creamy enough to melt easily, while an artisanal cheddar will be nutty and sharp (it becomes more sharp as it ages) and shot through with crunchy saltlike crystals of calcium lactate. It's an eye-opening comparison; it's hard to believe they're both the same cheese.

Hopefully, in time, the cheddars of New England will achieve a reputation that rivals their British counterparts. To support the efforts of these domestic cheesemakers, I buy as much of the good stuff as I can. It's a delicious (and worthy) mission.

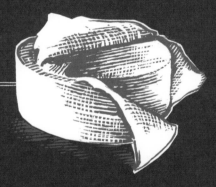

WHOLE ROASTED CHEESE
WITH BLACK GARLIC SPREAD AND GIARDINIERA

Taking a whole wheel of a luxurious cheese and baking it until it's molten is a party trick for the ages; the heat transforms an already good thing into something great, and it's visually exciting to present an entire wheel with a spoon stuck into it and watch people's eyes grow as big as saucers.

Harbison, a soft-ripened cow's-milk cheese with a bloomy rind made by my friends at Vermont's Jasper Hill Farm, is particularly well suited to the whole-roasted treatment. If it's not available where you live, you could substitute Rush Creek Reserve from Wisconsin or a nice Camembert.

You should serve the warm cheese with some crusty bread or crackers and, if you want to go to a bit of extra effort, this deeply savory black garlic spread. Black garlic is made by slowing caramelizing whole cloves of garlic over low heat over a period of several weeks until they're ink black and sticky, with a sweet-savory flavor. Good-quality black garlic can be purchased from Black Garlic City (see Resources, page 334). Crushed cloves of Roasted Garlic (page 166) could be substituted, if you're looking for an easier option.

Offset the richness of the cheese with homemade giardiniera (assorted pickled vegetables); the tanginess is a nice complement to the cheese, though you can substitute store-bought giardiniera if you don't want to wait two weeks for a homemade batch. | SERVES 6 AS A SNACK

1 whole wheel aged semisoft cheese, such as Harbison, Rush Creek Reserve, or Camembert (9 to 12 ounces)	Black Garlic Spread (recipe follows), for serving 1 cup giardiniera, homemade (page 238) or store-bought, for serving	Crusty bread or crackers, for serving SPECIAL EQUIPMENT: 16-inch pizza stone

Preheat the oven to 450°F and put a pizza stone on the middle rack of the oven.

When the oven is hot, lay a piece of aluminum foil on the pizza stone. Unwrap the whole cheese and set it on top of the foil. Roast the cheese for about 8 minutes, or until the interior of the cheese has melted. To test its readiness, gently press on the rind; it should be soft, and even cracking in spots.

CONTINUED

Remove the cheese from the oven and let cool slightly. With a very sharp chef's knife, gently slice off the top of the cheese rind with a lateral cut, revealing the melted interior. Discard the top rind.

Transfer the cheese to a platter and stick a spoon into the cheese. Serve with the black garlic spread, giardiniera, and crusty bread or crackers on the side.

BLACK GARLIC SPREAD
MAKES 1 CUP

1 shallot, unpeeled
1 head black garlic, peeled
2 garlic cloves, smashed
2 teaspoons fresh lemon juice
1 tablespoon extra-virgin olive oil
2 teaspoons kosher salt, plus more as needed
½ teaspoon freshly ground black pepper, plus more as needed
½ to ¾ cup vegetable stock or water

Preheat the oven to 425°F.

Place the shallot on a baking sheet and roast until easily pierced with the tip of a knife, about 50 minutes. (Pro tip: Roasted shallots are delicious and can be added to pasta, salad dressings, or sauces, so you may want to roast more than the one needed for this recipe.)

Peel the shallot and put it in a blender. Add the black garlic, fresh garlic, lemon juice, olive oil, salt, pepper, and ½ cup of the stock and blend until the mixture forms a spreadable paste; if the mixture looks too thick, thin with some of the remaining stock. Season to taste with salt and pepper. The black garlic spread will keep in an airtight container in the refrigerator for up to 2 weeks; let it come to room temperature before serving.

CHEDDAR AND SQUASH DUMPLINGS

The recipe for these dumplings was given to me by one of my former cooks who grew up in a Polish community in Pennsylvania. Similar in texture and spirit to pierogi, the dumplings are made with a simple dough that can be filled with many different combinations. In the fall, I like to stuff them with a combination of sharp cheddar and sweet squash filling, though that's just one idea—you could substitute blanched chopped asparagus and goat cheese, or braised and pulled chicken with a nutty Gouda, or sautéed mushrooms and Taleggio.

Practice will make perfect when forming these small purses, so take your time and pay attention to the thickness of the dough when you roll it out. Too thick, and the dumplings will be too chewy. Too thin, and they will fall apart when you cook them. It's important to keep the dough chilled while rolling it out, so take only a small amount of dough from the refrigerator at a time and keep it under a clean, damp kitchen towel so it doesn't dry out while you work.

The rich dumplings are first boiled, then sautéed in butter. You can serve them unadorned, but I like them with a spoonful of sour cream, some toasted sunflower seeds, and a drizzle of pure maple syrup.

MAKES ABOUT 50 DUMPLINGS; SERVES 6 AS A MAIN COURSE

FOR THE DOUGH
5 to 5½ cups all-purpose flour,
    plus more for dusting
1 cup whole milk
1 cup cold water
1 egg
2 tablespoons sour cream

FOR THE FILLING
1 pound butternut squash,
    peeled, seeded, and cut into
    ¼-inch cubes
1 tablespoon extra-virgin olive oil
Kosher salt and freshly ground
    black pepper
4 ounces aged cheddar cheese,
    grated
2 tablespoons whole-milk ricotta,
    homemade (page 17) or
    store-bought

½ teaspoon freshly grated nutmeg
½ teaspoon ground cinnamon

6 tablespoons (¾ stick) unsalted
    butter
¼ cup finely chopped fresh chives,
    for garnish
2 tablespoons toasted sunflower
    seeds, for garnish
Pure maple syrup, for drizzling
Sour cream, for serving

CONTINUED

Make the dough: In a large bowl, combine 5 cups of the flour, the milk, water, egg, and sour cream. Stir until the mixture comes together in a ball, adding more flour if the dough is sticky. Turn the dough out onto a well-floured work surface and knead gently with your fingertips, lifting the dough off the counter and dropping it down (the dropping technique is key for delicate and pliable dough). If the dough seems very sticky, add additional flour by the tablespoonful.

Knead until the dough is smooth on the outside and slightly sticky when poked, 2 to 5 minutes. Gather into a ball, wrap in plastic wrap, and let rest at room temperature while you make the filling.

Make the filling: Preheat the oven to 400°F. Line a rimmed baking sheet with aluminum foil.

Put the squash in a medium bowl, add the olive oil and a few pinches of salt and pepper, and toss to coat. Arrange the squash in a single layer on the prepared baking sheet. Roast, stirring frequently, until the squash is tender but not browned, about 20 minutes.

Remove the squash from the oven and let cool slightly, then transfer to a food processor. Add the cheddar cheese, ricotta, nutmeg, and cinnamon and process until pureed. Transfer to a bowl, season to taste with salt and pepper, and let cool.

Form and cook the dumplings: Preheat the oven to 250°F. Bring a large pot of salted water to a boil. Unwrap the dough and cut it into six even pieces. Working with one piece of dough at a time (keep the remaining pieces under a clean, damp kitchen towel so they don't dry out) and using a well-floured rolling pin, roll the dough to a thickness of ¼ inch.

Using a 2-inch round cutter, cut out circles from the dough. Spoon a small amount of the filling into the middle of a dough circle and, with a pastry brush, brush the edge of the dough with water. Carefully fold the dough over to form a half-moon, enclosing the filling inside. Crimp the edges with your fingers to seal. Set the dumpling on a baking sheet. Repeat until all the dough and filling have been used, gathering up and rerolling the scraps of dough as needed.

Add the dumplings to the boiling water and cook for about 90 seconds, until they float. Use a slotted spoon or spider to transfer them from the water to a rimmed baking sheet and let cool.

In a large skillet, melt the butter over medium heat. Add some of the dumplings and fry, turning frequently, until lightly browned on both sides, 4 to 5 minutes. Transfer to an ovenproof platter and keep warm in the oven while you fry the remaining dumplings.

Just before serving, sprinkle with chives and sunflower seeds, and drizzle with maple syrup. Serve with sour cream on the side.

DESIGNING THE PERFECT CHEESE BOARD

Use the rule of five. That is, choose five distinct styles of cheese, with five distinct textures and flavor profiles. Get one of each of the following styles of cheese to make a well-considered cheese board.

Fresh cheese: *Fresh* is used to describe cheeses that are unaged and have a high moisture content. They are usually mild and creamy and can be made from all types of milk. Examples include ricotta, mozzarella, and chèvre.

Soft-ripened cheese: This term is used to describe cheeses that are ripened from the outside in. They're typically very soft at room temperature, and many have a white, bloomy rind. Think: Camembert, Brie, and Pierre Robert.

Hard and natural rind cheeses: This is a broad category of cheeses, with flavors ranging from tangy to nutty and mild to sharp. They can be made from any milks. Hard cheeses include cheddar, Gouda, Gruyère, and Parmigiano-Reggiano. Natural rind cheeses can be made from any type of milk and typically age for a long period of time, during which they can develop thick rinds; some of my favorites include Stilton, Tomme de Savoie, and Mimolette.

Blue cheese: No cheese board can be truly complete without a blue. If you aren't a fan, I suggest trying something new. Start with mild, tangy, and sweet blues, like Bayley Hazen Blue or Berkshire Blue, and as your palate develops, expand into stronger-flavored versions, like Gore-Dawn-Zola or Red, White, and Blue (both from Vermont).

Washed rind cheese: These are the cheeses colloquially referred to as "stinky." Cheeses in this category are surface-ripened by washing the cheese throughout the ripening/aging process with brine, beer, wine, or brandy, which encourages the growth of bacteria. They are often creamy and, when ripe, quite aromatic. Try Taleggio, Époisses, or Alsatian Munster.

CHOOSE THE ACCOMPANIMENTS
To bring out the best in your cheese, choose great accompaniments. Fresh in-season fruit or dried fruit are good supporting players. A fruit preserve is also an excellent accompaniment—just serve it alongside (and not on) the cheese. Honey or honeycomb complements both fresh cheese and tangy blue cheese; toasted nuts are great paired with hard cheese.

DETAILS, DETAILS, DETAILS
Whenever possible, buy cheese from a store with a dedicated cheese counter staffed by a knowledgeable professional who will allow you to taste various styles of cheese and make recommendations. Avoid cheeses that are precut and shrink-wrapped or wrapped in plastic, which blocks the natural airflow to the cheese; if they sit too long, they begin to taste like the plastic in which they were wrapped, or can mold prematurely. If you have cheeses left over, wrap them in parchment paper, waxed paper, or even aluminum foil and store them in the vegetable drawer of your fridge.

Cheese should never, ever be served cold from the fridge—let it come to room temperature before serving, which improves both flavor and texture. If you're creating a cheese board for a party, do people a favor—cut the cheese and arrange it on the platter. Nobody wants to hack away at a wedge of hard cheese with a dull knife, and many people don't know how to properly cut that delicate, expensive wheel of goat cheese without hacking it to bits (you know how, of course, because you asked your cheesemonger).

In general, plan on about 1 ounce of each cheese per person. This means that for a group of six people, you'll want to serve 1½ to 2 pounds of cheese in total. There are cases where abundance is called for (say, the cheese board at a wedding reception), but in those cases I still don't recommend more than four or five varieties of cheese—just buy more of each type.

What to drink with your masterful cheese board? Dry Champagne or another similar style of sparkling wine is always welcome. Other types of wine that I think generally complement a wide variety of cheese styles include dry Riesling, a mineral-y white wine like a Chablis, or, if you're serving cheese as a final course in lieu of dessert, port, Madeira, or even an aged mezcal.

FARMSTEAD MAC AND CHEESE

My former restaurant, Farmstead, was a real hub for the food community in Providence and southern New England, and we took pride in sourcing high-quality, small-batch products, including lots of artisan New England cheeses, from producers we knew by name. It was only appropriate that we create a hallmark mac and cheese for the bistro.

This ultra-mac uses a blend of Gruyère, Brie, and cheddar (which you can supplement with any cheese bits or ends that have accumulated in your cheese drawer). You can alter the cheeses based on what you have on hand, but try to choose ones that are similar in texture and flavor to the ones I've suggested. The macaroni and cheese can be made up to a day ahead; see the Note below if you plan on doing that. | **SERVES 6 AS A MAIN COURSE**

1½ cups coarsely grated Gruyère cheese (about 5½ ounces) 1½ cups coarsely grated sharp cheddar cheese (about 6 ounces) 1½ cups diced rindless Brie (about 12 ounces)	5 tablespoons unsalted butter ¼ cup all-purpose flour 2 teaspoons chopped fresh thyme leaves Scant ¾ teaspoon freshly grated nutmeg	4 cups whole milk, at room temperature Kosher salt 1¾ cups fresh bread crumbs (about 3½ ounces) 1 pound dry penne pasta

Preheat the oven to 375°F. Bring a large pot of salted water to a boil.

In a medium bowl, combine the Gruyère, cheddar, and Brie. Set aside 1 cup; cover and chill.

In a large saucepan, melt 4 tablespoons of the butter over medium heat. Add the flour and stir until the mixture turns golden brown, about 4 minutes. Add the thyme and nutmeg.

Gradually whisk in the milk, bring to a simmer, and cook, whisking, until thickened and smooth, about 4 minutes. Add 3½ cups of the cheese and simmer, whisking, until melted and smooth. Season with salt.

In a large heavy skillet, melt the remaining 1 tablespoon butter over medium-high heat. Add the bread crumbs and stir to coat with the butter. Cook, stirring, until golden and crisp, about 2 minutes. Transfer to a plate.

Cook the pasta in the boiling water until al dente. Drain. Transfer the pasta to a large bowl, pour the cheese sauce over the top, and stir to coat.

Divide the pasta among eight 1¼-cup ramekins and sprinkle each with some of the reserved cup of cheese (alternatively, transfer to one 9 x 13-inch baking dish and sprinkle the reserved cheese over evenly).

CONTINUED

Place the ramekins on a rimmed baking sheet. Sprinkle with the bread crumbs and bake until the edges start to bubble and the tops are golden, about 20 minutes. Serve hot.

NOTE: The macaroni and cheese can be made 1 day ahead. Before adding the bread crumbs, cover the ramekins with aluminum foil and transfer to the refrigerator. When you're ready to bake the macaroni and cheese, drizzle each ramekin with 1 teaspoon heavy cream (if baking in a 9 x 13-inch pan, drizzle with all 8 teaspoons of cream) and cover with foil. Bake for 15 minutes. Uncover. Sprinkle with the bread crumbs and bake until the edges begin to bubble and the tops are golden, about 20 minutes more.

MILK-BRAISED CHICKEN LEGS
WITH SPICED RICE

Do you remember that ubiquitous chicken stew of the 1980s made with a can of Campbell's Cream of Mushroom soup? You'd pour the soup over browned chicken legs and simmer until the meat literally fell off the bone, then serve it over white rice.

I had that stew in mind when I created this comforting main dish. Milk may not seem a likely braising liquid, but it works beautifully, tenderizing the meat and combining with the chicken juices and spices to create the sauce.

One of the appealing things about braising chicken is that, unlike other braised meat, it cooks very quickly. You can brown the meat in advance, assemble the braise and refrigerate it, then pop it into the oven just before you want to eat; in under an hour you'll have a comforting main course that's perfect for a snowy evening. Don't be alarmed if your sauce curdles slightly—it's perfectly normal. If the appearance bothers you, you can always whiz the sauce with an immersion blender until smooth.

SERVES 6 AS A MAIN COURSE

FOR THE CHICKEN

12 bone-in, skin-on chicken thighs (about 4 pounds)

Kosher salt and freshly ground black pepper

2 tablespoons canola oil

1 tablespoon unsalted butter

18 pearl onions, peeled

3 celery stalks, sliced on an angle into 1-inch pieces

5 (2-inch-long) strips orange zest, removed with a vegetable peeler

2 whole star anise

1 (2-inch) cinnamon stick

2 tablespoons all-purpose flour

5 cups whole milk

1 bay leaf

FOR THE SPICED RICE

1 tablespoon canola oil

1 shallot, thinly sliced

2 garlic cloves, thinly sliced

1 teaspoon coriander seeds, toasted and ground

1 teaspoon cumin seeds, toasted and ground

1 teaspoon kosher salt

2 cups long-grain brown rice, rinsed under cold water

1 tablespoon unsalted butter

2 scallions, green parts only, thinly sliced, for garnish

Preheat the oven to 300°F. Season the chicken thighs on all sides with salt and pepper.

In a large Dutch oven, heat the canola oil and butter over medium-high heat. Once the butter has melted, add half the chicken thighs, skin-side down,

and cook until the skin has browned and the fat has rendered out, about 5 minutes. Flip and cook on the second side until golden brown, 4 minutes more. Transfer to a rimmed baking sheet or plate and repeat with the remaining thighs until they have all been browned. Set the chicken aside.

Reduce the heat to low and add the onions, celery, orange peel, star anise, and cinnamon stick to the pot. Cook, stirring, for 5 minutes. Add the flour to the pot and stir with a wooden spoon until lightly toasted, about 1 minute. Whisk in the milk and increase the heat to bring the milk to a simmer.

Return the chicken and any accumulated juices to the pot, skin-side up; they should be partially submerged in the liquid and tightly packed together in a single layer. Add the bay leaf. Cover the pot and transfer to the oven. Bake until the chicken is tender and cooked through, about 45 minutes.

While the chicken cooks, make the rice: Heat the canola oil in a 2-quart pot over low heat. Add the shallot, garlic, coriander, cumin, and salt and cook, stirring, until the shallots are slightly translucent, about 5 minutes. Add the rice and cook, stirring, for 1 minute, until toasted.

Add 3½ cups water, bring to a boil, stir, then cover, reduce the heat to low, and cook for 45 minutes. Uncover the pot, fluff the rice with a fork, and add the butter. Re-cover, remove from the heat, and let stand for 10 minutes.

Remove the chicken from the oven, uncover, and remove and discard the star anise, cinnamon stick, and bay leaf. Transfer the chicken thighs, onions, and celery to a platter and spoon the sauce over the top. Garnish with the scallions. Serve with the spiced rice alongside.

LAMB MEATBALLS WITH YOGURT SAUCE

Made with ground lamb and cooked in a tangy yogurt sauce, these are a delicious variation on a classic meatball. While meatballs aren't difficult to make, oftentimes they're tough or dry. Using rich ground lamb prevents the latter; to avoid the former fate, work the ground meat gently—don't knead it to death.

If you can't find or don't like ground lamb, you can substitute ground beef (opt for an 85/15 blend). Any leftover meatballs make a mean sandwich the next day. | **SERVES 4 AS A MAIN COURSE**

FOR THE YOGURT SAUCE
2 cups plain whole-milk yogurt
2 garlic cloves, finely minced
3 tablespoons finely chopped fresh dill
2 tablespoons finely chopped fresh mint
Salt and freshly ground black pepper

FOR THE MEATBALLS
1¼ pounds ground lamb
1 large egg, lightly beaten
½ cup fine fresh bread crumbs
1 large shallot, minced
1 tablespoon harissa
1 teaspoon kosher salt
½ teaspoon cumin seeds, toasted and ground

¼ teaspoon freshly ground black pepper
1 tablespoon extra-virgin olive oil

1 tablespoon toasted sunflower seeds, for garnish
Pickled chiles, homemade (page 241) or store-bought, for garnish

---

Make the yogurt sauce: In a medium bowl, whisk together the yogurt, garlic, 2 tablespoons of the dill, and 1 tablespoon of the mint. Season to taste with salt and pepper and set aside.

Make the meatballs: In a large bowl, combine the lamb, egg, bread crumbs, shallot, harissa, salt, cumin, and pepper and mix well with your hands. Shape into 24 small balls, dipping your hands in cold water as needed to keep the mixture from sticking.

In a 12-inch skillet, heat the olive oil over medium heat. When the oil is hot, add the meatballs in a single layer and fry, turning the meatballs so they brown on all sides, until cooked through, about 8 minutes. Using a slotted spoon, transfer the meatballs to a plate. Pour off and discard any fat in the pan.

Spoon some yogurt sauce into the bottom of four bowls. Top with a few meatballs, and garnish with the remaining dill and mint, the sunflower seeds, and a few pickled chiles.

GRILLED CORN FLATBREAD
WITH BURRATA

Flatbreads are a delicious way to clean out the fridge, as they can be topped with any number of things. But this combination is my particular favorite, especially because we wait all summer long in New England for the first local corn, which fortuitously debuts during peak grilling season. The combination of sweet corn and creamy burrata is a great one. If you can't find burrata, substitute fresh mozzarella.

The flatbread is made from a simple yeasted dough. Make it early in the day on the same day you plan to grill the flatbreads, or make a batch in advance and freeze it so you can have it on hand anytime the mood strikes. The dough will keep, frozen, for up to 3 months. Thaw it overnight in the refrigerator before using. | **SERVES 6 AS A MAIN COURSE OR 12 AS A SNACK**

FOR THE FLATBREAD DOUGH	FOR THE GRILLED CORN	
3 cups warm water	2 ears corn, husked	2 (8-ounce) balls burrata
1 (¼-ounce) packet active dry yeast (2¼ teaspoons)	Canola oil, for brushing	Extra-virgin olive oil, for drizzling
4¾ cups all-purpose flour, plus more for dusting	2 tablespoons extra-virgin olive oil	Aleppo or Maras pepper, for garnish (optional)
2¼ cups whole wheat flour	¼ cup chopped fresh basil	
2 tablespoons kosher salt	¼ cup chopped fresh cilantro	
½ cup sour cream	1 tablespoon minced shallot	
Canola oil, for the grill	1 tablespoon red wine vinegar	
	¼ teaspoon kosher salt	
	Freshly ground black pepper	

Make the dough: Pour the warm water into a large bowl and sprinkle the yeast over it. Let stand for 5 minutes. Add the all-purpose and whole wheat flours and mix with your fingertips until a rough dough forms. Cover the bowl with plastic wrap and let rest at room temperature for 20 minutes.

Sprinkle the salt over the dough, then add the sour cream; knead until the mixture is well incorporated and the dough pulls away from the sides of the

bowl and holds together in a loose, wet ball, about 5 minutes (the dough will be very soft and wet; lightly moisten your hands to prevent sticking if needed). Cover the bowl with plastic wrap and let the dough rise at room temperature until doubled, about 1 hour (the warmer and more humid your kitchen is, the faster it will rise).

Prepare the corn: Build a medium-hot fire in a charcoal grill, or heat a gas grill to high. Brush the corn with the canola oil and place it on the grill grate. Grill, turning frequently, until the corn is tender and blackened in spots, about 10 minutes. Let cool slightly, then cut the kernels from the cob into a bowl. Add the extra-virgin olive oil, basil, cilantro, shallot, vinegar, and salt and pepper to taste, and toss to combine. If using a charcoal grill, add coals to maintain the heat.

Divide the dough into six equal portions. Generously flour a work surface. Working with one or two portions at a time (depending on how many flatbreads will fit on your grill), roll out the dough into ovals, each about 8 x 4 inches and ¼ inch thick.

Lightly oil the grill rack. Transfer one or two flatbreads to the grill and grill until lightly charred on one side and no longer sticking to the grill, 2 to 3 minutes. With a spatula, flip the flatbreads. Top each with some of the burrata and the corn, and grill until the flatbreads are browned on the bottom and the burrata has melted, 1 to 2 minutes more.

Remove the flatbreads from the grill and drizzle with olive oil and Aleppo pepper (if using), then cut into wedges and serve. Repeat with the remaining balls of dough.

CLAM AND SQUID CHOWDER

New England is known for its chowder (or, as we like to call it, chowdah). I have certainly had my share over the years, but my favorite is the thick, creamy version served in a Styrofoam cup from the galley kitchen on the Nantucket ferry. I've passed many a crossing on the top deck of that boat, bundled up against the wind and spray, slurping chowder with a beer alongside while the boat navigated the fog banks and blinking buoys on the dark horizon.

My version takes some liberties: I add fresh squid to the broth, along with seaweed for some briny flavor. If you want a more traditional chowder, try my mom's recipe on page 51. Serve with Squid Ink Crackers (page 50) or oyster crackers. | **SERVES 6 AS A MAIN COURSE**

2 to 3 pounds medium-size top neck or littleneck clams, scrubbed	1 tablespoon unsalted butter	2 sprigs thyme
1 pound seaweed, well rinsed (ask your fishmonger)	1/3 pound salt pork, finely diced	1 bay leaf
4 whole squid, cleaned tubes and tentacles	3 small leeks, tops removed, halved, cleaned, and sliced into half-moons	2½ cups heavy cream
2 tablespoons extra-virgin olive oil, plus more for drizzling	2 celery stalks, finely diced	¼ cup chopped flat-leaf parsley, for garnish
1 tablespoon fresh lemon juice	2 large Yukon Gold potatoes, peeled and cut into ¼-inch cubes	1 tablespoon finely chopped chives, for garnish
Kosher salt and freshly ground black pepper, to taste	½ cup dry white wine	Squid Ink Crackers (recipe follows), for serving (optional)

Place the clams in a large pot or a heavy Dutch oven, add a quart of water and the seaweed, and set over medium-high heat. Cover and cook until the clams have opened, 10 to 15 minutes (discard any clams that do not open).

Separate the squid tentacles from the bodies, then add both the bodies and tentacles to a medium bowl. Add the olive oil and lemon juice, season with salt and pepper, and stir to combine. Set aside.

Drain the clams into a colander set over a bowl and reserve the cooking liquid. Strain the cooking liquid through a sieve lined with cheesecloth or doubled-up paper towels, and set aside the broth. Remove the clams from the shells and coarsely chop. Transfer the chopped clams to a bowl. Discard the shells and seaweed.

Heat the butter in the cleaned pot over medium-low heat. Once the butter has melted, add the salt pork

and cook, stirring occasionally, until the fat has rendered, about 5 minutes. With a slotted spoon, transfer the pork to a paper towel–lined plate.

Add the leeks and celery to the pot and cook, stirring frequently, until they are softened but not browned, about 10 minutes. Stir in the potatoes and wine and continue cooking until the wine has evaporated and the potatoes have just started to soften, about 5 minutes. Add enough of the reserved clam broth (about 3 cups) to just cover the potatoes (any extra broth can be reserved for another use). Add the thyme and bay leaf. Partially cover the pot and simmer gently until the potatoes are tender, about 10 minutes.

When the potatoes are tender, stir in the cream, the reserved chopped clams, and the salt pork. Season to taste with salt and pepper. Heat to a bare simmer (do not let the chowder come to a full boil). Remove and discard the thyme and bay leaf.

Prepare a gas or charcoal grill for direct high-heat grilling (alternatively, you can set a grill pan over high heat). Drain the squid bodies and tentacles from the marinade, and place on the hot grill grate or grill pan. Grill, turning once, about 1 minute per side.

Remove the squid to a cutting board and coarsely chop the bodies into medium to large dice and the tentacles into bite-size pieces. Stir the squid into the chowder and serve immediately. Ladle into bowls. Garnish with the chopped parsley and chives, a drizzle of olive oil, and Squid Ink Crackers crumbled over the top, if using. The chowder can be made ahead; let cool to room temperature, then cover and refrigerate. Reheat gently over low heat, stirring frequently.

SQUID INK CRACKERS
MAKES 2 DOZEN

1 cup rye flour
1 cup all-purpose flour, plus more for dusting
2½ tablespoons extra-virgin olive oil, plus more for brushing
2 teaspoons kosher salt
1½ tablespoons squid ink (ask your fishmonger)
1¼ cups warm water
Flaky salt, such as Maldon, for sprinkling

Preheat the oven to 425°F. Line a rimmed baking sheet with parchment paper.

In the bowl of a stand mixer fitted with the dough hook, whisk together both flours, olive oil, and kosher salt. Turn the mixer to low and add the squid ink, then gradually pour in the water. Mix until the dough is well combined and beginning to pull away from the sides of the bowl, about 5 minutes.

Turn the dough out onto a floured work surface and, with a lightly floured rolling pin, roll the dough into a rectangle that is about 1/16 inch thick.

Cut the dough into large rectangles, each about 12 inches long and 5 inches wide; transfer the pieces to the prepared baking sheet. Brush each rectangle with a little olive oil and sprinkle with flaky sea salt. Bake for 5 minutes, then flip and bake on the second side for 1 to 2 minutes more, until crispy. Remove from the oven and let cool on the baking sheet.

The crackers will continue to crisp as they cool. Break into irregular shards to garnish the chowder. The crackers will keep in an airtight container at room temperature for up to 2 days.

MY MOM'S CLAM CHOWDER

When I shared my nontraditional chowder recipe (page 48) with my mom, she fired off the following e-mail: "I make the best—no squid or other crap." And it's true—my mother's version of a classic chowder, thick with potatoes and dense with clams, is the gold standard. So this book includes both recipes—one nouveau, one old-school. Try both to see which you prefer, or make mine when you want something different, and save Mom's for when you crave the classic. If you'd like, you can substitute red potatoes for the Yukon Golds in the recipe. They do not need to be peeled.

| SERVES 5 OR 6 AS A FIRST COURSE, 3 OR 4 AS A MAIN COURSE

8 pounds quahog clams (littlenecks or cherrystones can be substituted)	1 heaping tablespoon all-purpose flour	1 cup heavy cream
Bottled clam juice, as needed	2 sprigs thyme	Kosher salt and freshly ground black pepper
4 thick-cut bacon slices, cut crosswise into ¼-inch pieces	2 bay leaves	Biscuits (page 210) or oyster crackers, for serving
2 small yellow onions, diced	1 pound Yukon Gold potatoes, peeled and cut into ½-inch cubes	

Bring 4 cups water to a boil in a heavy stockpot. Add the clams, cover, and steam for 5 to 10 minutes. When the clams open, they are done; do not overcook. Drain the clams in a colander set over a bowl and reserve the cooking liquid. Discard any clams that do not open. Remove the clams from the shells and coarsely chop; transfer the chopped clams to a bowl.

Pour the cooking liquid into a measuring cup, leaving behind any sediment that has settled to the bottom of the bowl. You need 5 to 6 cups of cooking liquid; add bottled clam juice as needed.

In a large Dutch oven, fry the bacon over medium heat until it begins to brown. Pour off all but 1 tablespoon of the fat from the pan, then add the onions and cook, stirring, until they begin to soften, about 5 minutes. Sprinkle the flour over the onions and cook, stirring, for 3 to 4 minutes, then pour in 5 cups of the clam cooking liquid, the thyme, bay leaves, and potatoes. Bring to a boil, then reduce the heat to maintain a simmer and cook until the potatoes are tender, about 8 minutes.

Add the chopped clams and cream and season with salt and pepper. Heat to a bare simmer (do not let boil), then remove from the heat and let stand, covered, for 1 hour.

Remove and discard the thyme and bay leaves and reheat the soup gently over low heat, stirring, until hot.

If the soup is too thick or your liking, thin with any remaining clam cooking liquid. Taste and adjust the seasoning. Serve with biscuits (page 210) or oyster crackers.

CHOCOLATE SILK PIE

I grew up on a version of this dessert, made perfectly every time by my stepmother, Pam; it was one of her old family recipes. It became a dish of folklore in my family, frequently requested by myself and my father, but saved for celebrations like birthdays or the holidays. That said, chocolate pie shouldn't be only a special-occasion dessert. Though time-consuming, it is fairly simple to make, particularly if you do it in stages—the crust one day, the filling the next, and the whipped cream topping just before you plan to serve it. | **MAKES ONE 9-INCH PIE; SERVES 6 TO 8**

FOR THE CACAO NIBS

2 tablespoons unsalted butter

5 tablespoons cacao nibs, lightly chopped

1½ teaspoons granulated sugar

1 recipe Pâte Brisée (recipe follows)

All-purpose flour, for dusting

FOR THE FILLING

3 ounces unsweetened chocolate, chopped

½ cup plus 2 tablespoons (1¼ sticks) unsalted butter, at room temperature

3 large eggs

1 cup plus 3 tablespoons granulated sugar

1½ teaspoons fine sea salt

1½ teaspoons pure vanilla extract

¾ teaspoon instant espresso powder (such as Medaglia d'Oro)

1 cup heavy cream

FOR THE WHIPPED CREAM TOPPING

½ cup heavy cream

1 tablespoon confectioners' sugar

½ teaspoon pure vanilla extract

Unsweetened cocoa powder, for dusting (optional)

SPECIAL EQUIPMENT: Instant-read thermometer

Make the cacao nibs: In a small skillet, melt the butter. Add the cacao nibs and granulated sugar and cook, stirring, until the nibs are toasted and lightly caramelized, about 5 minutes. Remove from the heat and set aside.

Put the pâte brisée on a lightly floured work surface and, using a lightly floured rolling pin, roll the pâte brisée into a 12-inch circle that is about ¼ inch thick. Transfer the dough to a 9-inch pie plate and decoratively crimp the edge. Transfer to the freezer and freeze for at least 2 hours or overnight.

Parbake the crust: Preheat the oven to 350°F. Remove the crust from the freezer and line it with parchment paper. Fill with pie weights and bake until the crust looks set, 20 to 25 minutes. Remove the pie weights and parchment, return the pie crust to the oven, and bake until golden brown, 10 to 15 minutes more. Transfer to a wire rack and let cool.

Make the filling: Put the chocolate in a medium heatproof bowl and set the bowl over a saucepan of simmering water; be sure the bottom of the bowl does not touch the water. Cook, stirring, until the chocolate is melted. Remove from the heat and let cool to room temperature; keep the water at a low simmer.

In the bowl of a stand mixer fitted with the paddle attachment, beat the butter on high speed until light and fluffy, about 3 minutes.

In a medium heatproof bowl, whisk together the eggs and 1 cup of the granulated sugar until combined. Set the bowl over the saucepan of simmering water (be sure the water does not touch the bottom of the bowl). Cook, whisking, until the mixture is pale, has increased in volume, and registers 165°F on an instant-read thermometer. Remove from the heat and stir in the melted chocolate.

With the mixer on low, slowly drizzle the chocolate-egg mixture into the beaten butter, scraping down the sides of the bowl as needed. Mix in the salt, then transfer to a large bowl and clean the mixer bowl.

In a small bowl, combine the vanilla and espresso powder and stir until the espresso powder dissolves. In the bowl of the mixer, now fitted with the whisk attachment, combine the cream, remaining 3 tablespoons granulated sugar, and the vanilla mixture and beat on medium-high speed until the cream holds medium peaks. With a rubber spatula, fold the cream into the chocolate-butter mixture in three additions. Fold in the toasted cacao nibs; the mixture should be fluffy and homogeneous. Pour the filling into the parbaked pie crust and refrigerate, covered, overnight.

Just before serving the pie, make the whipped cream topping: In the bowl of a stand mixer fitted with the whisk attachment, combine the heavy cream, confectioners' sugar, and vanilla and beat until the cream holds medium peaks. Spread the topping over the pie. Sift some cocoa powder over the top, if desired. Serve immediately, or refrigerate, uncovered, for up to 1 day before serving; top with the cocoa powder just before serving.

PÂTE BRISÉE

The key to a flaky, flavorful pie or tart crust is using a generous amount of butter and not overworking the dough; you should stop the mixer when the mixture is still quite crumbly. This crust can be made ahead, wrapped tightly, and refrigerated for up to two days or frozen for up to two months. Thaw overnight in the refrigerator before using. If you're using this crust for a savory pie, like Seafood Tourtière (page 123), double the recipe and omit the sugar.

MAKES ONE 9-INCH CRUST

3 cups all-purpose flour
1 tablespoon sugar
1½ teaspoons kosher salt
1 cup (2 sticks) plus 1 tablespoon cold unsalted butter, cut into cubes
¼ to ½ cup ice water

In the bowl of a stand mixer fitted with the paddle attachment, combine the flour, sugar, and salt. Add the butter and mix until the mixture is crumbly and resembles wet sand. Very gradually drizzle in half the water, then stop the mixer. Take a small handful of the mixture and gently squeeze it; if it forms a ball, you have added enough liquid. If not, gradually add more ice water until it holds together in a ball when squeezed.

Transfer the pâte brisée to a sheet of plastic wrap (it may be crumbly, which is okay) and use the plastic wrap to form the dough into a ball. Wrap tightly and refrigerate for a few hours or overnight.

SUMMER BERRY ETON MESS WITH PINK PEPPERCORN

When I was a kid, my grandmother made ambrosia salad each Thanksgiving. I thought the "salad"—a mixture of canned mandarin orange segments, canned pineapple, cherries in syrup, toasted almonds, coconut, and marshmallows, all folded into whipped cream—was weird and amazing, and couldn't imagine the holiday without it.

Eton mess is a classic English dessert, comprising macerated fruit and crumbled meringue folded into whipped cream, and it reminds me a bit of Grandma's ambrosia. Both are light and airy, owing to the whipped cream, and both have fruit folded in, though Eton mess also includes bits of crumbled meringue, which serves the same textural purpose as Grandma's toasted almond addition.

For this version, I like to use an assortment of summer berries, though any juicy fruit will work, meaning you can vary the fruit according to the seasons, swapping in stone fruit or poached cranberries (page 259) as the seasons march on. It may seem odd to use peppercorns in a dessert, but pink peppercorns have a fruity, floral flavor that adds dimension. | **SERVES 6**

FOR THE MERINGUE
4 large egg whites,
    at room temperature
1¼ cups granulated sugar
2 teaspoons cornstarch
1 teaspoon fresh lemon juice
¾ teaspoon crushed pink
    peppercorns
½ teaspoon pure vanilla extract

FOR THE MESS
12 strawberries, hulled and sliced
½ cup raspberries
½ cup blueberries
¼ cup blackberries, halved
¼ cup confectioners' sugar
2 cups heavy cream

1 quart Sour Cream Ice Cream
    (page 71) or Vanilla Ice Cream
    (page 70)
¼ teaspoon crushed pink
    peppercorns

Make the meringue: Preheat the oven to 200°F. In the bowl of a stand mixer fitted with the whisk attachment (or in a large bowl using a handheld mixer), beat the egg whites on low speed until they look foamy. Gradually increase the speed to high and beat until the whites hold soft peaks, then begin adding the granulated sugar 1 tablespoon at a time until all the sugar has been added. Beat until the egg whites are thick and glossy, about 7 minutes total. Fold in the cornstarch, lemon juice, peppercorns, and vanilla.

Line an 11 x 17-inch rimmed baking sheet with a silicone baking mat or parchment paper. Transfer the meringue to the prepared baking sheet and spread it into a thin, even layer. Bake for about 1 hour, until the meringue is dry to the touch but still a bit soft when pressed and lifts easily from the baking sheet in a single piece; it will continue to dry as it cools. Remove from the oven and let cool completely. Crumble half of the meringue into bite-size pieces. You need 2 cups of crumbled meringue for the "mess"; any extra meringue can be stored in an airtight container for snacking or use as a topping for ice cream.

Assemble the mess: In a small bowl, stir together the fruit and confectioners' sugar; let macerate until juicy, about 10 minutes. In the bowl of a stand mixer fitted with the whisk attachment (or in a large bowl using a handheld mixer), beat the cream on high speed until it holds soft peaks.

Put a scoop of ice cream in each of six bowls and spoon some of the macerated fruit alongside. Top each scoop with whipped cream and the crumbled meringue, dividing it evenly. Garnish with a sprinkle of pink peppercorns. Serve immediately.

COCONUT TAPIOCA
WITH MISO PEANUTS

I can recall many a night of my childhood sitting on the floor of my living room, eating bowlfuls of tapioca after dinner while my parents watched *Chronicle* (a local Boston TV news show). Back then, it was always the store-bought version made from a powdered mix that you whisked into hot milk. If my mom was feeling fancy, she would stir in a heaping tablespoon of powdered hot chocolate. This is my modern-day homage to that comforting childhood classic, simultaneously light but rich, sweet but not overwhelmingly so. I like the contrasting texture and flavor provided by the miso peanut garnish, but even without it, this is a great dessert. | **SERVES 4 TO 6**

⅓ cup small tapioca pearls 1 (14-ounce) can full-fat coconut milk ¼ cup whole milk 2 large eggs, separated	½ cup sugar 1 teaspoon pure vanilla extract ½ teaspoon kosher salt Miso Peanuts, for garnish (recipe follows)	½ cup unsweetened coconut chips, lightly toasted, for garnish ½ cup mandarin orange, tangerine, or navel orange segments, for garnish

In a small bowl, combine the tapioca pearls and ¾ cup water and let soak for 1 hour, then drain; the pearls will have absorbed most of the liquid.

In a medium saucepan, combine the tapioca, coconut milk, whole milk, egg yolks, ¼ cup of the sugar, the vanilla, and the salt. Cook over medium heat, whisking continuously, until the mixture thickens, about 8 minutes. Remove from the heat.

In the bowl of a stand mixer fitted with the whisk attachment (or in a large bowl using a handheld mixer), beat the egg whites on high speed until foamy. With the mixer running, gradually add the remaining ¼ cup sugar until it is all incorporated, then beat until the whites hold stiff peaks.

Return the tapioca mixture to low heat. Stir 1 cup of the hot tapioca into the egg whites, then pour the egg white mixture into the saucepan with the remaining tapioca and fold in with a rubber spatula until fully incorporated. Divide between four or six glasses and refrigerate until cold, 3 to 4 hours.

To serve, garnish each glass with some of the miso peanuts, coconut chips, and mandarin orange segments.

MISO PEANUTS

MAKES 1 CUP

1 cup raw unsalted peanuts
¼ cup wildflower honey
1 tablespoon white miso
1 teaspoon rice vinegar
¼ teaspoon kosher salt

Preheat the oven to 325°F. Line a rimmed baking sheet with a silicone baking mat.

Spread the peanuts on the prepared baking sheet, transfer to the oven, and bake until lightly toasted, 8 to 10 minutes.

Reduce the oven temperature to 300°F.

In a medium bowl, whisk together the honey, miso, vinegar, and salt. Add the toasted peanuts and stir to coat, then return to the baking sheet, transfer to the oven, and bake until caramelized and golden brown, 3 to 5 minutes, watching carefully to avoid scorching.

Remove from the oven and let cool completely. The peanuts can be made up to a week ahead; let cool completely and store in a tightly sealed container at room temperature. The recipe makes more peanuts than you will need for the tapioca; the remaining peanuts can be used as a topping for ice cream (see Ice Cream Social, page 68) or just eaten as a snack.

BOSTON CREAM WHOOPIE PIES

The official state dessert of Massachusetts, Boston cream pie—a pie in name alone—comprises two layers of yellow sponge cake sandwiched together with pastry cream and glazed with chocolate. Though accounts of its origin vary, its popularity is widely attributed to Boston's Parker House Hotel, which first began serving it in 1856. Now the combination of cake, cream, and chocolate glaze most often appears in doughnut form, likely first popularized by the Massachusetts-based chain Dunkin' Donuts, and found in every doughnut shop the country over.

Here the dessert is reimagined as a whoopie pie, the cream filling sandwiched between two tender cakes, glazed with semisweet chocolate. | MAKES 12

FOR THE FILLING
2 cups whole milk
1 tablespoon plus 1 teaspoon powdered gelatin, dissolved in ¼ cup warm water
¼ cup cornstarch
6 egg yolks
⅔ cup plus ¼ cup sugar
¼ teaspoon kosher salt
3 tablespoons unsalted butter, at room temperature
3 teaspoons pure vanilla extract
2 cups heavy cream

FOR THE CAKES
½ cup (1 stick) unsalted butter, at room temperature, plus more for greasing
1½ cups sugar
4 large eggs
2¾ cups all-purpose flour
1 tablespoon plus ½ teaspoon baking powder
1 teaspoon kosher salt
½ cup whole milk
2 tablespoons pure vanilla extract

FOR THE CHOCOLATE GLAZE
12 ounces semisweet chocolate (64% cacao), chopped
1 cup heavy cream
1½ teaspoons extra-virgin olive oil

SPECIAL EQUIPMENT: Piping bag with plain tip

Make the filling: In a medium saucepan, combine 1 cup of the milk and the gelatin mixture. Cook over medium heat until bubbles begin to form around the edges of the pan. Remove from the heat.

Prepare an ice bath by filling a large bowl with ice and water and set it nearby.

Put the cornstarch in a medium bowl. Whisk in the remaining 1 cup milk until smooth. Add the egg yolks, ⅔ cup of the sugar, and the salt and whisk until well blended. While whisking continuously, slowly pour one-third of the hot milk mixture into the egg yolk mixture. Gradually whisk in the rest of the hot milk. Return the mixture to the saucepan and bring to a boil over medium heat. Boil gently for 1 minute, stirring continuously; the mixture will thicken. Pass the mixture through a fine-mesh sieve into a clean bowl and whisk in the butter. Nest the bowl containing the pastry cream into the ice water bath. Let cool, stirring occasionally, until the cream is at room temperature; whisk in 2 teaspoons of the vanilla. Cover with plastic wrap, pressing it directly against the surface of the pastry cream to prevent a skin from forming, and refrigerate until cold, at least 2 hours or up to overnight.

In the bowl of a stand mixer fitted with the whisk attachment (or in a large bowl using a handheld mixer), beat the cream and the remaining 1 teaspoon vanilla on high speed until it holds stiff peaks. Stir one-third of the whipped cream into the chilled pastry cream to lighten it, then fold in the remaining two-thirds. Cover and refrigerate for at least 2 hours or up to 2 days.

Make the cakes: Preheat the oven to 350°F. Line two 11 x 17-inch rimmed baking sheets with silicone baking mats or parchment paper. If using parchment, grease the paper with butter or spray with nonstick cooking spray.

In the bowl of a stand mixer fitted with the paddle attachment (or in a large bowl using a handheld mixer), beat the butter and sugar together on high speed until fluffy and light. Reduce the mixer speed to medium, add the eggs, and beat until fully incorporated and the mixture looks creamy and very pale yellow. Reduce the mixer speed to low and beat in the flour, baking powder, and salt, followed by the milk and vanilla. Beat everything together on low for 30 seconds, and then on high for 3 minutes. Scrape down the sides of the bowl with a rubber spatula as needed.

Spoon 3-tablespoon mounds of the batter onto the prepared baking sheets, spacing them 2 inches apart. Bake in the upper and lower thirds of the oven, switching the position of the sheets halfway through baking, until the cakes are light golden with puffed tops and spring back when touched, 10 to 12 minutes. Once cool, use a spatula to transfer from the baking sheets to the rack.

While the cakes cool, make the glaze: Put the chocolate in a bowl. In a small saucepan, gently heat the cream to a simmer. Pour the cream over the chopped chocolate and let stand for 10 minutes, then gently whisk the cream and chocolate until smooth. Whisk in the olive oil.

Arrange the cakes flat-side up on a wire rack set over a rimmed baking sheet. Transfer the cream filling to a piping bag fitted with a plain tip. Pipe a generous layer of filling onto half the cakes, then top with a second cake to create a sandwich. Spoon some of the chocolate over each whoopie pie, letting the excess drip off, then transfer to a plate. Refrigerate for 10 minutes before serving.

COFFEE FRAPPE
WITH MAPLE WHIP AND TOFFEE CRUMBLE

There are no more Brigham's ice cream shops left in New England. For years, Brigham's set the gold standard for New England ice cream parlors, with old-school soda fountain–type seating at a long counter, and small booths you could pile into and eat grilled cheese sandwiches, turkey clubs, and patty melts, capping off the meal with a scoop of ice cream.

I always went for the coffee ice cream, which I tried long before I became a coffee drinker. Brigham's coffee frappe was the gateway drug.

It's important to discuss here the difference between a frappe and a milk shake. In New England, the term *milk shake* is traditionally used to describe a mixture of milk and syrup that has been blended until frothy. The term *frappe* is used to describe a blended combination of milk, syrup, *and* ice cream (which is referred to everywhere else as a milk shake). And to make matters more confusing, in Rhode Island (where coffee milk, a combination of coffee syrup and milk, is the unofficial state beverage), a frappe is called a cabinet, named for the place where the blender was kept.

Whatever you call it, this combination of coffee ice cream, syrup, and milk, topped with a cloud of whipped cream and a sprinkling of toffee crumble, is my homage to the late, great Brigham's. | MAKES 2 FRAPPES

½ cup heavy cream 2 tablespoons maple syrup, preferably dark amber	1 quart coffee ice cream, homemade (page 71) or store-bought	1 cup whole milk 2 tablespoons Toffee Crumble (page 72)

Place the glasses in which you plan to serve the frappes in the freezer to chill.

In the bowl of a stand mixer fitted with the whisk attachment (or in a large bowl using a handheld mixer), beat the cream and maple syrup on high speed until the cream holds stiff peaks. Set aside.

In a heavy-duty blender, combine 2 scoops of the ice cream with ½ cup of the milk and blend until smooth. Pour into one of the chilled glasses. Blend the remaining ice cream and milk and transfer to the second glass. Garnish each glass with half the whipped cream and a tablespoon of the toffee crumble. Serve each frappe with a spoon and a straw.

FEAST | ICE CREAM SOCIAL

For three-quarters of the year, it's hardly ice cream weather in New England. Maybe that explains our devotion to the frozen treat—when the long, hot days of summer finally arrive, we want to make the most of them. Eating a cone after a baseball game or snagging a chocolate-dipped ice cream bar off the Good Humor truck after a hot day at the beach was a childhood ritual, and trips to Brigham's (see page 66) were an adolescent rite of passage.

Ice cream is something people are happy to gather for, which is why hosting an ice cream social is so much fun. It goes without saying that kids love it, but adults do, too—there's something nostalgic about building your own sundae that appeals to the kid in all of us.

The key to a successful social is variety. I like to serve a few different flavors of ice cream and sorbet (a quart will serve 6 to 8 people), along with a couple of sauces, like chocolate, caramel, and a berry compote, and a nice array of toppings, both homemade and store-bought. Here's where you can get creative—you might try the caramelized miso peanuts (page 59) in place of the classic chopped peanuts, a bowl of chopped homemade toffee (page 72), crumbled pink peppercorn meringue (page 55), or a dollop of lime curd (page 74). Chopped-up brownies, crumbled cookies, and, of course, sprinkles go a long way with the kiddie set.

Arrange everything on one long table, preferably outside and lined with a plastic tablecloth for easy cleanup. Offer bowls and cones, provide a few scoops set in a container of warm water, and put the warmed sauces in squeeze bottles. Almost every element of an ice cream social can be made ahead; when your guests arrive, the only thing left to do is whip some cream and dig in!

VANILLA ICE CREAM

COFFEE ICE CREAM

SOUR CREAM ICE CREAM

CONCORD GRAPE SORBET

CHOCOLATE SORBET

TOFFEE CRUMBLE

DOUBLE CHOCOLATE SAUCE

CARAMEL SAUCE

BERRY COMPOTE

LIME CURD

WHIPPED CREAM

VANILLA ICE CREAM

MAKES 1 QUART

1¾ cups heavy cream

1¼ cups whole milk

1 vanilla bean, split lengthwise and seeds scraped

6 egg yolks

½ cup sugar

⅓ cup light corn syrup

¼ teaspoon kosher salt

2 teaspoons pure vanilla extract

SPECIAL EQUIPMENT: Ice cream maker; instant-read thermometer

1 In a medium saucepan, combine the cream, milk, and vanilla bean pod and seeds. Heat over medium-low heat until bubbles begin to form at the pan's edge. Remove from the heat.

2 Fill a large bowl with ice and water and set it nearby.

3 In a large bowl, whisk together the egg yolks, sugar, corn syrup, and salt until well combined. While whisking continuously, slowly add about 1 cup of the hot cream mixture to the egg yolks, then pour the egg mixture into the saucepan with the remaining cream. Heat over medium-low heat, stirring continuously, until the mixture thickens and coats the back of the spoon and registers 160°F on an instant-read thermometer.

4 Pour the mixture through a fine-mesh sieve into a clean bowl. Set the bowl in the ice water bath and let cool, stirring occasionally, until the custard is at room temperature. Stir in the vanilla extract, then remove the bowl from the ice water bath. Cover the custard with plastic wrap and refrigerate for at least 8 hours or up to overnight.

5 Transfer the chilled custard to an ice cream machine and freeze according to the manufacturer's instructions. Transfer to a freezer-proof container and freeze until solid, at least 2 hours.

For Caramelized Goat's-Milk Ice Cream: Substitute goat's milk for the cow's milk in the recipe, and substitute an equal amount of dark brown sugar for the granulated sugar. Follow the directions for vanilla ice cream.

For Lemon Ice Cream: Add the peel from ½ lemon (removed with a vegetable peeler) to the cream and milk and heat as described above. Before adding the hot cream to the egg mixture, remove the lemon peel. Follow the directions for cooking the custard in the vanilla ice cream recipe. When the custard is at room temperature, whisk in ⅓ cup fresh lemon juice and 1 teaspoon kosher salt.

COFFEE ICE CREAM

MAKES 1 QUART

2 cups heavy cream

1¼ cups whole milk

3½ ounces coarsely ground coffee (from about 1 cup whole beans)

6 egg yolks

½ cup sugar

⅓ cup light corn syrup

¼ teaspoon kosher salt

SPECIAL EQUIPMENT: Ice cream maker; instant-read thermometer

1 In a large bowl, combine the cream and milk. Whisk in the ground coffee, cover the bowl with plastic wrap, and refrigerate overnight. The next day, strain the liquid through a fine-mesh strainer into a large saucepan, pressing hard on the solids to extract as much liquid as possible.

2 Fill a large bowl with ice and water and set it nearby.

3 In a large bowl, whisk together the egg yolks, sugar, corn syrup, and salt until well combined. Heat the cream-milk mixture over medium-low heat until bubbles begin to form around the pan's edges. Remove from the heat. While whisking continuously, slowly add about 1 cup of the hot cream mixture to the egg yolks, then pour the egg mixture into the saucepan with the remaining cream. Heat over medium-low heat, stirring continuously, until the mixture thickens and coats the back of the spoon and registers 160°F on an instant-read thermometer.

4 Pour the mixture through a fine-mesh sieve into a clean bowl. Set the bowl in the ice water bath and let cool, stirring occasionally, until the custard is at room temperature. Remove the bowl from the ice water bath. Cover the custard with plastic wrap and refrigerate for at least 8 hours or up to overnight.

5 Transfer the chilled custard to an ice cream machine and freeze according to the manufacturer's instructions. Transfer to a freezer-proof container and freeze until solid, at least 2 hours.

SOUR CREAM ICE CREAM

MAKES 1 QUART

¾ cup whole milk

½ cup heavy cream

6 egg yolks

¾ cup sugar

½ teaspoon kosher salt

2 cups sour cream

Juice of ½ lemon

SPECIAL EQUIPMENT: Ice cream maker; instant-read thermometer

1 In a heavy saucepan, heat the milk and cream over medium-low heat until bubbles begin to form at the edges of the pan.

2 Fill a large bowl with ice and water and set it nearby.

3 In a large bowl, whisk together the egg yolks, sugar, and salt until well combined. While whisking continuously, gradually add the hot cream mixture to the egg yolks, then pour the egg mixture into the saucepan with the remaining cream. Heat over medium-low heat, stirring continuously, until the mixture thickens and coats the back of the spoon and registers 160°F on an instant-read thermometer.

4 Pour the mixture through a fine-mesh sieve into a clean bowl and whisk in the sour cream. Set the bowl in the ice water bath and let cool, stirring occasionally, until the custard is at room temperature. Whisk in the lemon juice, then remove the bowl from the ice water bath. Cover the custard with plastic wrap and refrigerate for at least 8 hours or up to overnight.

5 Transfer the chilled custard to an ice cream machine and freeze according to the manufacturer's instructions. Transfer to a freezer-proof container and freeze until solid, at least 2 hours.

CONCORD GRAPE SORBET

MAKES 1 QUART

1½ pounds Concord grapes, stemmed

⅔ cup Sorbet Syrup (recipe follows)

1 tablespoon fresh lime juice

SPECIAL EQUIPMENT: Ice cream maker; food mill

1 Fill a large bowl with ice and water. Set it nearby.

2 In a medium saucepan, combine the grapes and ¼ cup water. Bring to a boil, then reduce the heat, cover, and simmer for 5 minutes, until the grapes start to burst.

3 Process the grapes through a food mill set over a clean bowl. Measure the juice; you should have 1⅓ cups (save any surplus juice; it's great with sparkling water over ice). Set the juice-filled bowl in the ice water bath and let cool, stirring occasionally, until the juice is at room temperature. Remove the bowl from the ice water bath and stir in the sorbet syrup and lime juice. Transfer to the refrigerator and refrigerate until completely cold, about 2 hours.

4 Transfer the juice to an ice cream machine and freeze according to the manufacturer's instructions. Transfer to a freezer-proof container and freeze until solid, at least 2 hours.

Sorbet Syrup

MAKES ⅔ CUP

⅓ cup sugar

In a small saucepan, combine the sugar and ⅔ cup water and heat over high heat until the sugar has dissolved. Remove from the heat and let cool completely.

CHOCOLATE SORBET

MAKES 1 QUART

¼ cup light corn syrup

2 tablespoons sugar

8 ounces bittersweet chocolate (70% cacao), chopped

3 ounces milk chocolate, chopped

½ teaspoon kosher salt

SPECIAL EQUIPMENT: Ice cream maker

1 In a medium saucepan, bring 2 cups water to a boil over high heat, then remove from the heat and whisk in the corn syrup and sugar until the sugar has dissolved. Add the bittersweet and milk chocolates and the salt and whisk until smooth. Transfer to a bowl and let cool to room temperature, then cover the bowl with plastic wrap and refrigerate until very cold, at least 4 hours or up to overnight.

2 Transfer the chilled mixture to an ice cream machine and freeze according to the manufacturer's instructions. Transfer to a freezer-proof container and freeze until solid, at least 2 hours.

TOFFEE CRUMBLE

MAKES ABOUT 4 CUPS

2 cups sugar

1 cup light corn syrup

¼ teaspoon cream of tartar

2 cups slivered almonds, toasted

2 tablespoons unsalted butter

1 teaspoon baking soda

3 cups chopped bittersweet chocolate (70% cacao)

1 tablespoon unsalted butter

2 teaspoons flaky salt, such as Maldon

SPECIAL EQUIPMENT: Candy thermometer

1 Line a rimmed baking sheet with a silicone baking mat or parchment paper. If using parchment, spray with cooking spray or grease with butter.

2 In a heavy saucepan, combine the sugar, corn syrup, cream of tartar, and ½ cup water over medium heat. Cook, without stirring, until the caramel registers 290°F on a candy thermometer; the caramel will be a light amber color. Remove from the heat and stir in the almonds, butter, and baking soda—the mixture will bubble furiously. Immediately pour the mixture onto the prepared pan, tilting the pan so the toffee spreads into a thin, even layer. Let cool until hard.

3 Put the chopped chocolate in a medium metal bowl. Fill a medium saucepan halfway with water and bring to a boil, then turn off the heat and set the bowl of chocolate over the simmering water, making sure the bottom of the bowl does not touch the water. Add the butter and let stand, stirring occasionally, until the chocolate has completely melted. Remove the bowl of chocolate from the saucepan and let cool to 80°F. Pour the cooled chocolate over the toffee and, with an offset spatula, spread it into an even layer. Sprinkle with the flaky salt. Let cool completely, until the chocolate is solid, then break into pieces or finely chop. The toffee will keep in an airtight container at room temperature for up to 2 weeks.

DOUBLE CHOCOLATE SAUCE

MAKES ABOUT 3 CUPS

3 ounces semisweet chocolate (64% cacao), chopped

3 ounces unsweetened chocolate, chopped

1½ cups heavy cream

6 tablespoons sugar

3 tablespoons unsweetened cocoa powder

1½ tablespoons crème de cacao liqueur

¾ teaspoon pure vanilla extract

1 Put the chopped semisweet and unsweetened chocolate in a medium metal bowl and set the bowl over a saucepan of simmering water; make sure the bottom of the bowl does not touch the water. Let the chocolate melt, stirring occasionally, until smooth. Remove the bowl from the saucepan and set aside.

2 In a small saucepan, heat the cream and sugar over medium-low heat, whisking until the sugar has dissolved. Whisk in the cocoa powder, crème de cacao, and vanilla, then whisk in the melted chocolate. Cook until heated through. If using immediately, strain through a fine-mesh strainer into a plastic squeeze bottle and keep warm in a hot water bath. If not using immediately, strain through a fine-mesh strainer into a mason jar, let cool, then cover and refrigerate. The chocolate sauce will keep for up to 2 weeks. Reheat before using.

CARAMEL SAUCE

MAKES ABOUT 3 CUPS

2 cups sugar

1 cup heavy cream, warmed

4 tablespoons (½ stick) unsalted butter

1½ teaspoons fine sea salt

1 In a large heavy saucepan, combine the sugar and ½ cup water over medium heat. Cook, swirling the pan occasionally, until the mixture is a dark amber color. Slowly

pour in the warm cream. Be careful: the mixture will bubble furiously. When the bubbles subside, whisk in the butter and salt.

2 Strain the caramel through a fine-mesh strainer into a heatproof container and let cool for 30 minutes before using. The caramel will keep in an airtight container in the refrigerator for up to 2 weeks. Reheat gently over low heat before using.

BERRY COMPOTE

MAKES ABOUT 4 CUPS

4 cups mixed berries (strawberries, blueberries, blackberries, and raspberries)

¼ to ½ cup sugar

1½ teaspoons lemon zest

Juice of 1 lemon

Pinch of kosher salt

1 In a large bowl, combine the berries (if using strawberries, hull and halve or quarter them). Add ¼ cup of the sugar, the lemon zest, lemon juice, and salt and toss to combine. Taste the fruit and add additional sugar to taste (some berries are sweeter, others are more tart, so the amount of sugar you add will vary). Let stand at room temperature for 30 minutes.

2 The compote can be made a few hours ahead and refrigerated, though it will get juicier the longer it sits, so you may want to strain it before using.

LIME CURD

MAKES ABOUT 1 CUP

2 eggs

¾ cup sugar

6 tablespoons fresh lime juice

½ teaspoon powdered gelatin

6 tablespoons (¾ stick) unsalted butter

1 In a medium bowl, whisk together the eggs, sugar, and lime juice. Set the bowl over a saucepan of simmering water; make sure the bottom of the bowl does not touch the water. Cook, whisking, until the mixture just thickens (do not overcook or it will curdle). Remove the bowl from the saucepan, then sprinkle the gelatin over, whisking it into the hot mixture.

2 With an immersion blender, blend in the butter. Pass the mixture through a fine-mesh sieve into a clean bowl and cover with a sheet of plastic wrap, pressing it directly against the surface to prevent a skin from forming. Transfer to the refrigerator and refrigerate until thick and cold, at least 4 hours or up to 2 days.

WHIPPED CREAM

MAKES ABOUT 4 CUPS

2 cups cold heavy cream

¼ cup confectioners' sugar, sifted

½ teaspoon pure vanilla extract

In the bowl of a stand mixer fitted with the whisk attachment (or in a large bowl using a handheld mixer), beat the cream, confectioners' sugar, and vanilla together on high speed until the cream holds soft peaks. Serve immediately.

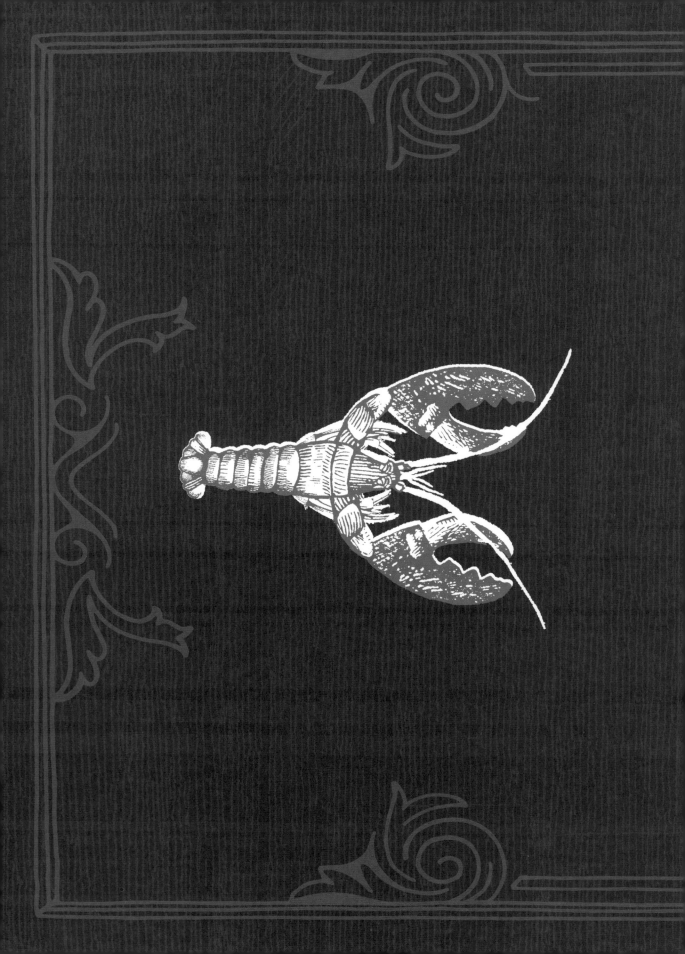

OCEAN

''Fish,'' he said softly, aloud,
''I'll stay with you until I am dead.''
—Ernest Hemingway, *The Old Man and the Sea*

When I was eight years old, I went digging for quahogs with my stepdad for the first time. We had gotten up early, packed a cooler, put the rusty clam rakes in the back of the Isuzu Trooper, deflated our tires to the perfect PSI for driving over the sand, and set out across the spit of sand that connects two inlet beaches on Smith Point, in Nantucket.

Within five minutes of walking out into the water, I sliced my foot open on a shell, cutting our trip short. I remember watching my blood create crimson clouds in the brackish shallows. Maybe this is how I was infected with a love for the ocean. Perhaps it was at this moment that the Atlantic entered my bloodstream. That's how I like to think it all happened, anyway.

The ocean has provided New England with sustenance for ages. The Atlantic, teeming with cod and shellfish, was one of the reasons the British colonized New England, and the seafood that colonists pulled from the cold waters sustained their settlements, both as a keystone of their diets and as a trade export. By the early 1800s, canneries dotted the entire eastern seaboard, packing the abundant runs of herring and sardines. By the 1840s, commercial fisheries specializing in lobster had opened in Maine; forty-five years later, that industry would catch 130 million pounds of the crustacean annually. Today, tourists still flood the New England coastline in summer with plans to eat piles of steamer clams, fried clam rolls, and boiled lobsters.

Growing up in a coastal community helped shape the person and the cook that I've become. I spent my summers on Nantucket Island as a young boy, staying at my grandmother's midcentury fishing shack in Siasconset—long before the island became known as the "Botox borough" it is today.

It was in Nantucket, its silver-shingled cottages as a backdrop, where I had my first experiences catching fish, angling for squid in the pitch-black night off the end of the pier, and watching my grandmother make beach plum jam.

Days off between prep sessions in the balmy back kitchens of seafood restaurants where I worked would be spent at Smith Point with my stepfather, heaving shiny lures into the rip, hoping for a mighty battle with a bluefish. If we were successful, at day's end we would pile buckets of the fish into the sandy trunk and head for home.

Today, overfishing and climate change have impacted our relationship with the ocean. Wild Atlantic salmon, once abundant, are scarce; silvery schools of herring that once choked waterways were on the brink of extinction in the 1970s, until a conservation effort restored the population. Atlantic cod, once a staple of the New England diet, is now in short supply.

It has become vitally important to be mindful not only of what species of fish we consume, but of how those species are fished. It's okay to ask questions of your fishmonger or at the seafood counter at the supermarket; sustainable seafood should be a priority for all of us.

These days, I don't get out fishing as much as I'd like. Instead, my phone chimes at four a.m.; it's a text from Matt Henderson of Wulf's Fish, a Boston outfit that connects New England fishermen with chefs. The text is a picture of a black tub of wild turbot on ice, with this message attached: "Real wild turbot! My halibut boat has never landed them before!! Gulf of Maine!" Matt's enthusiasm, and the quality of seafood that he sources from small commercial fishermen and -women throughout New England, eases the pain of not casting a rod myself.

The recipes in this chapter highlight the best of New England seafood, from lobster rolls (page 106) to mussels in a coconut-curry broth (page 117) to a stunning double-crusted seafood pie (page 123) and roasted oysters bathed with zabaglione (page 90). Desserts, too, take a cue from the ocean; you'll find recipes for delicate thumbprint cookies filled with beach plum jam (page 126) and a Meyer lemon ice (page 133) that is the ideal refresher after a day at the beach.

PEEKYTOE CRAB SALAD
WITH SCALLION PANCAKES

I first created a version of this recipe for the *New York Times* back in 2012 when they asked me to come up with a dish that reflected the seasonal nature of seafood in New England. I focused on a northern cold-water specialty, peekytoe crab (also known as mud or sand crab), with especially sweet, delicate meat.

These are basically little crab sandwiches. The pancakes, which are a lot like the ones you get at dim sum restaurants, should be about the size of a silver dollar; when you panfry them, they puff just enough to be split and stuffed with a crab salad bound with maple mayonnaise. These are a perfect small appetizer to pass around at a cocktail party: all components of the dish can be made ahead; assemble the bites when your friends and family walk in the door. | SERVES 6 AS A FIRST COURSE

FOR THE PANCAKES	FOR THE CRAB SALAD	
1½ cups warm water	1 pound peekytoe crabmeat (substitute Jonah crabmeat, if necessary)	Canola oil, for greasing the bowl and pan
2 (¼-ounce) packets active dry yeast (4½ teaspoons)	¼ cup Maple Mayonnaise (recipe follows)	Melted unsalted butter, for brushing
1½ teaspoons sugar	1 tablespoon thinly sliced fresh chives	
4 cups all-purpose flour, plus more for dusting	2 teaspoons fresh thyme leaves, coarsely chopped	
1 tablespoon kosher salt	Kosher salt and freshly ground black pepper	
1 tablespoon sesame oil		
1 tablespoon extra-virgin olive oil		
2 bunches scallions, light green and green parts only, thinly sliced		

Make the scallion pancakes: In a medium bowl, whisk together the warm water, yeast, and sugar. Let stand until foamy, 5 minutes. Transfer to the bowl of a stand mixer fitted with the dough hook attachment. With the mixer on low speed, gradually add the flour and salt, stopping the mixer occasionally and scraping down the sides of the bowl, until a soft, sticky dough forms. Drizzle in the sesame and olive oils, add the scallions, and mix until incorporated.

Turn the dough out onto a well-floured work surface and knead gently for a few minutes until smooth. Do not overwork the dough, as this will make the pancakes tough.

Lightly oil a bowl, set the dough in the bowl, and cover tightly with plastic wrap. Set the bowl in a warm place and let stand until it doubles in size, 40 minutes to 1 hour.

Make the crab salad: In a medium nonreactive bowl, combine the crabmeat, mayonnaise, chives, and thyme and season to taste with salt and pepper. Refrigerate while you prepare the pancakes.

Return the dough to a floured work surface and very gently roll it with a floured rolling pin to a thickness of ½ inch. With a 3-inch round cutter, stamp out as many pancakes as you can. Gather and reroll the scraps, adding flour if the dough is sticky, and stamp out more pancakes.

Heat a large cast-iron skillet or griddle over medium heat. Add a film of canola oil to the pan and panfry the pancakes in batches, turning once, until golden brown, puffed, and cooked through, about 2½ minutes total. Transfer to a rimmed baking sheet or a plate and brush with some of the melted butter; keep warm while you fry the remaining pancakes. Repeat with the remaining pancakes, adding more canola oil to the pan as necessary.

To serve, cut each pancake in half and fill with some of the crab salad. Serve immediately.

MAPLE MAYONNAISE
MAKES ABOUT ½ CUP

1 egg yolk
½ teaspoon whole-grain mustard
½ teaspoon fresh lemon juice
Dash of hot sauce
½ cup blended oil (or a 50/50 mix extra-virgin olive oil and canola oil)
2 tablespoons pure maple syrup
1 tablespoon warm water, plus more as needed
Kosher salt and freshly ground black pepper

In a small bowl, combine the egg yolk, mustard, lemon juice, and hot sauce. While whisking continuously, add the oil to the egg yolk mixture, drop by drop at first, until the mixture begins to thicken and emulsify. Add the remaining oil in a slow, steady stream (do not add the oil too quickly, or the mayonnaise won't emulsify and thicken). When all the oil has been added and the mayonnaise is thick, whisk in the maple syrup and warm water. The mayonnaise should look creamy; add another tablespoon of water if necessary. Season to taste with salt and pepper. Cover with plastic wrap and refrigerate until ready to use. The mayonnaise will keep in the refrigerator for up to 4 days.

BLUEFISH PÂTÉ
WITH LEMON PICKLE RELISH AND GARLIC CROSTINI

Bluefish is majorly underrated; like sardines and mackerel, it has oily flesh and a strong flavor, but it's precisely these characteristics that make it a good choice for so many treatments, including grilling, pickling, and smoking. Whenever my stepdad and I had a successful fishing trip, we'd always smoke some of our catch, which my mom would then use to make her now famous bluefish pâté. I serve it here on garlicky toasts garnished with some lemon pickle relish; I love how the acid from the relish contrasts with the creamy, smoky pâté. If you want to keep it simple, trust me when I tell you this stuff is just fine served unadorned, on a crusty baguette or cracker. | **SERVES 6 AS A SNACK**

FOR THE PÂTÉ

½ pound boneless, skinless smoked bluefish or mackerel

1 (8-ounce) package cream cheese, at room temperature

½ medium red onion, minced

¼ cup finely sliced fresh chives, plus more for garnish

1 tablespoon Worcestershire sauce

1 tablespoon fresh lemon juice

1 tablespoon finely chopped fresh flat-leaf parsley

2 teaspoons finely chopped fresh dill

5 dashes of hot sauce

Kosher salt and freshly ground black pepper

FOR THE LEMON PICKLE RELISH

1 preserved lemon, homemade (page 240) or store-bought

1 tablespoon sugar

1 tablespoon extra-virgin olive oil

1 tablespoon finely sliced fresh chives

1 baguette, cut on an angle into ¼-inch-thick slices

2 tablespoons extra-virgin olive oil

Kosher salt and freshly ground black pepper

1 garlic clove

Preheat the oven to 300°F.

Make the pâté: In a nonreactive medium bowl, combine the bluefish, cream cheese, onion, chives, Worcestershire, lemon juice, parsley, dill, and hot sauce. Using a rubber spatula, fold the mixture together until well combined. Season to taste with salt and pepper. Transfer to a bowl; the pâté will keep, covered, in the refrigerator for up to 3 days.

Make the lemon pickle relish: Rinse the preserved lemon well in cold water, remove and discard the pulp, and slice the lemon rind into very thin strips.

In a small saucepan, combine the sliced lemon rind, sugar, and ½ cup water. Bring to a simmer over medium-low heat, then reduce the heat to low and simmer gently until the syrup has thickened and almost all the liquid has evaporated, about

6 minutes. Remove from the heat and use a slotted spoon to transfer the lemon strips to a small bowl to cool. Once cool, finely chop and return to the bowl. Add the olive oil and chives and stir to combine.

Arrange the bread on a baking sheet and drizzle with the olive oil. Season the crostini with salt and pepper.

Bake the crostini for 10 minutes, rotating the baking sheet halfway through. The crostini should not brown, but they should be crisp. Remove from the oven and let cool to room temperature. Rub each slice of bread with the garlic clove. (The intent here is to merely perfume the crostini, not make them overwhelmingly garlicky, so swipe each piece just once.)

To serve, spread the bluefish pâté on the crostini and garnish with the lemon pickle relish and chives.

SAUTÉED SUMMER FLOUNDER
WITH TOMATO VIERGE

In the Atlantic, there is winter flounder and summer flounder. Summer flounder is actually fluke, just called by a different name. Winter flounder is, in fact, true flounder. Completely confused? Rest assured, you can use any mild, flaky fish for this recipe. Cod, bass, or halibut could all be substituted for the flounder. This is a light, refreshing, and healthy dish that highlights summer ingredients.

Tomato vierge is a classic French sauce typically made from olive oil, lemon juice, chopped tomato, and, often, chopped basil. This version swaps cherry tomatoes for the chopped tomatoes, and omits the basil in favor of crushed coriander seeds. Serve with grilled zucchini. | **SERVES 6 AS A FIRST COURSE**

FOR THE TOMATO VIERGE

1 pint mixed-color cherry tomatoes, halved

1 teaspoon sugar

½ teaspoon coriander seeds, toasted and ground

½ cup extra-virgin olive oil

2 tablespoons fresh lemon juice

1 tablespoon balsamic vinegar

Flaky salt, such as Maldon

8 fresh basil leaves, coarsely torn, for garnish

FOR THE FISH

2 tablespoons canola oil

6 skin-on flounder fillets (cod or halibut can be substituted), about 4 to 6 ounces each

Kosher salt and freshly ground white pepper

4 tablespoons (½ stick) cold unsalted butter, cubed

Make the tomato vierge: Preheat the oven to 400°F.

Put the cherry tomatoes in a baking dish and sprinkle with the sugar and coriander. Bake just until the tomatoes begin to soften and wilt, about 8 minutes. Remove from the oven and add the olive oil, lemon juice, and balsamic vinegar. Mix well and season with flaky salt. Set aside.

Make the fish: In a large nonstick skillet, heat 1 tablespoon of the canola oil over medium-high heat. Season the fillets on both sides with salt and white pepper, then add half the fillets to the pan, flesh-side down. Sear the fish until golden brown, about 3 minutes, then carefully flip the fillets and add 2 tablespoons of the butter to the pan.

Use a spoon to baste the fish with the butter as it melts. Cook until the fish is no longer opaque and is golden brown on the second side, about 3 minutes. Use a fish spatula to transfer the fillets to a paper towel–lined plate. Wipe the pan clean, then repeat with the remaining fish, olive oil, and butter.

Place a fillet onto each of six plates. Stir the basil into the tomato vierge and spoon some over each piece of fish. Serve with grilled zucchini, if you'd like.

ROASTED OYSTERS
WITH PARMIGIANO-REGGIANO RIND ZABAGLIONE

As a chef, I have some core beliefs: Use the best ingredients possible. Create dishes that reflect the seasons. Support local producers and growers. Waste nothing. Every single piece of food has a use. We ferment melon rinds into kimchi, dehydrate leek tops and transform them into a spice blend, save woody herb stems to use as a place to rest meats after they come off the grill. So, while others might view cheese rinds as garbage, I see possibility. Sometimes they end up in a broth to pour over pasta. Sometimes they're grated and added to whipped potatoes. Here you take leftover Parmigiano-Reggiano rinds and use them in a savory zabaglione to spoon over roasted oysters. These bites pair beautifully with Champagne; they'd be an elegant hors d'oeuvre for a New Year's Eve celebration. | **SERVES 6 AS AN HORS D'OEUVRE OR FIRST COURSE**

18 oysters, scrubbed well	3 tablespoons dry white wine, such as Sauvignon Blanc or Chenin Blanc	½ cup finely grated Parmigiano-Reggiano rind, grated with a rasp-style grater
FOR THE ZABAGLIONE	Kosher salt and freshly ground black pepper	1 tablespoon finely chopped fresh chives
¼ cup heavy cream		
2 egg yolks		

Preheat the oven to 400°F. (Alternatively, the oysters can be roasted on a gas or charcoal grill; preheat the grill for direct, high-heat grilling.)

If using the oven, line a rimmed baking sheet with aluminum foil, scrunching up the foil into irregular mounds to help hold the oysters in place. Place the oysters on the foil, cup-side down, arranging them so they are as flat as possible so none of their liquor spills out when the shells open. (If using the grill, place the oysters directly on the grates once the grill is up to temperature.) Roast the oysters in their shells until the shells have begun to open and you can see some steam escaping, about 8 minutes.

While the oysters roast, make the zabaglione: In a medium bowl, whisk the cream until it holds soft peaks. Set aside.

Bring 2 inches of water to a simmer in a large saucepan. In a large nonreactive bowl, whisk together the egg yolks and wine. Season with salt and pepper. Set the bowl over the simmering water; make sure the bottom of the bowl is not touching the water. Cook, whisking continuously, until the mixture has thickened and gained volume, about 4 minutes.

Remove the bowl from the heat. Whisk vigorously for another minute, then gently whisk in the grated Parmigiano-Reggiano rind. Season with salt and pepper.

Gently whisk in one-third of the whipped cream to lighten the mixture, then add the remaining cream, whisking very gently to incorporate without overworking the sauce.

Remove the oysters from the oven. Preheat the broiler. Using an oyster knife, carefully remove and discard the top shells of each oyster, separating the meat from the shell and taking care not to spill the liquid in the bottom shell. Return the oysters (still in the bottom shell) to the baking sheet and spoon some zabaglione over each. Place under the broiler and broil just until the zabaglione has a hint of color, 1 to 2 minutes. Carefully transfer to a serving platter and garnish with the chives. Serve immediately.

GRILLED SQUID
WITH YOGURT GREEN GODDESS AND AVOCADO

Point Judith, Rhode Island, is known for the quantity and quality of the squid found in the nearby waters, so it's always a treat to get squid from the fishermen in this area. In fact, the "secret" to this simple recipe, if there is one, is that it should only be made with pristine, freshly caught squid.

The toothsome, chargrilled squid is complemented by a Green Goddess dressing and enhanced by some chunks of luscious, ripe avocado—not a New England ingredient, sure, but a damn tasty addition to this dish.

This is a great first course to bust out for a summer dinner party—it can be plated family-style and passed around so your dinner guests can help themselves. Note that you need to marinate the squid for a few hours before grilling, and you can make the dressing up to a few days in advance. | **SERVES 6 AS A FIRST COURSE**

FOR THE SQUID

¼ cup olive oil, plus more for the grill

¼ cup dry white wine

6 garlic cloves, minced

1 tablespoon fresh oregano, coarsely chopped

1 teaspoon red pepper flakes

1 teaspoon sweet Spanish paprika

½ teaspoon kosher salt

2 pounds whole squid, cleaned, long tentacles trimmed if desired

FOR THE GREEN GODDESS DRESSING

½ cup mayonnaise

⅓ cup buttermilk

¼ cup chopped fresh chives

¼ cup coarsely chopped fresh flat-leaf parsley

1 tablespoon chopped fresh tarragon

1 tablespoon fresh lemon juice

2 oil-packed anchovy fillets, drained and chopped

1 garlic clove, chopped

Kosher salt and freshly ground black pepper

1 avocado, halved, pitted, and cut into thick slices

Extra-virgin olive oil, for drizzling

2 French breakfast radishes, greens removed and julienned, for garnish

1 teaspoon poppy seeds, for garnish

Make the squid: In a large bowl, whisk together the olive oil, wine, garlic, oregano, red pepper flakes, paprika, and salt. Add the squid, toss to coat, then cover and marinate in the refrigerator for 3 to 4 hours.

While the squid marinates, make the Green Goddess dressing: In a food processor, combine the mayonnaise, buttermilk, chives, parsley, tarragon, lemon juice, anchovy fillets, and garlic. Process until smooth, then transfer to a bowl and season with salt and black pepper. Cover and refrigerate until ready to use; the dressing will keep, refrigerated, for a few days.

Prepare a charcoal or gas grill for direct, high-heat grilling. Lightly oil a perforated grill pan or a cast-iron grill griddle and set it on the grill to preheat.

Remove the squid from the marinade and place on the preheated rack or griddle. Grill for 4 minutes, turning once, or until the squid are almost opaque all the way through and have crisped around the ends and tentacles. Do not overcook, or the squid will become rubbery, but don't undercook it, either—it should be cooked through, not just charred on the exterior and warm inside.

Smear the dressing onto a large platter and top with the grilled squid. Arrange the pieces of avocado alongside. Drizzle with a ribbon of olive oil, garnish with radishes and a sprinkle of poppy seeds, and season with salt. Serve immediately.

BEER-STEAMED LITTLENECK CLAMS WITH CHORIZO VERDE

Pork and clams go together so well. The Portuguese are known for dishes combining the two; *porco à alentejana*, a recipe for braised pork and clams, is among the most celebrated.

New England has a large Portuguese population centered around the coastal towns of New Bedford and Fall River, and there are plenty of restaurants where you can find *alentejana*, as well as shops selling salt cod, chorizo, and other essential Portuguese ingredients. Here, the pork takes the form of chorizo verde, a robustly spiced homemade fresh sausage that flavors the beer in which the clams are steamed. If you're nervous about making sausage, take heart: the chorizo verde is uncased, so it's no more difficult to make than meat loaf. This recipe makes more sausage than you will need for this recipe; freeze the rest for another use (it's great with eggs in a breakfast burrito). The addition of greens makes this a complete meal. If you don't want to grind the meat yourself, purchase coarsely ground fatty pork from your butcher; you'll need 2¾ pounds. | SERVES 6 AS A MAIN COURSE

FOR THE CHORIZO

3 poblano peppers

2 pounds lean pork shoulder, cut into 4 x ½-inch strips

¾ pound pork fatback, cut into large dice

6 tablespoons apple cider vinegar

4 tomatillos, husked, rinsed well, and coarsely chopped

½ cup fresh cilantro leaves, coarsely chopped

2 tablespoons white sesame seeds, toasted

2 tablespoons raw pumpkin seeds, toasted

2 serrano chiles, halved, seeded, and coarsely chopped

3 canned chipotles in adobo, coarsely chopped

6 garlic cloves, minced

1 tablespoon dark brown sugar

1 tablespoon finely chopped fresh oregano

1 teaspoon cayenne pepper

1 tablespoon kosher salt

1 teaspoon freshly ground black pepper

FOR THE CLAMS

3 tablespoons canola oil

4 garlic cloves, thinly sliced

4 pounds littleneck clams, cleaned well

2 (12-ounce) bottles lager or light ale (such as Narragansett or Pacifico)

1 cup chicken stock

2 pounds fresh mustard greens or spinach, coarsely chopped

2 tablespoons Chinese black vinegar or balsamic vinegar (see Note)

Kosher salt and freshly ground black pepper

SPECIAL EQUIPMENT: Meat grinder

CONTINUED

Make the chorizo: If you have a gas stove, set the poblanos directly on the burner and char them, turning occasionally, until blackened on all sides. (Alternatively, place the poblanos on a baking sheet and blacken under the broiler.) Transfer to a paper or plastic bag, seal the bag, and let the peppers steam for 10 minutes. Peel and seed the poblanos. Set aside.

Put the pork shoulder and fatback on a rimmed baking sheet and place it in the freezer for 15 minutes.

In a food processor, combine the poblanos, apple cider vinegar, tomatillos, cilantro, sesame seeds, pumpkin seeds, serranos, chipotles, garlic, brown sugar, oregano, cayenne, salt, and black pepper. Process until the mixture is well combined and smooth; it should have the consistency of a very thick salsa. Transfer to a saucepan and cook over medium heat, stirring, until most of the liquid has evaporated and the mixture has the consistency of a thick paste. Transfer to a bowl and let cool to room temperature, then place in the freezer while you grind the meat.

Assemble a meat grinder and fit it with a ⅜-inch plate. Set a large bowl beneath the grinder. Grind the chilled pork shoulder and fatback directly into the bowl. Transfer the ground meat to the bowl of a stand mixer fitted with the paddle attachment. Mix on low speed until a film begins to form on the bowl, then add the chilled chile pepper mixture and mix until well incorporated.

Pinch off a small amount of meat (about the size of a quarter), form it into a patty, and cook it in a dry pan until cooked through but not browned. Taste and adjust the seasoning of the sausage, cooking additional test patties as needed. Once the sausage is seasoned to your liking, transfer the mixture to the refrigerator. The sausage can be made up

to a day ahead; press a piece of parchment paper directly onto the surface of the meat, then cover the bowl with plastic wrap. The sausage can also be transferred to plastic freezer storage bags and frozen for up to 1 month. Thaw completely in the refrigerator before using.

Make the clams: In a large pot or Dutch oven, heat the canola oil over medium-high heat. Once hot, add 1 pound of the sausage (save the rest for another use; it's great with eggs or beans, or with cheese in a quesadilla, or it can be used for another batch of clams) and stir with a wooden spoon, breaking up any large chunks, until the sausage is almost completely cooked through, 4 to 5 minutes. Add the garlic and clams and stir to combine.

Pour in the beer and bring to a boil. Add the stock, reduce the heat to low, cover, and cook the clams until they open, about 5 minutes.

When all the clams have opened (discard any that do not open), add the greens to the pot. Cook, stirring, until the greens wilt, about 5 minutes.

With a slotted spoon, portion about ten clams into each of six bowls, leaving the pot liquor, greens, and sausage in the pot. Once you have plated the clams, ladle some of the pot liquor, greens, and sausage into each bowl.

Sprinkle each serving with a teaspoon of black vinegar and serve immediately, while the bowls are still steaming, with an empty bowl set in the center of the table to collect the clamshells.

NOTE: Chinese black vinegar, also called Chinkiang vinegar, is a dark vinegar from China's Jiangsu province. It's made from glutinous rice and malt. It's available at Asian grocery stores; if you can't find it, use balsamic vinegar instead.

EAST COAST CLAMOLOGY 101

Littleneck, count neck, top neck, steamer, mahogany . . . the shellfish industry is filled with confusing terms for clams, some of which refer to the variety, some to the size of the clam, and some even to the cooking method. To make it easier to understand, here's a little clamology to help you navigate these delicious bivalves.

On the East Coast, you are most likely to find hard-shell Atlantic clams. These are also known locally as quahogs (KOH-hogs), which is the clam typically featured in clam chowder, clam cakes, fried clams, and linguine with clam sauce. Quahogs are categorized by size:

Littlenecks: 10 to 12 clams per pound

Middle necks: 8 to 10 clams per pound

Top necks: 5 to 7 clams per pound

Cherrystones: 3 clams per pound on average

Chowders: 1 to 2 clams per pound (these are huge!)

Small-size quahogs, including littlenecks, middle necks, and top necks, are great for any dish that requires whole clams, such as pastas, soups, or stews, and can also be eaten raw.

Larger-size quahogs, including cherrystones and chowders, are best when they are chopped or ground prior to using. The meat tends to be a little tougher, so cutting the protein structure, which helps tenderize the meat, is a good move. These big boys are best for chowders, clam cakes, and ragouts.

Mahogany clams are another variety of Atlantic hard-shelled clam. These beauties have a more pronounced flavor; they're a little brinier, with a robust meatiness. You can easily substitute mahogany clams for any quahog of the same size. On account of their stronger flavor, I love using them in pan-roasted dishes. Along with some bacon, tomato, saffron, strong herbs, garlic, or other highly flavored ingredients, these clams will shine.

Aptly named for their elongated, straight-razor shape, razor clams are very briny and delicious. They tend to be a little tougher, but if prepared properly, they can be silky smooth and creamy when raw, or toothsome and tender when cooked. I prefer to either tenderize them with a Jaccard (a tool with tiny sharp blades that move up and down), chop, and then dress the raw meat with a lime vinaigrette; or steam the razor clams, remove the meat from the shells and chop it, and then sauté the meat with garlic and toss it with pasta (see Northern Carbonara, page 118).

Soft-shell steamer clams are sweet, creamy, and tender, with an elongated neck (also called a siphon) that peeks out from the shell and allows the clam to feed. Because of this siphon, the thin, brittle shells of steamer clams never fully close, which is the primary distinction between soft-shell and hard-shell varieties of clams. Eating steamers is a New England rite of passage; I cannot count the number of times I have sat on the back porch in summertime with a huge bucket of these freshly steamed beauties. Try it yourself: don't forget a bowl of drawn butter, lemon wedges, and some cold beer to drink alongside.

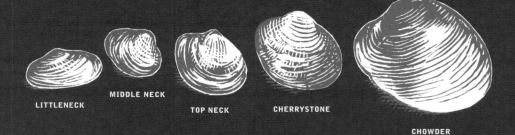

LITTLENECK MIDDLE NECK TOP NECK CHERRYSTONE CHOWDER

NEW ENGLAND CLAM ROLL
WITH TARTAR SAUCE

After a day spent on one of the beaches on Massachusetts's North Shore, it's a family ritual to make a detour to my favorite seafood spot, Woodman's (see page 104). The golden, crisp, whole-belly clams (never strips!) are piled so high that you can barely see the roll beneath, sided by a mammoth pile of French fries. Once or twice a year, on a hot summer day, this meal is worth the splurge. Note that the clams need to soak overnight before frying. | MAKES 6

---

3 pounds shucked whole-belly clams

3 cups buttermilk

6 cups canola oil, for frying

3 cups fine cornmeal

2 cups all-purpose flour

1½ cups grated Parmigiano-Reggiano cheese

1 tablespoon garlic powder

1 tablespoon sweet Spanish paprika

Kosher salt and freshly ground black pepper

6 split-top Potato Rolls (recipe follows) or hot dog buns

6 tablespoons (¾ stick) unsalted butter, melted

6 tablespoons tartar sauce, homemade (recipe follows) or store-bought

2 cups shredded iceberg lettuce

1 lemon, cut into wedges, seeds removed

SPECIAL EQUIPMENT: Deep-fry thermometer

Place the clam bellies in a nonreactive bowl, add the buttermilk, cover, and soak in the refrigerator for at least 8 hours or overnight.

Pour the oil into a very large, deep, straight-sided pot (a stockpot works well) and heat over high heat until it registers 365°F on a deep-fry thermometer. Line a rimmed baking sheet with paper towels and set it nearby.

In a large bowl, combine the cornmeal, flour, Parmigiano-Reggiano cheese, garlic powder, and paprika. Using a slotted spoon, transfer the clam bellies from the buttermilk mixture (discard the buttermilk) to the flour mixture and toss to coat.

When the oil is at temperature, transfer a third of the clams to the oil and fry until golden brown, 2 to 3 minutes. With a spider or slotted spoon, transfer the clams to the prepared baking sheet and season immediately with salt and pepper. Fry the remaining clams in two batches, letting the oil come to temperature between each batch.

Heat a large skillet or griddle over medium heat. Brush the potato rolls on both sides with the melted butter and place them butter-side down in the pan. Toast the rolls until golden brown on one side, about 3 minutes, then flip and toast on the second side. Transfer the rolls to plates. Spread about 1 tablespoon of the tartar sauce on each roll, stuff each with some of the lettuce, and pile high with clams. Serve immediately with the lemon wedges alongside.

POTATO ROLLS

MAKES 12

1 large Yukon Gold potato, peeled and cut into quarters
¼ cup warm water
1 (¼-ounce) packet active dry yeast (2¼ teaspoons)
4 tablespoons (½ stick) unsalted butter, at room temperature, plus more for greasing
¼ cup sugar
1½ teaspoons kosher salt
1 cup warm milk
2 eggs
4 egg yolks
4½ to 5 cups all-purpose flour, plus more as needed
Canola oil, for the bowl
Flaky salt, such as Maldon, for sprinkling

Place the potato in a medium saucepan and add cold water to cover. Bring to a boil, then reduce the heat so the water is simmering and simmer until the potato pieces are tender, about 15 minutes. Drain and mash with a potato masher. Measure out ½ cup of the mashed potato and set aside.

Pour the warm water into a large bowl and sprinkle the yeast over it. Let stand until the yeast is foamy, about 5 minutes.

In a separate bowl, stir together the ½ cup mashed potato, butter, sugar, and kosher salt. Add the yeast mixture, milk, eggs, and 2 of the egg yolks and stir to combine. Stir in 2 cups of the flour until incorporated, then add 2½ to 3 cups of the remaining flour, stirring until a soft dough forms.

Turn the dough out onto a lightly floured surface and knead until smooth and elastic, about 7 minutes, adding additional flour if the dough is sticky. Place the dough in a lightly oiled bowl, turning to coat all sides of the dough with oil. Cover the bowl with plastic wrap and set in a warm place until the dough has doubled in size, about 1 hour.

Lightly grease a rimmed baking sheet with butter and set nearby.

Punch the dough down, turn out onto a lightly floured work surface, and use a bench scraper or knife to portion the dough into twelve 4-ounce pieces. To shape, gently press each piece of dough into a 5 x 3-inch rectangle. Orient the rectangle so the long side is facing you, then roll the dough toward you to create a seamless log. Transfer to the prepared baking sheet, arranging the rolls crosswise into two rows of six rolls, leaving 1 inch of space between each roll. When all the dough has been formed, cover the rolls with a sheet of plastic wrap greased with butter and let stand in a warm place until almost doubled in size, about 1 hour.

Preheat the oven to 400°F.

In a small bowl, whisk together the remaining 2 egg yolks and 2 tablespoons water until combined. Brush each roll lightly with the egg wash and sprinkle with flaky salt. Transfer to the oven and bake for 15 minutes, then rotate the pan and bake for 10 to 15 minutes more, until golden brown. The rolls will grow together as they bake, which is normal. Let cool, then gently pull the rolls apart and slice each roll directly down the middle to create a "split" top-loading bun.

TARTAR SAUCE

MAKES 1 CUP

1 cup mayonnaise, preferably Hellmann's or Best Foods
2 tablespoons pickle relish
½ red onion, minced
1 tablespoon fresh lemon juice
Kosher salt and freshly ground black pepper

In a small bowl, whisk together the mayonnaise, pickle relish, onion, and lemon juice. Season to taste with salt and pepper. Refrigerate for at least 1 hour before serving. Tartar sauce will keep in an airtight container in the refrigerator for up to 3 weeks.

NEW ENGLAND'S BEST CLAM SHACKS

Clam shacks are the hallmark of New England summers. When the weather begins to warm, shacks from Cape Cod all the way up the coast of Maine come out of hibernation to greet tourists and locals alike who understand that pints of fried clams are as essential to the season as are dips into the ice-cold Atlantic. Dug from the flats during low tide using a simple, oversize, three-pronged iron fork, the humble clam is the very heart and soul and the defining identity of communities throughout coastal New England. Regardless of whether the natives are harvesting clams for their supper or selling them to others, nearly everyone living in these coastal communities is somehow influenced by this historic industry.

This is by no means an exhaustive list of the best shacks in New England, but includes all my favorites, pulled from over forty years of intensive summer research. Get your Wet-Naps ready and hit the road.

MAINE
The Clam Shack, Kennebunkport
Sitting directly above the Kennebunk River, this humble wood-shingled shack serves proper lobster rolls, hulking slabs of fried dough sprinkled with powdered sugar, freshly squeezed lemonade, and, of course, its namesake: fried clams, clam strips, and clam cakes. Everything is packaged to go on paper plates, so you can take your order across the street to watch the boats come and go from the boardwalk. Originally opened in 1968, with a lease signed over a handshake, this place is timeless.

Red's Eats, Wiscasset
Located on the shoulder of the tidal Sheepscot River, Red's Eats—part honky-tonk, part mecca, and 100 percent pure New England original—has been in operation for over eighty years. Red's prides itself on its lobster roll (made with the meat from a whole lobster), but it is the clams that keep me coming back. A brimming pint of fried clams, coated in a crispy, thin batter, is served with a side of French fries and coleslaw, and is one of my favorite summer lunches. Don't fear the ever-present line—it moves quickly.

NEW HAMPSHIRE
Ceal's Clam Stand, Seabrook
Ceal's may not have a website, but they've got a reputation—they've been serving guests since 1948. The enormous portions of fried clams are handed over in a paper bag, which quickly becomes spotted with grease. Hampton Beach State Park is just across the bridge, so my recommendation is to head there with your loot, park on the shore, and people-watch while you dig into the exceptional sweet, plump mollusks, fried to a perfect golden brown. Don't sleep on the onion strings, either.

MASSACHUSETTS
Woodman's of Essex, Essex
With its claim to have invented the fried clam, there is no need to visit any other clam shack in my home state. Woodman's founder, Lawrence "Chubby" Woodman, introduced his clams—hand-shucked, coated with cornmeal, and deep-fried in a kettle—during the Fourth of July parade in Essex in the summer of 1916. The move here is an order of the "Chubby's Original" fried clams, along with a cup of clam chowder, a few ears of corn, and some coleslaw, which is presented on a cafeteria tray. Seat yourself outside at a community picnic table. Woodman's is open year-round, but summer is the time to go, particularly after a day at the beach. Pro tip: There is no liquor license here, so if you need some beer with those clams, you better pour some into your thermos. Tell them I said it was okay.

RHODE ISLAND
Evelyn's Drive-In, Tiverton
Alongside a tidal pond on the drive to Tiverton and Little Compton, you'll spot the red-and-white building with the crushed shell parking lot. Pull in, step up, and order with confidence. After all, they've been perfecting the art of the fried clam at Evelyn's for

close to sixty years. The service isn't much—the veteran waitstaff will get to you when they can (or feel like it), but no matter. It's the whole-belly clam plate that makes it all worth it. And the clam cakes. Take your lunch out to one of the covered picnic tables overlooking the harbor and Nanaquaket Pond. If you're lucky enough to come at dusk, you can catch the sunset while eating your bulging basket of glistening, golden clams.

Aunt Carrie's, Narragansett

Since 1920, the Cooper family has been in charge of these parts, perfecting a simple menu of seasonal specialties. Stuffies (baked stuffed clams) are a Rhody standby and specialty here, as well as flounder fresh from nearby waters. But I go for the clam cakes, a variation of Aunt Carrie's original corn fritter recipe, the fried clam plate, and an icy lemonade. Winner of many awards, including a prestigious James Beard Foundation American Classic award, Aunt Carrie's is known as the state's finest seafood joint.

CONNECTICUT
Johnny Ad's, Old Saybrook

"The Little Seafood Restaurant with the Big Ocean Taste" is the motto at Johnny Ad's, and it's a fitting one. While my two sons may prefer the jumbo hot dogs here, it's only because they haven't learned to appreciate the almighty clam . . . yet. But I've got my order down: A clam roll, please. Anchored with creamy slaw and crinkle-cut fries, this is the only place I go for clams in Connecticut. The fried calamari isn't half bad, either—get it "local style" with a side of marinara if you're feeling frisky. Get your order to go and drive a few minutes down the coast to Plum Bank Marsh, where you can sit and take in the views.

CLASSIC LOBSTER ROLLS

Plenty of visitors make summertime pilgrimages to the New England coast just to eat as many lobster rolls as they can, and with good reason—super-fresh lobster salad, stuffed into a soft, buttery roll, is one of the greatest things to eat, period. Cooking lobster at home is not difficult, though cracking the shells and extracting the meat is sort of a project. If you're not up for it, you can purchase shelled lobster meat. It's very expensive, but it saves you a lot of work. This is the lobster roll of my dreams: ice-cold meat, combined with mayonnaise, celery, and chives, piled onto a potato roll with some shredded iceberg lettuce for crunch. | **MAKES 6**

6 (1- to 1¼-pound) live lobsters (or 1¼ pounds cooked, picked lobster meat)	½ cup finely diced celery	Kosher salt and freshly ground black pepper
½ cup plus 2 tablespoons mayonnaise, preferably Hellmann's	2 tablespoons fresh lemon juice	6 split-top Potato Rolls (page 102) or hot dog buns
2 tablespoons tobiko roe (see Note)	1 tablespoon finely sliced fresh chives	6 tablespoons (¾ stick) unsalted butter, melted
	Pinch of cayenne pepper	2 cups shredded iceberg lettuce

If using live lobsters, fill a large bowl with ice and water and set it nearby. Bring a large pot of salted water to a boil. When the water is boiling, add the lobsters and cook until they turn bright red, about 10 minutes. With tongs, remove the lobsters from the boiling water and transfer to the ice water bath, adding more ice as necessary. Let stand in the ice bath until cool, then transfer to a rimmed baking sheet.

Twist the lobster tails and claws off the bodies and remove the meat from the shells. Discard the shells (or save for stock). Remove and discard the vein in the center of each lobster tail. Chop the lobster meat into ½-inch pieces and pat dry with paper towels, then transfer to a strainer set over a bowl and refrigerate until very cold, about 1 hour.

In a large bowl, gently fold together the lobster meat, mayonnaise, tobiko, celery, lemon juice, chives, and cayenne. Season to taste with salt and black pepper.

Heat a large skillet or griddle over medium heat. Brush the potato rolls on both sides with the melted butter and place butter-side down in the pan. Toast the rolls until golden brown on one side, about 3 minutes, then flip and toast on the second side, about 3 minutes more. Transfer the rolls to plates, fill them with the shredded lettuce and the chilled lobster salad, and serve immediately.

NOTE: Tobiko roe, bright orange eggs sourced from flying fish, is inexpensive and can be purchased from any seafood shop or special ordered at your supermarket's seafood counter.

THE "BIG ONE'S" GRILLED BLUEFISH

This recipe has been handed down through the generations of my family. I remember my grandfather making this dish when I was young, and later my father, and now I carry on the tradition, hoping that someday my boys will make it, too. Though I'm not afraid to mess with tradition, when it comes to this dish, I stick to the family recipe.

For this dead-simple preparation, only Hellmann's mayonnaise will do (for you West Coasters, use Best Foods brand). The mayonnaise gets smeared on a fresh bluefish, which is then sprinkled with gin, topped with lemon slices, and grilled. That's it. When the fish comes off the grill, serve it alongside a cucumber or green salad, some sweet summer corn, and, of course, a gin and tonic. Or two. | **SERVES 6 TO 8 AS A MAIN COURSE**

1 tablespoon canola oil, for the foil 1 whole skin-on side of bluefish (about 4 pounds), scaled ½ cup Hellmann's or Best Foods mayonnaise	¼ cup Beefeater or other dry London-style gin Kosher salt and freshly ground black pepper	1 or 2 lemons, sliced into ¼-inch-thick rounds ¼ cup fresh dill fronds

Prepare a charcoal or gas grill for direct, medium-heat grilling. Cover a rimmed baking sheet with a piece of heavy-duty aluminum foil, then drizzle the foil with the canola oil and use a pastry brush to brush the oil all over the foil.

Place the fish skin-side down on the foil. Spread the mayonnaise over the flesh side of the fish, then sprinkle with the gin. Season generously with salt and pepper, then place the lemon slices evenly over the fish. There should be enough lemon slices to cover the fish. If not, slice another lemon.

Transfer the fish—with the foil still beneath it—to the grill grate. You may need help to do this; an extra set of hands helps complete this step with ease. With a pair of tongs, curl the edges of the foil around the fish, but do not completely enclose the fish in the foil.

Cover the grill (if using charcoal, open the vents) and cook until the fish flakes easily when the tip of a paring knife is inserted into the fleshy side, 10 to 12 minutes. Carefully transfer the fish (still on its sheet of foil) back onto the rimmed baking sheet.

Let the fish cool for a minute, then use a spatula to transfer it to a platter. Remove and discard the lemon slices, garnish with the fresh dill, and serve immediately.

GIN AND TONICS FOR A CROWD

I'll forever associate pitchers of gin and tonics with my late stepfather, who was fond of the expression "It's always five o'clock somewhere." If I close my eyes I can see him there, in his Nantucket red pants and button-down shirt, mixing up a batch. | SERVES 6 TO 8

2 quarts ice
2 cups Beefeater or other dry
    London-style gin
	3 limes, cut into ¼-inch slices, plus
	    2 limes, quartered, for garnish
	Tonic water (preferably Schweppes)	

In a large pitcher, combine the ice, gin, and lime slices. Top with tonic water, stir to combine, and serve immediately.

WHEY-BRINED STRIPED BASS
WITH SUMMER VEGETABLE CAPONATA

Whey, the liquid left over from cheese-making, is an overlooked ingredient with great potential. If you get into the habit of making fresh ricotta at home, you'll have plenty of whey. Instead of dumping it down the drain, save it for this recipe.

The lactic and sour flavors of whey are a good flavor base for brine. Not all fish benefit from brining, but striped bass, a meaty fish with a thick protein structure, is well suited to this treatment. If you don't have whey, you can skip the brining step; simply season the fish generously with salt before cooking. Pair the fish with a caponata loaded with summer vegetables. If you'd like, finish the dish with some crumbled feta cheese. | **SERVES 6 AS A MAIN COURSE**

---

2 cups cold fresh whey, left over from making ricotta (page 17)

6 skin-on striped bass fillets (about 2 pounds), scored gently on the skin side

3 tablespoons extra-virgin olive oil

1 large eggplant, cut into ¼-inch cubes

3 cubanelle peppers, seeded and diced

1 large zucchini, cut into ¼-inch cubes

6 cipollini onions, quartered

2 garlic cloves, thinly sliced

Kosher salt and freshly ground black pepper

½ cup chicken or vegetable stock

2 slightly underripe heirloom tomatoes, cored and cut into medium dice

10 white anchovy fillets, coarsely chopped

2 tablespoons minced fresh oregano

1 teaspoon minced fresh rosemary

1 teaspoon red pepper flakes

½ cup oil-cured black olives, pits removed, coarsely chopped

2 teaspoons fresh lemon juice

2 tablespoons cold unsalted butter

¼ cup fresh parsley leaves, minced

¼ cup fresh basil leaves, minced

Oregano leaves, for garnish (optional)

Pour half the whey into a glass or plastic storage container large enough to accommodate the fish. Place the fillets into the container, skin-side down (if you need to stack the fillets, stack them flesh side together; in other words, the second layer would be skin-side up). Pour the remaining whey over the top. Ideally, the fillets will be submerged in whey, though they don't need to be swimming. Cover and refrigerate for at least 30 minutes but not more than 3 hours.

Preheat the oven to 350°F.

In a medium saucepan, heat 1 tablespoon of the olive oil over medium heat. Add the eggplant, cubanelle peppers, zucchini, onions, and garlic to the pan. Season with salt and black pepper and sauté for 4 to 5 minutes, until the vegetables begin to sweat and soften.

CONTINUED

Reduce the heat to low and cover with a tight-fitting lid. Cook, stirring occasionally, for about 10 minutes. When you open the saucepan to stir the vegetables, check the amount of liquid in the pan; if the vegetables are sticking to the pan and seem dry, add the stock as necessary.

Remove the lid and stir in the tomatoes, anchovy fillets, oregano, rosemary, red pepper flakes, olives, and lemon juice. Season with salt and black pepper and cook over low heat, stirring occasionally, for 6 minutes. Set the caponata aside.

Heat an ovenproof 12-inch skillet over medium heat. Remove the fish fillets from the brine and pat dry with paper towels. Discard the whey.

Heat the remaining 2 tablespoons olive oil in the skillet. When the oil is hot, add the fillets to the pan, skin-side down. Gently press down on the fillets one at a time with a spatula, to flatten and help crisp the skin, about 3 minutes.

Flip the fillets and add the butter to the pan. When the butter melts, use a spoon to baste the fish repeatedly. Cook, basting the fish, until the butter begins to brown, about 1 minute. Check the fish; the fillets should bounce back when pressed. Depending on the thickness of your fillets, you may need to finish cooking them in the oven. If this is the case, transfer the pan to the oven and cook until the fish bounces back to the touch and the flesh flakes easily.

Remove the pan from the oven. Remove the fillets from the pan one at a time using a fish spatula, and transfer each to a plate.

Fold the chopped parsley and basil into the caponata, divide the caponata among six plates, and garnish with oregano, if using. Top with a fillet and serve immediately.

YANKEE GUMBO

I know I'm taking some liberties by calling this recipe gumbo. Down South, gumbos are traditionally thickened with a roux and either okra or filé powder (made from dried sassafras leaves). This recipe, which was passed down to me from my mother, is instead thickened only with the brown roux, which also lends a nutty flavor to the finished stew. The specific combination of seafood that you add to the gumbo doesn't much matter, but an assortment makes this stew feel especially luxurious. | SERVES 6

1 pound chorizo sausage, removed from casing 2 celery stalks, finely diced 1 large red bell pepper, finely diced 1 large leek, white and light green parts only, split lengthwise and thinly sliced 2 garlic cloves, minced 2 tablespoons unsalted butter 1 tablespoon extra-virgin olive oil	⅓ cup all-purpose flour 2 cups bottled clam juice 2 cups chicken stock 1 (15-ounce) can whole plum tomatoes, crushed by hand 2 bay leaves ½ teaspoon cayenne pepper Kosher salt and freshly ground black pepper	¾ pound skinless swordfish or halibut, cut into 1-inch pieces ¾ pound medium shrimp, peeled and deveined ¾ pound sea scallops, halved if large 1 medium zucchini, cut into ½-inch cubes ½ cup chopped fresh parsley Cooked white rice, for serving (optional)

Heat a large Dutch oven over medium heat. Add the chorizo and fry, breaking up the large chunks with a wooden spoon, until just cooked through, about 6 minutes. Remove from the pan with a slotted spoon, leaving the fat in the pan, and transfer to a bowl. Set aside.

Add the celery, bell pepper, leek, and garlic to the pan and cook, stirring occasionally, until the vegetables are softened and beginning to brown, about 6 minutes. Transfer the vegetable mixture to another bowl and set aside.

Add the butter and olive oil to the pan. When the butter has melted, whisk in the flour, reduce the heat to low, and cook, stirring occasionally with a wooden spoon, until the roux is nut brown and

smells like toasted bread, about 20 minutes. Whisk in the clam juice, chicken stock, and the crushed tomatoes and their juices. Add the bay leaves and cayenne and stir in the cooked vegetable mixture. Bring to a boil, then reduce the heat so the liquid is gently simmering. Cover and simmer, stirring occasionally, for about 40 minutes. Season to taste with salt and black pepper.

Return the chorizo to the pot and add the fish, shrimp, scallops, and zucchini. Cover and simmer until the fish is just cooked through, about 6 minutes. Season to taste with salt and black pepper and stir in the parsley. Divide among warmed bowls and serve, accompanied by white rice, if you'd like.

MUSSELS WITH RED CURRY BROTH AND LEMONGRASS

Inexpensive and easy to cook, mussels are a great meal for a group. I like to use mussels from Bang's Island, a small mussel producer in Casco Bay, Maine, that sells rope-raised mussels from the northern Atlantic (see Resources, page 331). Bang's Island mussels are small, plump, and incredibly flavorful. But if you can't get Bang's Island mussels, you can substitute mussels from your local source. The red curry broth is flavorful but not too spicy—it has a little kick but is also fruity and nuanced, with coconut milk taming and sweetening the broth. Serve with crusty bread to sop up all that love in the bottom of the bowl. | **SERVES 6 AS A MAIN COURSE**

4 pounds mussels, rinsed and debearded	8 ounces sweet Italian pork sausage (if cased, removed from casing)	2 tablespoons gochujang (Korean chile paste; see Resources, page 331)
2 tablespoons canola oil	1 large yellow onion, julienned	3 tablespoons shoyu (white soy sauce)
1 tablespoon toasted sesame oil	5 tablespoons prepared Thai red curry paste	1 tablespoon honey
3 shallots, thinly sliced	1 cup dry white wine	2 (14-ounce) cans full-fat unsweetened coconut milk
4 garlic cloves, thinly sliced	2 cups fish or shellfish stock	Kosher salt
1 stalk lemongrass, top and bottom trimmed and outer leaves discarded; bottom third of stalk thinly sliced	3 tablespoons fish sauce	Cilantro leaves, for garnish
	1 tablespoon oyster sauce	Baguette or crusty bread, for serving

Pick through the mussels and discard any that have open shells.

In a large high-sided skillet or pot, heat the canola and sesame oils over medium heat. When the oil is hot, add the shallots, garlic, and lemongrass and cook, stirring, until aromatic, about 2 minutes. Add the sausage and onion and cook, using a wooden spoon to break up the chunks of sausage as it cooks, until the sausage is no longer pink and the onion is translucent, about 5 minutes. Stir in the curry paste, then pour in the wine and cook until almost all the liquid has evaporated, 3 to 4 minutes. Add the stock, fish sauce, oyster sauce, gochujang, shoyu, and honey. Pour in the coconut milk and stir to combine, then season to taste with salt and add the mussels. Cover the pot and cook until the flavors have married and all the mussel shells have opened, about 5 minutes. Discard any mussels that do not open.

Divide the mussels among six serving bowls. Pour the liquid from the pot over each dish and garnish with cilantro. Serve immediately with a crusty baguette alongside to sop up the juices.

NORTHERN CARBONARA
SPAGHETTI WITH RAZOR CLAMS AND SALT PORK

Sometimes classics aren't meant to be messed with, and one could argue that spaghetti carbonara, the classic Roman pasta, is one of them. So I'll beg for your forgiveness for this recipe, which draws inspiration from the traditional pasta but then takes some Yankee deviations, becoming a sort of *spaghetti alle vongole*/carbonara hybrid.

Razor clams are a special bivalve, only available when the muddy sandbars from which they are harvested are accessible. In recent winters, it has been so cold in New England that the harbors have been freezing over, making the sandbars inaccessible and cutting razor clam season short. So when razor clams are available, eat them while you can.

The combination of clams and pork is a stalwart New England pairing, one that is complemented by the eggs and Parmigiano-Reggiano that make this pasta especially creamy and satisfying. If you can't track down lovage, use celery leaves in its place. | SERVES 6 AS A MAIN COURSE

2 pounds razor clams, scrubbed (littleneck or manila clams can be substituted)	4 garlic cloves, thinly sliced	Kosher salt and freshly ground black pepper
1 pound dry spaghetti	1 egg	1 tablespoon unsalted butter
½ pound salt pork or pancetta, cut into ¼-inch cubes	4 egg yolks	½ cup finely chopped fresh flat-leaf parsley
1 medium yellow onion, julienned	¾ cup grated Parmigiano-Reggiano cheese	½ cup chopped lovage leaves or celery leaves (optional)
	¼ teaspoon freshly grated nutmeg	

Fill a medium saucepan with a ½-inch depth of water. Bring the water to a boil. When the water is boiling, add the clams, cover, and steam until the shells open, about 8 minutes. Remove from the heat and use a slotted spoon to remove the clams from the pot, reserving the liquid in the pot. Discard any clams that do not open. Remove the clams from their shells, discard the shells, and coarsely chop the meat into pieces about the size of a nickel. Set aside. Strain the clam liquid through a fine-mesh strainer into a large measuring cup.

Bring a large pot of salted water to a boil and add the strained clam liquid. Add the spaghetti and boil until al dente. Drain, reserving 1 cup of the cooking water.

While the spaghetti cooks, heat a 12-inch skillet over medium heat. Add the salt pork and sauté for about 10 minutes, until the fat has rendered and the pieces of salt pork are browned and crisp. Remove from the pan with a slotted spoon and let drain on a paper towel–lined plate. Add the onion and garlic to the pan and sauté for 5 minutes, until the onion is soft. Add the chopped clams and sauté for 2 minutes more, then add the spaghetti and toss until the spaghetti is warmed through and the mixture is well combined.

In a small bowl, whisk together the whole egg, egg yolks, Parmigiano-Reggiano, and nutmeg. Remove the spaghetti from the heat and carefully drizzle in the egg mixture, tossing the noodles as you go to prevent the egg from scrambling, until fully incorporated. Add a splash of the reserved pasta cooking water and toss until the pasta looks silky. Season with salt and a generous amount of pepper, then stir in the butter, parsley, and lovage, if using. Transfer to a platter or serving plates and serve warm.

SEAFOOD TOURTIÈRE

A Quebeçois savory pie, *tourtière* is typically made with spiced ground pork and potato and is often served on Christmas Eve. This version includes a filling of five different types of seafood, along with mushrooms and potatoes, and honors the long Yankee tradition of seafood pies. Both the filling and the crust can be made in advance, so when you're ready to eat, all that's left to do is assemble and bake the pie. Like the recipe that inspired it, this is the perfect dinner for an icy winter night. Serve fat wedges of it with a green salad alongside. | **MAKES ONE 7-INCH PIE; SERVES 6 TO 8 AS A MAIN COURSE**

½ cup (1 stick) unsalted butter

½ cup all-purpose flour, plus more for dusting

1 cup whole milk

Pinch of freshly grated nutmeg

2 tablespoons canola oil

8 ounces cremini mushrooms, sliced

1 small yellow onion, thinly sliced

2 garlic cloves, thinly sliced

½ cup dry white wine

1 medium russet potato

½ pound medium raw shrimp, peeled, deveined, and coarsely chopped

½ pound shelled cooked lobster meat

½ pound skinless cod, coarsely chopped

½ pound fresh sea scallops, feet removed and coarsely chopped

Pinch of saffron

Kosher salt and freshly ground black pepper

1 pound shelled cooked crabmeat

¼ cup finely chopped fresh flat-leaf parsley

2 tablespoons finely chopped fresh tarragon

Zest and juice of 1 Meyer lemon

1 recipe Pâte Brisée (page 54), sugar omitted

1 egg

Green salad, for serving

SPECIAL EQUIPMENT: 7-inch springform pan or 9 x 3-inch removable bottom tart pan

---

Preheat the oven to 400°F.

In a medium saucepan, melt the butter over medium heat. When the butter has melted, whisk in the flour and cook, whisking, until the flour is golden brown, about 5 minutes. Pour in the milk and add the nutmeg. Bring to a simmer and cook, whisking, until the béchamel thickens, about 5 minutes. Remove from the heat.

In a large high-sided skillet, heat the canola oil over medium-high heat. Add the mushrooms, onion, and garlic to the pan, reduce the heat to medium, and cook, stirring occasionally, until the mushrooms have released their liquid and the onion is soft, about 7 minutes. Add the wine to the pan and use a wooden spoon to scrape up any browned bits from the bottom of the pan. Bring to a boil and cook until the liquid has reduced by half, about 5 minutes.

CONTINUED

Peel the potato and grate it on the large holes of a box grater. Add the potato to the pan with the mushrooms and stir to combine, then stir in the shrimp, lobster, cod, and scallops. Cook, stirring gently, until the shrimp is bright pink and the cod is beginning to flake, about 5 minutes. Add the saffron and stir to incorporate, then season with salt and pepper. Remove from the heat.

Stir in the crabmeat, béchamel, parsley, tarragon, lemon zest, and lemon juice. Taste and adjust the seasoning. Let the mixture cool completely.

On a floured work surface, divide the pâte brisée dough into two pieces; one piece should be larger, about two-thirds of the dough. With a lightly floured rolling pin, roll the larger piece of dough into a 12-inch circle. Carefully transfer to a 7-inch springform pan, gently pressing it in so the pan is lined with dough on the bottom and sides, with some overhang. Spoon the cooled seafood mixture into the pan and gently tamp it down. Roll the second piece of dough into an 8-inch circle and top the pie, crimping the edges to seal.

In a small bowl, whisk together the egg and 2 tablespoons water. Brush the top crust with the egg wash and cut a few slits in the crust to allow steam to escape. Set the pan on a rimmed baking sheet, transfer to the oven, and bake for 25 minutes.

Reduce the oven temperature to 350°F and bake until the pastry is golden brown, about 30 minutes more. Remove from the oven and let cool for 20 minutes; it will contract as it cools, making it easier to remove from the pan. Carefully remove the springform pan ring and let cool for 10 minutes more.

The tourtière should be served warm, not hot. Cut into wedges and serve with a green salad alongside.

HOW TO ASSEMBLE SEAFOOD TOURTIÈRE

1. Transfer the dough to the springform pan.

2. Spoon the cooled fish mixture into the crust and tamp it down with the back of a spoon.

3. Use a rolling pin to transfer the second piece of dough on top.

4. Use a fork to crimp together the edges of the pie to form a seal.

5. Brush the top with egg wash and cut a few slits in the crust to allow the steam to escape.

LEMON BEACH PLUM THUMBPRINT COOKIES

Every summer, the arrival of the beach plums in coastal New England communities signifies the end of one season and the arrival of another. I remember this transition well, as I would walk past these plants, their thick, tasseled leaf sets springing from sandy soil, on my way to work in local restaurants in Nantucket during high school. For me, the sight of those plums meant school was coming. It was a sign that my freedom was waning and my opportunity to save some pocket change was almost over.

My stepfather's mother, though not a skilled cook by any means, took jam-making seriously. At the end of each summer, she'd make large batches of beach plum jam, its smell permeating the small fishing cottage where she lived. This recipe for tender lemon thumbprint cookies uses a similar jam made from the beach plum, a fleeting, seasonal delight. But if you don't have beach plums growing nearby, don't sweat it: the cookies can be filled with any type of jam you like, homemade or store-bought. Make sure you chill the dough well before rolling. | **MAKES ABOUT 30 COOKIES**

1½ cups all-purpose flour 1¼ teaspoons baking powder 1 teaspoon cornstarch ½ teaspoon kosher salt ½ cup granulated sugar	1 tablespoon lemon zest ½ cup (1 stick) unsalted butter, at room temperature ¼ cup packed light brown sugar 1 egg 1 tablespoon fresh lemon juice	½ teaspoon pure vanilla extract ½ cup Late-Summer Beach Plum Jam (recipe follows) or store-bought plum jam (other flavors can be substituted) Confectioners' sugar, for dusting

In a small bowl, whisk together the flour, baking powder, cornstarch, and salt. Put the granulated sugar and lemon zest in a food processor and pulse to combine, about 1 minute.

In the bowl of a stand mixer fitted with the paddle attachment (or in a large bowl using a handheld mixer), combine the butter and brown sugar and beat on medium speed until light and creamy. Add the egg, lemon juice, and vanilla and beat until combined. Reduce the speed to low and gradually add the flour mixture; mix just until incorporated. Cover the bowl with plastic wrap and refrigerate for at least 3 hours or up to overnight.

CONTINUED

Preheat the oven to 350°F. Line two baking sheets with silicone baking mats or parchment paper.

Using your hands, roll the dough into 1¼-inch balls and space them 2 inches apart on the prepared baking sheets. With the handle of a wooden spoon or your thumb, press down in the middle of each cookie to form an indentation.

Bake, rotating the pans halfway through, for 7 minutes, until golden. Remove from the oven and spoon ½ teaspoon of the jam into the indentation in each cookie. Return to the oven and bake for 3 minutes more, until golden brown. Let cool for 2 minutes on the baking sheets, then transfer the cookies to a wire rack and dust with confectioners' sugar while still warm.

Store the cookies in an airtight container at room temperature for up to 3 days.

LATE-SUMMER BEACH PLUM JAM
MAKES ABOUT 2 CUPS

2 pounds beach plums, pitted
1 to 1¼ cups sugar
Juice of ½ lemon
1 teaspoon pectin
Pinch of kosher salt

In a large heavy saucepan, combine the plums, 1 cup of the sugar, the lemon juice, pectin, and salt. Bring to a simmer over medium heat and cook, stirring occasionally, until the plums have broken down and the mixture has thickened, about 10 minutes, then taste the mixture and add some or all of the remaining sugar as desired.

Using an immersion blender, lightly blend the jam (it should not be perfectly smooth). Transfer to a bowl and let cool.

The jam can be made ahead and refrigerated for up to 1 week or frozen for up to 1 month.

CHOCOLATE–SEA SALT SHORTBREAD SANDWICH COOKIE

Sometimes simple is best. Shortbread has all the identifiers of simple perfection: it's rich, tender, and keeps well, and is made with basic ingredients. I'd often find it stuffed into the bottom of my stocking at Christmas, wrapped in its red Scottish tartan packaging.

Sandwich these brown sugar shortbread cookies with bittersweet chocolate ganache to create an addictive little cookie. Though they're great any time of year, if you're looking for an elegant sweet to add to your holiday baking repertoire, try these. | **MAKES 36 SANDWICH COOKIES**

1 cup (2 sticks) unsalted butter, at room temperature ¾ cup packed light brown sugar ¼ teaspoon sea salt, plus a pinch	1 egg yolk 1½ teaspoons pure vanilla extract 2 cups all-purpose flour Flaky salt, such as Maldon, for sprinkling	4½ ounces bittersweet chocolate (70% cacao), chopped ½ cup heavy cream **SPECIAL EQUIPMENT:** Piping bag with plain tip

In the bowl of a stand mixer fitted with the paddle attachment (or in a large bowl using a handheld mixer), combine the butter, brown sugar, and sea salt. Beat on high speed until light and creamy, about 4 minutes. Reduce the speed to low and add the egg yolk and vanilla.

Gradually add the flour and mix until combined. Cover the bowl with plastic wrap and refrigerate for at least 2 hours or up to overnight.

Preheat the oven to 325°F. Line two rimmed baking sheets with silicone baking mats or parchment paper.

Roll the dough into ½-inch balls and set them on the prepared baking sheets, spacing them about 1 inch apart. Gently flatten each ball and sprinkle with flaky salt. Bake for 10 minutes, until lightly golden on the edges. Remove from the oven and use a spatula to transfer the cookies to a wire rack to cool completely.

Put the chocolate in a medium bowl. In a small saucepan, warm the cream over medium heat until bubbles begin to form around the edges of the pan. Pour the hot cream over the chocolate and let stand for 5 minutes, then whisk until smooth. Whisk in a pinch of sea salt. Let the mixture cool completely.

Transfer the chocolate ganache to a piping bag fitted with a plain tip. Pipe a nickel-size amount of ganache on the underside of one cookie, then top with a second cookie to form a sandwich (alternatively, you can use a small spoon to spoon some of the ganache onto the cookies). The cookies will keep in an airtight container at room temperature for up to 3 days.

CASHEW-TOGARASHI BRITTLE

This unusual brittle is the perfect host or hostess gift; it's made with *togarashi*, a Japanese blend of seaweed and dried spices. The exact mixture of spices varies from maker to maker, but usually includes red pepper flakes, black pepper, sesame seeds, dried mandarin orange peel, dried seaweed, and Sichuan peppercorns. It is nutty and savory, with some lingering heat and fruitiness. Fold it into custards or yogurt, sprinkle it onto ice cream, or crumble it over salads or veggies. | MAKES ABOUT 4 CUPS

2 cups sugar 1 cup light corn syrup ¼ teaspoon cream of tartar 2 tablespoons unsalted butter 1 teaspoon baking soda	1½ cups roasted unsalted cashews, coarsely chopped ¼ cup finely crumbled nori (about 3 sheets) ¼ cup togarashi spice blend, homemade (recipe follows) or store-bought	Flaky salt, such as Maldon, for sprinkling SPECIAL EQUIPMENT: Candy thermometer

Line a rimmed baking sheet with a silicone baking mat.

In a medium saucepan, combine the sugar, corn syrup, cream of tartar, and ½ cup water. Bring to a boil over medium-high heat and cook, swirling the pan occasionally, until the mixture is a light amber color and registers 290°F on a candy thermometer.

Add the butter, baking soda, cashews, nori, and togarashi; the mixture will bubble up. Cook, stirring with a rubber spatula, until the cashews look toasty and the mixture registers 280°F on a candy thermometer, then pour onto the prepared baking sheet and, using an offset spatula, quickly and gently spread it into a thin layer. Sprinkle with flaky salt while still warm. Let cool completely.

When the brittle is cool, break it into large pieces with your hands. The brittle will keep in an airtight container at room temperature for up to 3 weeks.

TOGARASHI SPICE BLEND
MAKES ABOUT ¼ CUP

1½ tablespoons Sichuan peppercorns, toasted
1 tablespoon dried orange peel (see Resources, page 331)
2 teaspoons gochugaru (ground red Korean chile pepper; see Resources, page 331)
2 teaspoons finely crumbled nori
2 teaspoons black sesame seeds
2 teaspoons white sesame seeds, toasted
2 teaspoons poppy seeds

In a spice grinder, combine the peppercorns and orange peel and grind into a coarse powder. Transfer to a bowl and stir in the chile pepper, nori, and seeds. Transfer to an airtight container; the togarashi will keep at room temperature for up to 2 weeks.

MEYER LEMON ICE

Del's frozen lemonade is an iconic summer treat in Rhode Island. First served from a pushcart in 1948, the brand has grown; now there are franchises throughout Rhode Island and the United States selling the tangy frozen ice. This Meyer lemon version is my homemade ode to Del's, and it's so refreshing on a hot summer's day. I like the sweet-tart flavor of Meyer lemons. If you can't find them, substitute ubiquitous Eureka lemons. | **SERVES 6 TO 8**

1 cup sugar Zest of 2 Meyer lemons (Eureka lemons can be substituted)	½ teaspoon kosher salt ½ teaspoon pure vanilla extract	¾ cup Meyer lemon juice (Eureka lemon juice can be substituted)

In a medium saucepan, combine the sugar and 2½ cups water and cook over medium heat, stirring, until the sugar has dissolved. Stir in the lemon zest, salt, and vanilla.

Transfer the liquid to a bowl and refrigerate until completely cold. Whisk in the lemon juice, then pour into a 9 x 13-inch ceramic or glass baking dish and transfer to the freezer. Freeze for 1 hour, then remove the pan from the freezer and use a fork to scrape the surface, breaking up the ice crystals. Return the pan to the freezer and freeze until solid, at least 4 hours, scraping the ice with the tines of a fork every 30 to 40 minutes.

When the granita is completely frozen, use a fork to rake it into glittery snow. Spoon into chilled glasses and serve immediately.

FEAST | KITCHEN CLAMBAKE

Should you have access to a beach and lots of time on your hands, a traditional New England clambake is a nice way to spend a summer Sunday. You dig a pit, line it with rocks, build a big fire in the pit, let it burn down to coals, and layer in lobsters, clams, corn, potatoes, and sausage between sheets of seaweed. Then you cover the pit. And wait. Approximately a case of beer later, you go in for the buried treasure, unearthing the seafood and its trimmings, steamed to perfection. But if you find yourself with less time and no beach access, you can still get all the flavors of a clambake with this stovetop version. It applies the same basic layering principles, with a pot standing in for the pit, and the seafood added to the pot in stages so everything is cooked to perfection. The indoor clambake may not be quite as folkloric, and it doesn't provide you with an easy excuse for a day on the beach drinking beer, but the results taste just as good.

To make cleanup easy, serve this on a newspaper-lined table (outdoors or in). Make your guests cornbread with seaweed butter to eat alongside—a crusty baguette would be good, too. And don't scrimp on the drawn butter, either.

KITCHEN CLAMBAKE
CORNBREAD
SEAWEED BUTTER

KITCHEN CLAMBAKE

SERVES 8

3 medium yellow onions, peeled and cut into 6 wedges

6 garlic cloves

1 (12-ounce) bottle pale ale or other medium-bodied beer

Fresh seaweed, well rinsed, for layering (optional; ask your fishmonger)

1½ pounds small new potatoes (white, red, or a combination)

1 pound hot dried chorizo, cut into ½-inch pieces

Coarse salt

3 lobsters (1½ pounds each)

36 littleneck clams, scrubbed well

4 ears of corn, husked and halved crosswise

2 pounds mussels, debearded and scrubbed well

1½ pounds large shell-on shrimp (about 30)

2 tablespoons unsalted butter

2 lemons, halved

Crusty bread or Cornbread (recipe follows), for serving

Drawn butter, for serving

1 In a 16-quart stockpot, combine the onions, garlic, beer, and 1 cup water. Cover with a layer of seaweed (or place a steamer basket on top of the onions). Add the potatoes, chorizo, and 1 tablespoon salt. Bring to a boil over high heat.

2 Once boiling, add the lobsters, cover, and cook over high heat for 15 minutes. Add the clams and corn, re-cover, and cook for 6 minutes more. Add the mussels and shrimp, re-cover, and cook until the clams and mussels open and the shrimp are cooked through, 4 to 8 minutes more.

3 With tongs, remove the seafood, corn, potatoes, and chorizo and transfer to large platters or rimmed baking sheets. Discard the seaweed and any unopened clams and mussels. Strain the liquid through a fine-mesh sieve into a bowl and add the butter, swirling to melt. Squeeze the lemon halves over the seafood and serve immediately, with the buttery liquid and crusty bread or cornbread alongside.

CORNBREAD

MAKES ONE 9 X 13-INCH PAN; SERVES 12

1 cup (2 sticks) unsalted butter, melted, plus more for greasing

½ cup granulated sugar

½ cup packed light brown sugar

4 eggs

2 cups all-purpose flour

2 cups fine yellow cornmeal

1 teaspoon baking soda

1 teaspoon baking powder

1 teaspoon kosher salt

2 cups buttermilk

¾ cup honey

Seaweed butter, for serving (recipe follows), optional

1 Preheat the oven to 350°F. Grease a 9 x 13-inch pan with butter.

2 In a medium bowl, whisk together the melted butter, both sugars, and the eggs until well combined.

3 In a separate bowl, mix together the flour, cornmeal, baking soda, baking powder, and salt.

4 Add the dry ingredients to the wet in two batches, alternating with the buttermilk. The mixture should be smooth.

5 Transfer to the prepared pan and drizzle the honey over the top. Bake about 30 minutes, until a tester inserted into the center comes out clean. Let cool on a wire rack, then cut into squares and serve with seaweed butter alongside, if desired.

SEAWEED BUTTER

MAKES 1 CUP

½ ounce dried nori sheets (about 5 sheets), thinly sliced

1 cup (2 sticks) unsalted butter, cut into ½-inch pieces, at room temperature

½ teaspoon kosher salt

1 In a dry wide skillet over medium heat, toast the nori, stirring, until aromatic and crisp, about 7 minutes. Remove from the heat and let cool.

2 In the bowl of a food processor, combine the butter, salt, and toasted nori. Process until the mixture is smooth and the nori has broken down into small flakes. If serving right away, transfer to a bowl, cover, and keep at room temperature. The butter will keep in a refrigerated lidded container for up to a week. Let it come to room temperature before serving.

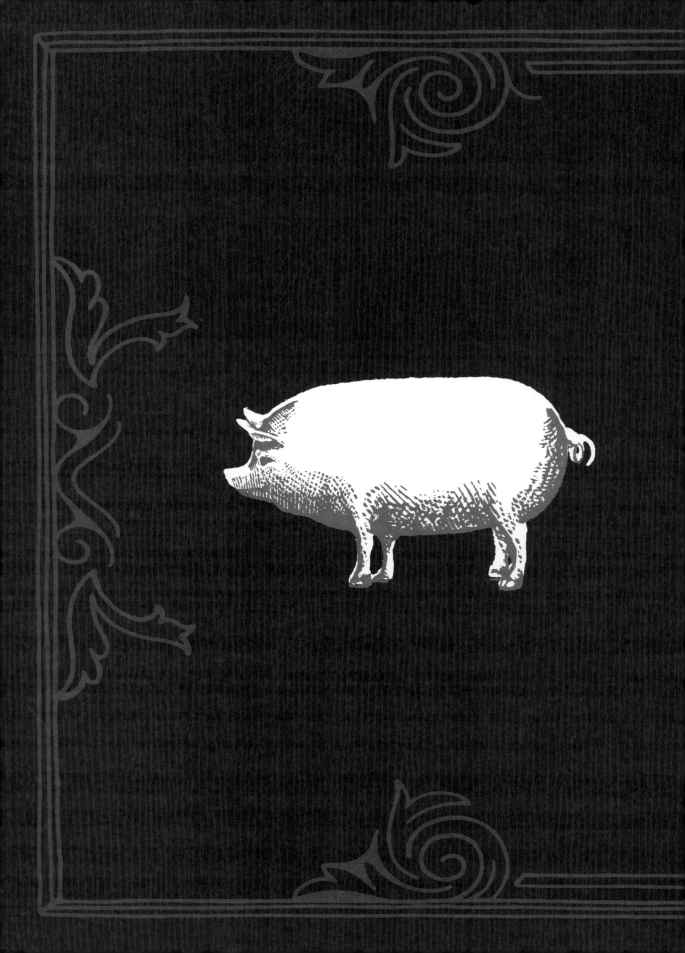

FARM

Good farmers, who take seriously their
duties as stewards of Creation and of their
land's inheritors, contribute to the welfare
of society in more ways than society usually
acknowledges, or even knows.

—Wendell Berry

In 2000, after I'd been working at Formaggio Kitchen for a few years, the owner, Ihsan, sent me on a sourcing trip to Italy, where I spent a few weeks scouting for new products and cheeses to import back to the shop. One of the first stops in Tuscany was Antica Macelleria Cecchini to pay a visit to the famed "butcher of Panzano," Dario Cecchini.

When I walked into the shop, the scent of lavender filled the air and a deep baritone opera singer belted from the small radio. And behind the raised butcher case, almost reminiscent of a stage, was a large, square man with spiky hair, dressed from head to toe in red and white, wrapped in a bloodstained apron, with hands as big as bags of potatoes engulfing a wood-handled cleaver. He spun around and grinned from ear to ear. "*Buongiorno!*" he bellowed.

In all ways, Dario was larger than life. His oversize hands were matched only by his oversize personality: he recited Dante to customers who walked into the shop, and his energy and affection for his craft were both evident and infectious. I intended to spend only a day in Panzano, but I ended up spending a week. While Dario rambled on in Italian (a language I do not speak), I made bouquets of herbs, zested and chopped citrus, and tied roasts. I watched as he arranged the butcher case each morning, setting coils of sausages beside a bowl of whipped, herb-flecked lardo piled so high it resembled a snowcapped mountain, nestled next to giant T-bones cut from those massive white Chianina cows that dot the Tuscan landscape.

I had never seen a butcher shop like this, nor had I met a butcher with such respect and reverence for animals, who paid such methodical and intricate attention to the details of every project. It was a watershed moment in my development as a cook, and I returned to the States determined to find farmers who were raising animals with the same care I'd seen in Italy, and to further hone the craft I'd begun to learn from Dario.

Fifteen or so years ago, most Americans weren't talking about whole-animal butchery, or heritage breeds of pigs, or chickens that laid blue eggs. Only a handful of restaurants made their own charcuterie, and there were only a few American artisan meat companies making salami. But over the last decade or so, that's changed. Cooks are more concerned with flavor now, and traceability, and as a result small farms that sustainably raise livestock have proliferated, and, in turn, have led to the rise of artisan butcher shops and charcuterie makers.

Now it seems like every time I go to the farmers' market, there's a new farmer under a tent, selling Vermont-raised lamb shanks or pork chops from pigs raised just outside the city limits.

My respect for farmers and their animals has only grown since that trip to Tuscany. Now I buy humanely raised meat from local farmers and ranchers, both because I think it tastes better and because I appreciate the care with which it was raised.

The consumption of meat is both a privilege and, if you're doing it right, a responsibility. Quality meat raised sustainably is always going to be more expensive than its commercial alternative. But I'd rather have less of the best stuff, sourced from a farm that I trust, than a huge steak of dubious provenance. And when you understand all the work that goes into raising, slaughtering, and butchering an animal, you will try very hard not to waste that product.

An economical home cook should learn how to cook more than just the prime cuts. There is no greater or lesser part of the animal; all parts of a beast can be delicious if butchered and cooked properly.

This chapter is a collection of meat and egg recipes. It includes braised short ribs for wintry evenings (page 175), an easy weeknight grilled chicken (page 164), and my tips for making bistro-quality beef tartare (page 143) and juicy sausages (page 161) at home. I couldn't resist the challenge of creating some farm-centric desserts, so this chapter includes those, too: a rhubarb and strawberry crisp capped with a crumble topping enriched by pork fat (page 193) and cranberry-filled hand pies made with a lard pastry crust (page 196).

Make these recipes and eat them, as Dario Cecchini recommends, *in convivio*—with friends and family gathered around the table.

TARTARE 101

There are some simple, essential guidelines for making the best beef tartare at home.

First, buy the absolute best quality beef you can afford. This is something you should always do, but it's especially important if you are serving beef raw. Use a combination of sirloin and hanger steak.

Freeze the meat. Placing the beef in the freezer for 15 to 20 minutes will not only make it easier to chop, but also ensure that the fat doesn't smear when you're chopping it. You want the fat within the inner fibers of the protein to become evenly distributed throughout the tartare, not melted, streaky, or separated from the lean protein.

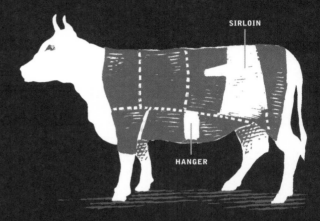

Chop the meat by hand or finely grind it. Hand mincing will always create a better quality tartare, and if you're making a small batch that is always the method I recommend. But I'd be lying if I told you that I hand cut every batch of tartare we serve at the restaurant. If you have a grinder attachment for your electric mixer, this will work, too; chill all the parts of the grinder in the freezer overnight, and grind the meat into a small stainless-steel or glass bowl nested into a larger bowl full of ice. When grinding the meat, the colder you can keep it, the better. A small, pebble-size grind is ideal, so use the smallest die on your grinder.

Customize your tartare. The greatest tartare is as much about what gets mixed in as it is the quality of the beef. Minced cornichon pickles or shallots, a splash of pickle juice, a teaspoon of hot mustard, pulverized dried smoky chile peppers, grated Parmigiano-Reggiano, minced raw garlic, finely minced chives or flat-leaf parsley, a squeeze of lemon juice—these and more are all terrific additions (though, it should be said, not all of them together). Play around. Find a combination of add-ins that you like and doctor your tartare to your taste.

Garnish away. At Townsman, we serve our tartare with freshly fried potato chips. Maybe you prefer a bright, crispy salad on top? A grilled slice of baguette alongside? A poached egg? The sky's the limit.

Eat. Tartare is best eaten right away. You can prepare the meat up to a few hours in advance and refrigerate it, covered (do not prepare it more than a few hours in advance, however, or the meat will oxidize), but don't mix in the remaining ingredients until just before you plan to serve it.

BEEF TARTARE

Simple and elegant, beef tartare might be something you're accustomed to ordering in a restaurant and have never attempted to make at home. But it couldn't be simpler to whip up in your own kitchen. Use the very best beef you can find for this recipe. | SERVES 6

8 ounces beef sirloin, fat cap and sinew removed	1½ tablespoons finely chopped fresh flat-leaf parsley	2 or 3 dashes of hot sauce, such as Tabasco, plus more as needed
4 ounces hanger steak	1 tablespoon extra-virgin olive oil	Kosher salt and freshly ground black pepper
¼ cup capers, drained and coarsely chopped	2 teaspoons minced fresh chives	Crème fraîche, for serving
1½ tablespoons minced shallot	1 teaspoon red miso	Potato chips, for serving
	2 egg yolks	

Put the meat on a plate and place it in the freezer for 15 minutes (this makes it easier to chop and prevents the fat from smearing). Place a platter or large plate in the refrigerator.

Once the meat is chilled, use a sharp knife to finely mince it (alternatively, you can cube the chilled meat and pass it through the coarse ⅜-inch plate of a meat grinder), then transfer it to a bowl and refrigerate until very cold, about 30 minutes.

Remove the meat from the refrigerator and stir in the capers, shallot, parsley, olive oil, chives, miso paste, and one of the egg yolks and mix well to combine. Season to taste with hot sauce, salt, and pepper. Transfer the tartare to the chilled plate and use the back of a fork to spread it into a thin layer. Top with the remaining egg yolk and a few dollops of the crème fraîche (if using). Serve immediately, while the meat is still very cold, accompanied by potato chips.

TONNATO-STYLE DEVILED EGGS
WITH LEMON AIOLI AND CRISPY CHICKEN SKIN

This dish pays homage to the classic picnic staple, but it stands out among all the other variations out there. The soft-boiled eggs are enrobed in a creamy, cold, mayonnaise-based sauce that's similar in style to the one that accompanies the Italian dish *vitello tonnato*, cold sliced veal cloaked in a rich tuna sauce. The crispy chicken skin garnish gives the dish a crunchy textural element that contrasts with the sauce and egg. You could make the eggs without this garnish, but I encourage you to try it at least once.

There are a million tricks out there for how to make peeling eggs easier. The only one I can attest to is to use older eggs; farm eggs are often too fresh and their shells haven't had time to cure, making peeling very difficult, so buy them well in advance of when you plan to make this dish. A little baking soda in the water helps, too. | SERVES 6 AS A SNACK

6 ounces chicken skin	1 teaspoon finely grated lemon zest	1 tablespoon minced fresh chives
Kosher salt and freshly ground black pepper	1 to 2 tablespoons fresh lemon juice	Capers, for garnish
½ teaspoon baking soda	1 teaspoon Dijon mustard	Maras or Aleppo pepper, for garnish
6 large eggs	1 garlic clove, minced	Shaved celery, for garnish (optional)
½ cup Basic Aioli (recipe follows)	Freshly ground white pepper	Marigold petals, for garnish (optional)

Preheat the oven to 350°F. Line a rimmed baking sheet with parchment paper.

Trim the meat and excess fat from the chicken skin and cut the skin into 3-inch pieces. Lay the skin on the prepared baking sheet, flesh-side down. Season with salt and black pepper, then top with another sheet of parchment and a second baking sheet (this prevents the skin from curling when it's baked). Bake until browned and crisp, about 1 hour. Remove the top baking sheet and parchment and let cool for 10 minutes.

In a large saucepan, bring 2 quarts water to a rapid simmer and add the baking soda. Fill a large bowl with ice and water; set it nearby. Gently lower the eggs into the boiling water with a slotted spoon. Set a timer for exactly 5 minutes and 15 seconds for soft-boiled eggs; the white will be set but the yolks will be runny. Remove the eggs from the boiling water and transfer to the ice water bath. Let the eggs stand in the ice water bath for 20 minutes, then remove and carefully peel.

CONTINUED

While the eggs chill, in a small bowl, whisk together the aioli, lemon zest, 1 tablespoon of the lemon juice, the mustard, and the garlic. Season with additional lemon juice, salt, and white pepper. Fold in the chives. The sauce should be thin enough to cloak the eggs; if necessary, add water to thin it to the proper consistency.

To serve, slice the eggs in half lengthwise, taking care that the yolk does not squirt out. Place the egg halves onto a platter yolk-side down and spoon the sauce over the top, enrobing each egg half completely. Garnish with crispy chicken skin and capers, as well as a pinch of Maras pepper. Serve immediately.

NOTE: Maras pepper is a deep red, dried Turkish chile pepper with a fruity flavor and lingering heat (see Resources, page 331).

BASIC AIOLI
MAKES ABOUT 1 CUP

1 large egg yolk
1 small garlic clove, minced
¼ teaspoon kosher salt, plus more as needed
¾ cup extra-virgin olive oil (or a 50/50 mix extra-virgin olive oil and canola oil)
1 tablespoon warm water
Fresh lemon juice
Freshly ground black pepper

Set a medium mixing bowl on a kitchen towel (this will prevent the bowl from moving as you whisk). Whisk together the egg yolk, garlic, and salt. Whisking constantly, slowly drizzle in the oil, drop by drop at first, until the mixture begins to thicken, then in a slow, steady stream until all the oil has been incorporated and the mixture is very thick. Whisk in the warm water to thin the aioli, then season to taste with additional salt, the lemon juice, and pepper. Serve right away or transfer to a lidded jar and refrigerate; the aioli will keep for up to 3 days in the refrigerator.

FARM EGG OMELETS
WITH WILD MUSHROOM CONSERVA

I was taught how to cook an omelet by chef Michel LeBorgne, who was an instructor when I was a student at the New England Culinary Institute in Montpelier, Vermont. I was intimidated by Chef LeBorgne. He was a small, pear-shaped man with a tall toque, a sharp Breton accent, and a level of energy at five a.m. matched only by that of a three-month-old puppy. Chef LeBorgne taught me that omelet-making is perfected with practice. Keep your heat low and don't rush it—the eggs should never brown.

Serving an omelet for dinner is a perfectly acceptable thing to do; it is quick to make and uses ingredients you probably have on hand. On a weeknight, you might serve the omelet with a green salad and some toast. When you have more time, try it with a spoonful of these herby olive oil–poached mushrooms and a bright herb salad. | **SERVES 6 AS A MAIN COURSE**

FOR THE MUSHROOM CONSERVA

2 cups extra-virgin olive oil

2 fresh bay leaves

4 sprigs thyme

1 sprig rosemary

1 teaspoon Maras or Aleppo pepper (see Note)

2 pounds assorted wild mushrooms, such as small shiitakes, morels, chanterelles, small porcini, hen of the woods, trumpet, and oyster

3 tablespoons sherry vinegar

Kosher salt and freshly ground black pepper

FOR THE HERB RELISH

¾ cup fresh herb leaves (a mixture of flat-leaf parsley, basil, mint, and chives)

1½ tablespoons capers, drained and rinsed

2 garlic cloves, minced

1 Fresno chile, minced (optional)

Zest and juice of 1 lemon

½ cup extra-virgin olive oil

FOR THE OMELETS

12 eggs

9 tablespoons unsalted butter, melted

Kosher salt and freshly ground black pepper

SPECIAL EQUIPMENT: Deep-fry thermometer

CONTINUED

Make the mushroom conserva: In a large wide pot, combine the olive oil, bay leaves, thyme, rosemary, and Maras pepper. Heat over medium-high heat until the oil registers 170°F on a deep-fry thermometer (it may be necessary to tilt the pot and pool the oil to get a correct reading on the thermometer).

Add the mushrooms to the oil and gently stir. The mushrooms will not initially be submerged in the oil, but as they cook, they will wilt and be covered by oil. Cook the mushrooms, occasionally stirring gently, for 5 minutes. Remove the pan from the heat, stir in the vinegar, season with salt and black pepper, and let the mushrooms steep in the oil for 45 minutes. The mushrooms can be eaten right away, or you can transfer the mushrooms, oil, and herbs to a quart-size mason jar; the mushrooms should be completely covered by the oil. Cover the jar and refrigerate. The mushrooms will keep for up to 1 month. Let come to room temperature or gently warm over low heat before serving.

Make the herb relish: Finely chop the herbs and transfer to a bowl. Add the capers, garlic, chile (if using), lemon zest, and lemon juice, then add the olive oil and stir to combine. Set aside.

Make the omelets: Heat a 12-inch nonstick skillet over medium-low heat. Crack four of the eggs into a small bowl and whisk thoroughly to combine (there should be no strands of egg white remaining, but don't aerate the eggs when whisking). Add 3 tablespoons of the melted butter to the pan. When the butter easily slides across the pan as you gently shake it, pour in the egg; it should not sizzle (if it does, turn down the heat).

With a fork, stir the eggs continuously in a figure-eight pattern until the eggs begin to set, about 2 minutes. Keep stirring until the eggs are nearly cooked through on the bottom (but not browned) but still runny on top, about 1 minute. Remove the pan from the heat and let sit for 1 minute to help the omelet release from the pan.

Starting at the edge of the omelet closest to you, roll the omelet away from you, using a rubber spatula to guide the egg. Tilt the pan slightly and continue to roll the egg until it's a cylinder at the edge of the pan. Turn out onto a plate. Make two more omelets the same way. Cut the omelets in half and transfer one half to each serving plate. Season with salt and black pepper and serve immediately, with the mushroom conserva and herb relish alongside.

CHICKEN LIVER SPIEDINI
WITH SWEET BEER MUSTARD

Chicken livers have an incredibly balanced flavor—a bit sweet and rich, with a musty, mineral tang. They're incredibly versatile and totally underrated (read: inexpensive). Celebrating the whole animal is part of being a good cook. These bits and pieces—the organ meats, the odd cuts—should be as much a part of your diet as steaks and burgers. The key with chicken livers is not to overcook them. You're aiming for medium-rare, when the livers are still tender and juicy. | **SERVES 6 AS A SNACK**

12 cipollini onions, quartered 24 chicken livers 12 cherry tomatoes 1 cubanelle or red bell pepper, cut into 1½-inch pieces	2 tablespoons extra-virgin olive oil Kosher salt and freshly ground black pepper Sweet beer mustard, homemade (recipe follows) or store-bought, for serving	**SPECIAL EQUIPMENT:** Six 8-inch metal or bamboo skewers (if using bamboo, soak in water to cover for 1 hour)

Bring a small saucepan of water to a boil and add the onions. Boil the onions until just tender, about 4 minutes, then drain and rinse with cold water.

Onto each skewer, thread the onions, livers, tomatoes, and bell pepper pieces, alternating; each skewer should have two of each vegetable and four livers. Set on a plate, drizzle with olive oil, and season with salt and black pepper.

Prepare a gas or charcoal grill for direct, high-heat grilling. Grill the skewers, turning once, until the chicken livers are browned on the outside but still pink within and the vegetables are lightly charred, about 5 minutes. Transfer to a platter and serve immediately, with beer mustard alongside.

SWEET BEER MUSTARD
MAKES ABOUT 1 CUP

1 cup dark beer
¾ cup brown mustard seeds
¼ cup yellow mustard seeds
½ cup apple cider vinegar
¼ cup honey
1 tablespoon light brown sugar
2 garlic cloves, minced
1 teaspoon kosher salt, plus more as needed
Freshly ground black pepper

In a medium bowl, combine the beer and brown and yellow mustard seeds. Cover and refrigerate overnight. Transfer to a food processor and add the vinegar, honey, brown sugar, garlic, and salt. Pulse until the mixture is slightly creamy (there will still be many whole mustard seeds). Transfer to a lidded jar and season to taste with salt and pepper. The mustard will keep, refrigerated, for many months.

COUNTRY-STYLE PORK PÂTÉ

A country-style pâté is no more difficult to make than a meat loaf, and it's a wonderful snack to prepare for a crowd, as it feeds many and can be made far in advance.

Apples and pork are a classic pairing, and this pork pâté showcases the fruit in two forms—hard apple cider and finely diced fresh apple. I like to eat pâté with a spoonful of homemade maple jelly, a product I discovered when dining out in Montreal (see Resources, page 331), though you can also serve it with a swipe of grainy mustard instead.

| MAKES ONE 9 X 5 X 3-INCH LOAF, ABOUT 20 SLICES

¾ cup hard apple cider	12 ounces bacon (8 to 10 slices), finely chopped, plus 16 bacon slices for lining the pan	1 teaspoon freshly ground black pepper
3 tablespoons unsalted butter		½ teaspoon sodium nitrite (Insta Cure #1; see Note; optional)
1 cup finely minced onion	1 (6-ounce) piece smoked ham, finely diced	
½ cup finely diced firm-tart apple, such as Fuji	3 garlic cloves, finely minced	2 large eggs, lightly beaten
2½ pounds coarsely ground pork shoulder (if grinding at home, use a ⅜-inch plate and follow the instructions on pages 161–62)	2½ teaspoons kosher salt	⅓ cup heavy cream
	2½ teaspoons fresh thyme leaves, chopped	Maple jelly, for serving (optional)
	1½ teaspoons Pâté Spice (recipe follows)	SPECIAL EQUIPMENT: Instant-read thermometer; foil-wrapped brick or similar size weight

Preheat the oven to 350°F. Set a rack in the lowest position in the oven.

In a small saucepan, bring the cider to a boil and cook until it has reduced to ½ cup. Remove from the heat and let cool.

In a heavy medium skillet, melt the butter over medium heat. Add the onion and sauté until soft and translucent but not brown, 5 to 6 minutes. Add the diced apple, reduce the heat to low, and cook, stirring occasionally, until the apple is slightly softened, 2 to 3 minutes. Remove from the heat and let cool.

In a large bowl, combine the ground pork, chopped bacon, and diced ham. With a fork or your hands, mix together until well blended. Add the cooled onion-apple mixture, the garlic, salt, thyme, pâté spice, pepper, and sodium nitrite (if using) and mix to combine. Add the eggs, cream, and reduced cider and stir until well incorporated.

CONTINUED

Line a 9 x 5 x 3-inch glass or metal loaf pan or a 6-cup capacity ceramic terrine mold with the bacon slices, arranging 8 slices across the width of the pan and 3 slices on each short side of the pan (do not trim the overhang). With your hands, lightly and evenly press the meat mixture into the pan.

Lay the remaining two slices of bacon lengthwise down the center of the meat mixture, then fold the overhanging bacon slices over so the meat mixture is entirely enclosed in bacon and cover the pan tightly with aluminum foil. Place the pan in a 9 x 13-inch baking pan. Pour boiling water into the baking pan to come halfway up the sides of the loaf pan. Transfer to the oven and bake the pâté until an instant-read thermometer inserted through the foil into the center of the pâté registers 155°F, about 2 hours.

Remove the loaf pan from the water bath. Carefully drain off any fat and juices that have accumulated in the loaf pan, then transfer the pan to a rimmed baking sheet. Place a foil-wrapped brick or similar-shaped weight on top of the pâté to weigh it down. Transfer the pâté to the refrigerator and chill overnight. The pâté will keep in the refrigerator for up to 1 week.

When you're ready to serve the pâté, remove the weight and place the loaf pan in a larger pan of hot water for about 3 minutes, which will allow the pâté to be easily removed from the pan. Invert the pâté onto a cutting board. With a sharp knife, cut the pâté crosswise into ½-inch-thick slices and serve with maple jelly alongside, if desired.

NOTE: Sodium nitrite prevents the meat from oxidizing and discoloring. It is available by mail order (see Resources, page 331).

PÂTÉ SPICE
MAKES ABOUT 1½ TABLESPOONS

1 teaspoon ground cloves
1 teaspoon freshly grated nutmeg
1 teaspoon ground ginger
1 teaspoon ground coriander
1 teaspoon ground cinnamon
¼ teaspoon freshly ground white pepper

Combine the spices in a small skillet and toast over low heat, stirring frequently, until the mixture is aromatic and darkens slightly, about 1 minute. Remove from the heat and let cool. The spice mixture will keep in a tightly lidded jar at room temperature for up to 1 month.

GRILLED CHICKEN WINGS
WITH CIDER BARBECUE SAUCE

I'm going to let you in on a secret: contrary to what every sports bar in America asserts, the best chicken wings don't come out of the deep fryer, but off the grill. These wings are marinated overnight in spiced citrus juice, which tenderizes and flavors the meat, and the sugar in the marinade caramelizes when the chicken is cooked.

Though the wings are flavorful enough on their own, serve them with a tangy apple cider and molasses barbecue sauce alongside, since every wing deserves a dip. Because the marinating and sauce-making are done ahead (and because wings are crowd-pleasers for adults and kids alike), this is a great recipe for a party. | SERVES 6

2½ cups fresh orange juice	2 tablespoons shoyu (white soy sauce)	5½ pounds chicken wings, wing tips removed
1 cup pineapple juice	2 sprigs oregano	1 tablespoon freshly ground black pepper
¾ cup fresh lime juice	2 sprigs thyme	1 teaspoon cayenne pepper
½ cup rice vinegar	1 tablespoon whole black peppercorns	¼ cup fresh cilantro leaves, for garnish
½ cup plus 2 tablespoons kosher salt	2 lemons, halved	Cider-Molasses Barbecue Sauce (recipe follows), for serving
8 garlic cloves, smashed	1 teaspoon cumin seeds, toasted and ground	
2 tablespoons brown sugar		

In a large pot, combine the orange juice, pineapple juice, lime juice, vinegar, ½ cup of the salt, the smashed garlic, brown sugar, shoyu, oregano, thyme, peppercorns, lemon halves, cumin, and 2 cups water and bring to a boil. Remove from the heat and let cool to room temperature. Pour the marinade into a gallon-size zip-top plastic bag or large bowl. Add the chicken wings to the cooled marinade, cover, and refrigerate overnight.

Prepare a gas or charcoal grill for direct, medium-high-heat grilling. Line a rimmed baking sheet with paper towels.

In a small bowl, combine the remaining 2 tablespoons salt, the ground black pepper, and the cayenne. Remove the chicken wings from the marinade and lay them on the paper towel–lined pan; blot them dry with more paper towels. Sprinkle the wings with the salt mixture on all sides and grill, turning often, until charred and cooked through, about 20 minutes.

Transfer the chicken wings to a serving platter and sprinkle with the cilantro. Serve with the barbecue sauce alongside.

CONTINUED

CIDER-MOLASSES BARBECUE SAUCE

MAKES ABOUT 4 CUPS

3 tablespoons canola oil

1 medium yellow onion, thinly sliced

2 garlic cloves, thinly sliced

2 tablespoons ancho chile powder

1½ pounds plum tomatoes, halved, seeded, and chopped

½ cup tomato paste

2 cups apple cider

1 cup chicken stock, plus more as needed

½ cup red wine vinegar

½ cup packed dark brown sugar

3 tablespoons blackstrap molasses

Kosher salt and freshly ground black pepper

In a large saucepan, heat the canola oil over medium heat. When the oil is hot, add the onion and cook, stirring, until lightly caramelized, about 15 minutes. Add 2 tablespoons water to the pan and use a wooden spoon to scrape up the browned bits from the bottom of the pan. When the water has cooked off, add the garlic and chile powder and cook, stirring frequently, for 2 minutes more, then add the chopped tomatoes and tomato paste, reduce the heat to low, and cook, stirring frequently, for 4 to 5 minutes more.

Add the cider, stock, vinegar, brown sugar, and molasses. Bring the mixture to a boil, then reduce the heat to low and simmer, stirring occasionally, until the sauce has thickened and has the texture of ketchup, about 30 minutes.

Working in batches, carefully transfer the sauce to a blender and puree until smooth (alternatively, you can blend the sauce directly in the pot using an immersion blender). If the sauce is too thick, thin it with an extra splash of stock; if it's too thin, return it to the pot and cook over low heat until it reaches the desired consistency.

Season the sauce with salt and pepper and strain through a fine-mesh strainer into a clean bowl, pushing the sauce through the strainer with a rubber spatula.

The sauce can be used immediately or transferred to a lidded jar and refrigerated for up to 2 weeks. Warm the sauce over low heat before using it on the wings or brushing it onto grilled chicken or pork chops.

CALABRIAN CHILE SAUSAGE

Though there are plenty of great store-bought sausages available now, preparing sausage from scratch is one of my favorite kitchen tasks. Once you get the hang of sausage-making (and have the proper equipment), it's easy to whip up a batch quickly and to customize a sausage recipe to suit your taste. The important thing to remember is that sausage must have the proper ratio of fat to lean meat, and you must keep the meat cold when grinding, mixing, and stuffing it; this prevents the emulsion from breaking, which results in grainy sausage. Follow those guidelines and you're ensured juicy sausages with great texture. I've given instructions for casing the sausage, but you could also keep it uncased and form it into patties, which is simpler and no less delicious.

This sausage is similar to an Italian-style link, though it includes spices beyond the typical fennel seeds, and the heat comes from oil-packed Calabrian chiles, which are fruity and spicy. If you can't find them, you could substitute red pepper flakes, minced jalapeños, or even smoky chipotle chiles in adobo sauce. Note that making this sausage is a three-day process, so plan accordingly. | **MAKES ABOUT 5 POUNDS SAUSAGE MEAT OR 12 MEDIUM SAUSAGES**

---

4 pounds pork shoulder or Boston butt, trimmed of sinew and cut into roughly 1 x 3-inch strips

1 pound pork fatback, cut into ½-inch cubes

2 or 3 oil-packed Calabrian chiles (see Resources, page 331), drained and minced

5 garlic cloves, coarsely chopped

3 tablespoons kosher salt

1 teaspoon fennel seeds

1 teaspoon coriander seeds, toasted and ground

1 teaspoon juniper berries, toasted and ground

½ teaspoon sodium nitrite (Insta Cure #1; see Note, page 156; optional)

10 feet hog casings, cleaned (see Note)

2 teaspoons canola oil

2 tablespoons unsalted butter

SPECIAL EQUIPMENT: Meat grinder; sausage stuffer; sausage teaser, pin, or metal skewer

---

In a large bowl, combine the pork shoulder, fatback, chiles, garlic, salt, fennel, coriander, juniper, and sodium nitrite (if using). Mix until evenly coated. Cover with plastic wrap and refrigerate overnight. Put the metal pieces of your meat grinder (the auger and the coarse ⅜-inch plate) into the freezer and freeze overnight.

An hour before you plan to make the sausage, put the bowl of your stand mixer in the freezer.

CONTINUED

Assemble the grinder and position the chilled bowl underneath. Grind the meat through the coarse plate of the grinder directly into the chilled bowl. Fit the stand mixer with the paddle attachment and paddle the ground meat on low speed until it starts to look sticky and leaves a white film along the sides of the bowl, about 5 minutes.

With a rubber spatula, fold the meat mixture to make sure all the ingredients are uniformly incorporated. Pinch off a small amount of meat (about the size of a quarter), form it into a patty, and cook it in a dry pan until cooked through but not browned. Taste and adjust the seasoning of the sausage to your liking, cooking additional test patties as needed.

Press a sheet of parchment paper or plastic wrap directly onto the surface of the meat mixture to prevent oxidation, then cover the bowl tightly with another piece of plastic wrap and refrigerate overnight.

The next day, stuff the sausages into the casings. Gently turn on the water on the kitchen sink. Hold one end of a piece of hog casing up to the faucet nozzle and support it with your other hand. Let the water run through the casing to rinse it and check for holes. Repeat with the remaining casings. (If there are any holes in the casings, cut out the pieces with holes.) Put the rinsed casings in a bowl of cold water and refrigerate until ready to use.

Load the sausage mixture into a sausage stuffer, compressing it gently to remove air bubbles. Have ready a sausage teaser (a pin works, too) and a bowl of water. Moisten the nozzle of the sausage stuffer with water, then load the casings onto the nozzle, keeping them straight and taking care not to overlap them. Crank or turn on the stuffer; when the meat just starts to come out of the nozzle, stop cranking or turn the machine off. Pull 4 to 5 inches of casing off the end of the nozzle but don't knot it. Moisten your work surface with water to prevent the sausages from sticking. With one hand, crank or turn on the sausage stuffer.

Once the sausage mixture starts to fill the casing, remove the air by pinching and tying a knot at the end of the casing. Keep your free hand on the casing as the sausage fills. (If you see air pockets, prick the casing with the teaser or pin.) If the casing splits, cut the damaged bit of casing and discard. Reserve the sausage mixture that burst and add it back to the stuffer. Once stuffed, knot the end of the sausage rope.

Pinch the sausage about 5 inches from the end to make your first link and twist the link forward for about seven rotations. Form the second link: this time, pinch firmly and twist it backward. Repeat this process, alternating forward and backward, until you reach the open end of the casing. Twist the open end right at the last bit of filling to seal off the whole coil, and then tie a knot. Transfer the links to a rimmed baking sheet and refrigerate, uncovered, overnight. Uncooked sausages will keep for up to 2 days in the fridge or they can be frozen. To freeze, arrange on a baking sheet in a single layer, not touching. When frozen solid, transfer to a plastic freezer storage bag. Frozen sausages will keep for up to 2 months; thaw before cooking.

To cook, separate the links from one another by cutting them where you twisted the casings. In a large heavy skillet, heat the canola oil over medium heat. When the oil is hot, add the sausages and brown on all sides. Once browned, add the butter to the pan and cook, basting the sausages with the hot fat to help them cook on all sides, until an instant-read thermometer reads 145°F when inserted into the center of a sausage, about 10 minutes. (Do not cut into them to determine doneness or all the juices will leak out.) Alternatively, you can cook the sausages on a grill, first over direct heat until browned, then move them to more indirect heat until cooked through.

NOTE: Hog casings can be special ordered from your butcher shop; any leftover casings can be packed in kosher salt and refrigerated; they will keep for up to 6 months but should be soaked overnight and rinsed thoroughly before using.

HOW TO MAKE SAUSAGE

1. The farce (seasoned ground meat), ready to be stuffed into casings.

2. Load the casings onto the nozzle of the sausage stuffer.

3. Stuff the farce into the casings.

4. Prick the casings all over with a sausage teaser, metal skewer, or pin to eliminate air pockets.

5. Pinch the casing at 5-inch intervals, then twist to form links.

MAPLE-LIME GRILLED CHICKEN LEGS WITH BEAN SALAD

Grilling season comes on fast in New England. When the cold spring mornings finally give way to the first days of short sleeves and iced coffee, we waste no time rolling our grills out from the garage, knowing it's only a matter of time before the weather turns again and drives us back indoors.

Grilled chicken with a simple side salad can be a weeknight staple during the summer. Marinate the chicken in a combination of maple syrup and fresh lime juice, amped up with hot sauce and smoky Spanish paprika. For easy cleanup, make the marinade in a zip-top plastic bag and then add the chicken. The genius of this marinade is that the lime juice tenderizes the meat, and its tartness is balanced out by the addition of the maple syrup. This recipe calls for whole chicken legs, but you can also use boneless, skinless chicken thighs, which will cook quickly but stay juicy. If you prefer, you can substitute breasts and reduce the grilling time accordingly. A simple bean salad, which can be made up to a day ahead, rounds out this summer supper. | SERVES 4 TO 6

FOR THE CHICKEN
¾ cup fresh lime juice
¼ cup hot sauce, preferably Cholula
3 tablespoons maple syrup
2 teaspoons sweet Spanish paprika
2 large garlic cloves, minced
1 tablespoon chopped fresh oregano
1 tablespoon kosher salt
1½ teaspoons freshly ground black pepper
6 whole chicken legs (drumsticks and thighs)

FOR THE BEAN SALAD
2 cups cooled cooked chickpeas, or 1 (15-ounce) can chickpeas, drained and rinsed
2 cups cooled cooked pinto beans, or 1 (15-ounce) can pinto beans, drained and rinsed
3 scallions, thinly sliced
½ medium red onion, finely diced
2 small carrots, coarsely grated on a box grater
6 radishes, thinly sliced
¼ cup chopped fresh dill
¼ cup chopped fresh parsley
¼ cup full-fat Greek yogurt
3 tablespoons extra-virgin olive oil
Juice of 1 lemon
4 cloves Roasted Garlic (recipe follows), mashed to a paste
1 teaspoon kosher salt, plus more as needed
Freshly ground black pepper
½ cup crumbled queso fresco

SPECIAL EQUIPMENT: Instant-read thermometer

Marinate the chicken: In a gallon-size zip-top plastic bag, combine the lime juice, hot sauce, maple syrup, paprika, garlic, oregano, salt, and pepper. Add the chicken to the bag and turn to coat with the marinade. Seal the bag and refrigerate for at least 2 hours or up to overnight.

CONTINUED

While the chicken marinates, make the bean salad: In a large bowl, combine the chickpeas, pinto beans, scallions, red onion, carrots, radishes, dill, and parsley.

In a small bowl, stir together the yogurt, olive oil, lemon juice, roasted garlic paste, salt, and pepper to taste. Pour over the beans and mix to coat. Add the queso fresco and stir gently to combine. Season to taste with salt and pepper, then transfer to a serving bowl.

Prepare a charcoal or gas grill for indirect grilling. If using a charcoal grill, light 50 to 60 briquets and let burn until just covered with ash, 20 to 30 minutes. Mound them to one side, leaving a cleared area for indirect cooking. If using a gas grill, turn all burners to high and close the lid. When the temperature reaches 400°F, lift the lid and turn off one of the burners, creating the indirect heat zone.

Remove the chicken from the marinade (reserve the marinade) and place skin-side down, on the hot side of the grill. Cook until the skin begins to brown, 2 to 3 minutes. Flip and cook 2 to 3 minutes more on the second side. Then move the chicken to the indirect heat zone. Continue cooking, flipping and basting with the reserved marinade occasionally, until well browned and an instant-read thermometer inserted into the joint between the leg and thigh registers 165°F, about 35 minutes. Transfer to a platter and serve hot or at room temperature with the bean salad alongside.

ROASTED GARLIC
MAKES 1 HEAD

1 head garlic, unpeeled
2 teaspoons olive oil

Preheat the oven to 400°F.

Peel most of the papery skin off the garlic, leaving the head itself intact with all the cloves connected. Trim about ¼ inch off the top of the head to expose the garlic cloves. Place on a sheet of aluminum foil and drizzle with the olive oil. Wrap the foil around the garlic, enclosing it completely, and roast until the garlic cloves are soft and golden brown, 45 minutes to 1 hour. The exact roasting time will depend on the size, age, and variety of the garlic head.

Use immediately or let cool slightly, then press on the bottom of each clove to push it out of its papery skin into an airtight container. It will keep in the refrigerator for up to 2 weeks or in the freezer for up to 3 months.

ORECCHIETTE BOLOGNESE

A meaty ragù is a back-pocket recipe: universally beloved (even, I've found, by picky children), it requires a tiny bit of effort and a decent investment of time, but it can be made well in advance and freezes beautifully, then defrosted for a weeknight dinner.

There are as many variations on ragù Bolognese as there are cooks making it. Some use a few different types of meat, including veal, pork, or lamb; others are fortified with chicken livers or prosciutto. For simplicity's sake, I use ground beef, simmered for a long time in a combination of milk and tomatoes until it becomes a silky, rich sauce. I like to serve the sauce with orecchiette, because the little ears capture and hold the sauce, but you could substitute (fresh or dried) pappardelle or tagliatelle. | **SERVES 6 AS A MAIN COURSE**

3 tablespoons unsalted butter	Kosher salt and freshly ground black pepper	1 (14.5-ounce) can diced San Marzano tomatoes
1 tablespoon canola oil	1 cup dry red wine	1 bay leaf
½ cup finely diced yellow onion	1¼ cups whole milk	1 pound dry or fresh orecchiette, pappardelle, or tagliatelle
¾ cup finely diced celery	Pinch of freshly grated nutmeg	Grated Parmigiano-Reggiano cheese, for serving
¾ cup finely diced carrot		
1 pound ground beef chuck		

In a medium pot, heat the butter and canola oil over medium heat. When the butter has melted, add the onion and cook, stirring, until it begins to soften, about 6 minutes. Add the celery and carrot and cook, stirring, for 3 to 4 minutes.

Add the ground beef, a large pinch of salt, and a few grindings of pepper. Cook the meat, breaking up the large chunks with a wooden spoon as it cooks, until the beef is just cooked through, about 5 minutes. Pour in the wine and cook, stirring occasionally, until almost all the wine has evaporated. Pour in the milk, add the nutmeg, and bring to a gentle simmer. Add the tomatoes and their juices and stir to combine. Bring to a

boil, then reduce the heat so the sauce is at a very slow simmer, barely bubbling. Add the bay leaf and cook, uncovered, for 2½ to 3 hours, until the meat is very tender and the sauce is rich and concentrated, stirring from time to time with a wooden spoon. If the sauce begins to look too dry, add a bit of water; you don't want the sauce to break or become too dry, but the goal is a reduced, concentrated sauce, so don't overwater it.

Season to taste with salt and pepper. Bolognese can be made ahead; let cool to room temperature, then transfer to the refrigerator. It will keep for up to 1 week or can be frozen for up to 3 months. Thaw before using.

Bring a large pot of salted water to a boil. When the water is boiling, add the orecchiette and cook until al dente. Drain, reserving 1 cup of the pasta cooking water. Add the pasta to the pot containing the Bolognese sauce (if you've made the Bolognese sauce in advance, rewarm it gently over low heat

before adding the pasta) and stir to combine, adding some of the reserved pasta water to help the sauce cling to the pasta.

Transfer to a platter and garnish with the Parmigiano-Reggiano. Serve immediately.

ROASTED LEG OF LAMB
WITH BLUEBERRY CHERMOULA

We think of lamb as a special-occasion meat (in my family it was always served on Easter), but roasting a leg of lamb is no more difficult than roasting a chicken. I'll roast a bone-in leg of lamb on holidays, but it's simpler to purchase a boneless leg of lamb. Purchase one that's on the smaller side, then use a sharp knife to butterfly the leg so it's an even thickness all over; it will give you more surface area on which to smear the garlicky rub, and it'll be easier to roll into a roast. Note that the lamb can also be grilled—if you opt for that method, it does not need to be rolled and tied. Grill the butterflied lamb over moderate coals, turning occasionally, until an instant-read thermometer inserted into the thickest part of the meat registers 130°F.

Chermoula is a Moroccan herb sauce traditionally served with grilled fish, but I love it with lamb and think it complements the distinct flavor of the meat wonderfully. I add fresh blueberries to this chermoula; it's a seasonal New England twist that pairs well with the meat. | SERVES 6

1 (4- to 5-pound) boneless leg of lamb, butterflied	**FOR THE CHERMOULA**	1 to 2 teaspoons fresh lemon juice
5 garlic cloves, minced	1 cup coarsely chopped fresh flat-leaf parsley	1 teaspoon cumin seeds, toasted
1 small bunch rosemary, half the leaves removed and coarsely chopped	1 cup coarsely chopped fresh cilantro leaves and tender stems	5 tablespoons extra-virgin olive oil
Zest of 1 lemon	3 garlic cloves, minced	Freshly ground black pepper
2 tablespoons extra-virgin olive oil	1 tablespoon sweet Spanish paprika	1 cup blueberries, halved
Kosher salt and freshly ground black pepper	2 teaspoons kosher salt, plus more as needed	**SPECIAL EQUIPMENT**: Instant-read thermometer
3 tablespoons canola oil	2 teaspoons sambal chile paste	

Set the lamb on a work surface. If the lamb leg is netted or tied, cut off the net or twine. Dry the exterior and the inside seam of the leg with paper towels. With a sharp knife, trim any large pockets of fat from the meat and remove any blood vessels or glands. Reserve the trimmed fat. Do not cut off all the fat; you want to leave some, which will baste the meat as it roasts.

In a small bowl, mix together the garlic, chopped rosemary, lemon zest, and olive oil. Season the lamb on both sides with salt and pepper, then rub the garlic mixture all over the meat. Transfer to a baking dish, cover loosely with plastic wrap, and refrigerate for at least 6 hours or up to overnight.

Remove the lamb from the refrigerator and let it come to room temperature. Preheat the oven to 375°F.

Lay the lamb out on your work surface, fat-side down, then roll it up so the fat is on the exterior. Set the meat seam-side down. With butcher's twine, tie the roast at 1-inch intervals. Set the lamb in a roasting pan and drizzle with the canola oil.

Roast for 20 minutes, then reduce the oven temperature to 325°F and roast until an instant-read thermometer inserted into the thickest part of the meat registers 130°F (for medium-rare), 25 to 30 minutes longer. Then, if you prefer

medium, roast until an instant-read thermometer registers 140°F, 10 to 15 minutes more. Remove the roast from the oven and transfer to a cutting board. Tent with aluminum foil and let rest for 15 minutes before carving.

While the meat roasts, make the chermoula: In a mini food processor (or with a mortar and pestle), combine the parsley, cilantro, garlic, paprika, salt, chile paste, 1 teaspoon of the lemon juice, and the cumin seeds. Process until the parsley is finely chopped. With the processor running, drizzle in the olive oil. Transfer to a bowl and season to taste with additional lemon juice, salt, and pepper. Gently fold in the blueberries. The sauce can be made up to 1 day in advance. Cover tightly and refrigerate; bring to room temperature before using.

To serve, carve the lamb into thick slices and transfer to a platter. Garnish with the remaining rosemary sprigs and serve the blueberry chermoula alongside.

A REGION OF BEAN EATERS

A staple of the Native American diet, protein-rich beans were quickly adopted by early colonists, who followed the example set by the natives, cooking them in pots, flavored with a bit of meat and maple syrup. Later, molasses—a major Boston export—became the sweetener, and salt pork became the meat of choice. Baked beans became the classic Saturday night supper, often accompanied by hot dogs and brown bread. Leftovers were warmed and served again on the Sabbath, when cooking was forbidden. Owing to the ubiquity of the dish in kitchens throughout the city, Boston got its nickname, Beantown.

Nutritional powerhouses, beans were also a staple of Maine lumber camps, where they were often cooked in pits in the ground. The bean hole tradition persists in some parts of the state today, and beans are still often served at church suppers, town hall meetings, and barbecues throughout New England. Today Maine has the largest number of growers of dry beans in New England.

The baked beans of choice, including Jacob's Cattle, Yellow Eye, and Marfax beans, are the same as those that were once favored by the colonists. These so-called heirloom beans are open pollinated—the seed is selected, saved from year to year, and replanted so that the next generation will inherit the same characteristics. The varieties that are most prevalent in New England are those that have been perpetuated by gardeners over decades. Hardy; well adapted to the local climate; producing a good yield; and oh yes, tasty, these heirloom varieties are distinctive in both flavor and appearance and are worth seeking out. And while heirloom beans can be more expensive than their supermarket counterparts, they also tend to be fresher (some supermarket beans can be up to 10 years old!), so they cook more quickly and evenly and have a creamier texture and richer taste.

Creamy, nutty, sweet, fatty, earthy, tender, toothsome: heirloom beans can possess all these attributes and more. They are a foodstuff with a long tradition, but I find myself discovering new favorite varieties—and finding new ways to use them—all the time. For more information about purchasing heirloom beans, see Resources (page 331). Here are some of my favorite bean varieties:

Bert Goodwin: Resembling a kidney bean, these bush beans have a tight skin and almost winelike flavor.

Boston Roman: This white bean with purple speckles is large and has a deep, earthy flavor.

Marfax: Perfect for baked beans, Marfax keep their shape when cooked and are rich and velvety.

Scarlet Beauty: My favorite bean for using in chili, these meaty deep-red beans were first developed by a plant breeder in New Hampshire.

Vermont Cranberry: A variety of bean that dates back to the 1700s, the Vermont cranberry is light in flavor and perfect in a brothy soup.

Yellow Eye: Melt-in-your-mouth smooth, these beans are especially good when paired with pork; I like to cook them with a smoky ham hock. They are also an excellent (and classic) choice for baked beans.

VERMONT CRANBERRY

BERT GOODWIN

SCARLET BEAUTY

BOSTON ROMAN

YELLOW EYE

MARFAX

BRAISED SHORT RIBS
WITH MOXIE BEANS

Long, cold New England winters would be unbearable if it weren't for braises. There's a solid six months between picking the last of the summer's tomatoes and trimming the first spear of asparagus, and during that time I turn to sturdy long-cooked recipes like these short ribs, which have the added benefit of warming your kitchen as they cook. This is a recipe intended for a cold day, when the wind is blowing sideways and the snow shoveling feels never-ending.

Moxie soda is a beloved New England soft drink first created in 1876 as a medicinal beverage (and is the official soft drink of Maine, where the founder was born). It's flavored with gentian root, giving it a bitter flavor, with hints of cola, root beer, and Dr Pepper, which is what you should substitute if you can't find Moxie where you live. It's the secret ingredient in these beans, giving them a complex, sweet, and fruity flavor.

A mustard jus, reduced until it coats the back of a spoon, finishes the dish. It adds a tangy, acidic element to the mellow, tender meat. Like all braises, these short ribs improve upon sitting, so make them the day before you plan to eat them if you're able; the beans can also be made a day ahead and reheated. | SERVES 6

FOR THE BEANS
2 cups dried kidney beans
Canola oil, for the dish
2¾ teaspoons kosher salt
2 to 3 cups Moxie soda (substitute Dr Pepper if necessary)
⅓ cup tomato paste
1 tablespoon apple cider vinegar
¼ teaspoon freshly ground black pepper
3 thick-cut bacon slices, quartered crosswise

FOR THE SHORT RIBS
4 pounds bone-in beef short ribs, cut crosswise into 4-inch pieces (have your butcher do this)
Kosher salt and freshly ground black pepper
¼ cup plus 3 tablespoons extra-virgin olive oil
3 celery stalks, chopped
2 carrots, chopped
1 medium onion, chopped
1 large tomato, cored and quartered

6 garlic cloves
¼ bunch fresh thyme
2 cups beef stock
1½ cups dry red wine
2 tablespoons whole-grain mustard
4 tablespoons chopped fresh flat-leaf parsley

CONTINUED

Make the beans: Put the beans in a bowl and add enough cold water to cover by a few inches. Soak at room temperature overnight.

Preheat the oven to 375°F and lightly oil an 8-inch square baking dish.

Drain the beans and transfer to a heavy-bottomed pot or Dutch oven. Add enough fresh water to cover and 2 teaspoons of the salt, then bring to a boil over high heat and cook until the beans are just tender, about 20 minutes. Drain and transfer to a large bowl.

Add 2 cups of the soda, the tomato paste, vinegar, the remaining ¾ teaspoon salt, and the pepper and stir to combine.

Transfer the beans to the prepared baking dish and top with the bacon. The beans can be made up to this point, covered, and refrigerated overnight, or baked, cooled, and refrigerated, then reheated before serving. Bake until the bacon is crisp and the beans are hot and bubbling, about 1 hour, adding more soda to the dish if the beans are beginning to look dry. If, after an hour, the beans are still not tender, cover with aluminum foil and cook until they are (older beans take longer to soften). When the beans are tender, remove from the oven and reduce the oven temperature to 275°F.

Make the short ribs: Heat a large cast-iron skillet over high heat. Season the short ribs with salt and pepper and drizzle with 3 tablespoons of the olive oil. When the pan is hot, add the short ribs (in batches, if necessary) and sear, turning, until well browned on all sides, about 10 minutes. Transfer to a plate.

In a food processor, combine the celery, carrots, onion, tomato, and garlic and process until the mixture is finely, evenly chopped.

Heat a large Dutch oven or heavy-bottomed pot over medium-high heat. Add the remaining ¼ cup olive oil and the thyme to the pot. Add the vegetables, season with salt and pepper, and cook, stirring frequently, until lightly browned, about 10 minutes.

Pour in the stock and wine and bring to a boil. Add the browned short ribs to the pot; the liquid should almost cover the meat. Reduce the heat to bring the liquid to a simmer, cover the pot, and transfer to the oven. Uncover and check after 15 minutes; the liquid should be just simmering. Adjust the oven temperature, if necessary, then re-cover and cook. Cook until the meat is very tender, 2 to 2½ hours. Remove the short ribs from the oven and return the beans to the oven to warm through. The short ribs can be prepared to this point, cooled to room temperature, then transferred to the refrigerator. The following day, scrape the congealed fat from the surface and rewarm gently, covered, over low heat.

Transfer the short ribs to a rimmed platter. Pour the short rib braising liquid through a fine-mesh strainer into a large measuring cup or bowl. Let stand until the fat rises to the top, then skim off and discard. Transfer 2 cups of the braising liquid to a small saucepan (discard any remaining braising liquid). Stir in the mustard, then bring to a boil over high heat. Boil the sauce until it has reduced to ¾ cup, about 15 minutes. Spoon the mustard jus over the short ribs, sprinkle the parsley over, and serve, accompanied by the warm beans.

GRILLED HANGER STEAK
WITH CHARRED ORANGE AND FENNEL RELISH

Hanger steak is a cut that's well suited to grilling. It's incredibly flavorful, with a pronounced beefiness and chewy texture befitting a cut derived from a working muscle, and is best when cooked just shy of medium. The relish on this dish is dumb simple. Made from charred wheels of orange, rind and all, and fresh fennel, it's sweet and herbaceous, a refreshing counterpoint to the grilled meat. | SERVES 6

---

2 pounds hanger steak (flank or deckle can be substituted)
2 tablespoons canola oil
Kosher salt and freshly ground black pepper

FOR THE RELISH
1 tablespoon canola oil
½ medium fennel bulb, fronds removed and reserved, root cut out, cut into 4¼-inch slices
1 orange, cut into ½-inch-thick rounds
Kosher salt and freshly ground black pepper

3 tablespoons extra-virgin olive oil
2 tablespoons white verjus (see Note)
1 tablespoon fresh lemon juice
1 tablespoon honey
1 tablespoon finely sliced fresh chives

SPECIAL EQUIPMENT: Instant-read thermometer

Remove the meat from the refrigerator, drizzle with the canola oil, season generously with salt and pepper, and let it come to room temperature.

Make the relish: Prepare a gas or charcoal grill for direct high-heat grilling. Drizzle the canola oil over the fresh fennel and orange slices. Season well with salt and pepper.

Lay the fennel and orange slices on the grill. Grill, turning them every 60 to 90 seconds, until well charred on all sides, about 6 minutes. Remove from the grill and let cool. When cool enough to handle, dice the fennel and the orange slices into small pieces and transfer to a bowl. Coarsely chop the reserved fennel fronds and add to the bowl, along with the olive oil, verjus, lemon juice, honey, and chives, and stir gently to combine. Season to taste with salt and pepper.

Lay the steak on the grill, watching for flare-ups (if the flames threaten to char the steak, move the steak to a cooler part of the grill for a few moments, until the fire calms). Grill the steak, turning it once, until it registers 125°F on an instant-read thermometer, 8 to 9 minutes per side.

Transfer the steak to a cutting board, tent it with aluminum foil, and let rest for 10 minutes. Slice the steak thinly against the grain, transfer it to a platter, and garnish with the relish.

NOTE: Verjus is the fresh, tart juice of unripe wine grapes. Though milder in flavor, white wine vinegar can be substituted in recipes that call for verjus. See Resources, page 331.

ON MEAT

Lately I've become a bit more sensible about my diet, and while I really enjoy meat, I no longer center my diet around it the way that I used to. And when I do eat meat, the quality is what's most important to me.

I prefer not to eat factory-farmed meat. Instead, I seek out meat from small farms that I know are raising their livestock humanely and sustainably. Yes, it's more expensive. But because I eat it less frequently and in smaller quantities, I'm able to spend more (and paying more also makes me more conscious of waste).

Both the quality of your meat and your cooking technique play huge roles in the final outcome of a dish. Certain cuts of meat are better suited to certain applications, and picking the right cut for the job is a fundamental part of successful meat cookery. Here are some guidelines.

IF IT'S TENDER, COOK IT HOT, FAST, AND DRY

Relatively speaking, tender cuts of meat from the loin sections—such as beef tenderloin, pork chops, lamb saddle, or chicken breasts—can be cooked over high and direct heat, either on the stovetop or grill, in what can be considered a quick cooking method. Use preparations that can add flavor to these cuts, including simple marinades, brines, and spice rubs.

IF IT'S TOUGH, COOK IT WET, SLOWLY, AND COVERED

The "working" muscles of the animal (whether it's beef, pork, lamb, or chicken) are muscles that see more movement and are tougher because of it. These cuts include the shoulder, belly, breast, shank, and leg. For these cuts, a longer cooking time at a lower temperature in liquid will yield the most tender, flavorful meat. Braising, steaming, or even smoking are the best methods for these cuts.

LAYER FLAVORS BY BROWNING

Whenever possible, browning a piece of meat (known as the Maillard reaction) is an excellent way to boost the flavor of almost any cut. This might mean you brown a steak on the stovetop in a hot pan before sliding it into the oven to finish, or that you brown a hunk of pork shoulder before settling it into its braising liquid. The important part about the Maillard reaction is not that it adds color to the meat, but that it unlocks flavors and aromas that wouldn't exist otherwise.

FAT IS YOUR FRIEND

Fat is not something to be afraid of. Seek cuts like steaks and chops and even brisket and rib sections that have a high proportion of marbling. As the meat cooks, the fat will render out, basting, moistening, and tenderizing the meat. Once it's cooked, you can always trim away some of the visible exterior fat if you prefer.

BEEF RIB EYE WITH CHANTERELLE
MUSHROOMS AND BEEF FAT BÉARNAISE

This is a sexy, rich, showstopping dish that rivals what you might order at a great steakhouse. It's also a relatively simple one, with the focus squarely on great beef with a great (classic) sauce. Purchase the best quality rib eye you can find, from a good butcher or a favorite farmers' market purveyor, someone who knows the provenance of the steak and who will cut your meat to order, to the requisite thickness.

The béarnaise sauce is made with a combination of melted butter and rendered beef fat. If your steak has an ample fat cap, you can trim some and render it over low heat in the same pan in which you plan to cook the steaks, then use that rendered fat in the béarnaise. Otherwise, you can ask your butcher for a small piece of supplemental beef fat, or make the béarnaise with all butter.

If chanterelles are not in season, the steak would be equally delicious with fresh porcini, cremini, matsutake, or even well-roasted button mushrooms. You could also substitute a different cut of steak for rib eye, if you desire— a New York strip steak or sirloin would be a good alternative. Allow the steak to come to room temperature before cooking it, which will help it cook evenly, and keep your béarnaise warm while you cook the meat to prevent it from separating. | SERVES 4 TO 6 AS A MAIN COURSE

---

2 (2-inch-thick) boneless rib eye steaks (about 3 pounds)

3 tablespoons toasted sesame oil

½ cup doenjang (Korean soybean paste; see Resources, page 331)

Kosher salt and freshly ground black pepper

2 tablespoons canola oil

4 tablespoons cold unsalted butter, cut into cubes

3 garlic cloves, thinly sliced

2 cups small chanterelle mushrooms (small porcini or oyster mushrooms can be substituted)

FOR THE BÉARNAISE SAUCE

2 tablespoons dry white wine

1 tablespoon white wine vinegar

1 medium shallot, quartered

1 sprig tarragon

½ teaspoon whole black peppercorns

3 egg yolks

⅓ cup unsalted butter, melted

4 tablespoons cold unsalted butter, cut into cubes

Flaky salt, such as Maldon, for finishing

Chinese black vinegar (see Note, page 98) or balsamic vinegar, for finishing

CONTINUED

Remove the steaks from the refrigerator and trim some of the excess fat and any silver skin; leave a thin layer of fat on each steak. Reserve the trimmed fat.

Transfer the steaks to a plate. Drizzle with the sesame oil, then slather with the doenjang and dot some of the garlic slices on both sides of each steak. Let stand at room temperature for at least 1 hour or up to 2 hours. With a paper towel, wipe off the doenjang and discard the garlic slices. Rinse the steaks under cold water and pat dry. Season with salt and pepper.

In a medium skillet, cook the reserved beef fat over medium-high heat until the fat has melted, about 5 minutes. Pour the fat into a bowl and set it on the back of the stove. Return the skillet to the heat and add 1 tablespoon of the canola oil and 2 tablespoons of the cold butter. When the butter stops foaming, add the garlic and mushrooms and cook, stirring occasionally, until the mushrooms and the butter are lightly browned, 5 minutes. Season with salt and pepper. Keep warm on the back of the stove.

Make the béarnaise sauce: In a small saucepan, combine the wine, vinegar, shallot, tarragon, and peppercorns and bring to a boil over medium-high heat. Cook until the liquid has reduced to 1 tablespoon. Strain into a medium bowl, discarding the aromatics.

Fill a medium saucepan with water to a depth of 1 inch and bring to a simmer over medium-high heat. Set the bowl containing the vinegar mixture over the simmering water; be sure the bottom of the bowl does not touch the water. Whisk the egg yolks into the mixture, one at a time, until well blended. Cook, whisking continuously, until the mixture begins to thicken, about 2 minutes. Whisk in the melted butter and 2 tablespoons of the rendered beef fat (if you do not have enough beef fat, add additional melted butter) and whisk until smooth. Season with salt and pepper and keep warm on the back of the stove while you cook the steaks. The sauce will thicken as it sits; if necessary, whisk in a few tablespoons of warm water just before serving—the béarnaise should have the consistency of thin mayonnaise.

In a large heavy skillet (preferably cast-iron), heat the remaining 1 tablespoon canola oil over medium-high heat. Add the steaks and panfry until well browned and cooked to the desired doneness, 6 to 8 minutes per side for rare (use a meat thermometer to check the internal temperature—125°F for medium-rare), reducing the heat to medium if the crust is becoming too dark. Halfway through the cooking, add the 4 tablespoons butter to the pan and baste the steaks with some of it as it melts. Transfer the meat to a cutting board, tent with aluminum foil, and let rest for 7 to 9 minutes.

Slice the steaks into ½-inch-thick slices. Spoon some of the mushrooms onto each plate and top with some of the sliced meat. Garnish the meat with some flaky salt and a few drops of black vinegar. Serve immediately with the béarnaise sauce alongside.

BEEF AND PORK MEAT LOAF
WITH CRISPY ONION RINGS

I'll admit, there are some unusual ingredients in this meat loaf. It's made with a combination of ground beef and pork, plus anchovies, Spanish paprika, and Korean chile paste, all of which add umami. The result is a robustly seasoned meat loaf that's deeply savory and, I think, a blue plate special for a modern age.

One key tip: Don't overmix the meat or the meat loaf will be tough. Blend the ingredients by hand just until combined, then form into a loaf. The loaf can be refrigerated up to four hours in advance. Let it come to room temperature before you cook it, and let it rest before slicing; otherwise, the slices may crumble.

The only thing better than a hot plate of meat loaf is a cold meat loaf sandwich, fully loaded with pickles, mayonnaise, and crunchy onion rings. You can make individual sandwiches or create a sort of meat loaf hero on a large baguette to serve the masses (or take to a picnic). This sandwich, and a cold beer? Heaven. | **SERVES 6**

---

1 small onion, coarsely chopped

1 small carrot, coarsely chopped

1 celery stalk, coarsely chopped

4 ounces button mushrooms, cleaned well and coarsely chopped

3 oil-packed white anchovy fillets (boquerones), coarsely chopped

2 garlic cloves, coarsely chopped

¼ cup finely minced fresh parsley

2 tablespoons unsalted butter

1 tablespoon canola oil

1 teaspoon sweet Spanish paprika

½ cup chicken stock

¼ cup heavy cream

2 teaspoons soy sauce

1 teaspoon Worcestershire sauce

1½ pounds ground beef (preferably 80% lean)

¾ pound ground pork

2 large eggs

1 cup finely grated sharp cheese, such as Vella Dry Jack or aged cheddar

2 slices white bread, crusts removed, cut into small cubes

2 teaspoons chopped fresh rosemary leaves

1 teaspoon chopped fresh thyme leaves

1 tablespoon Dijon mustard

2 teaspoons kosher salt

½ teaspoon freshly ground black pepper

FOR THE GLAZE

¾ cup ketchup

½ cup apple cider vinegar

¼ cup packed light brown sugar

½ teaspoon freshly ground black pepper

Crispy Onion Rings (recipe follows), for serving

SPECIAL EQUIPMENT: Instant-read thermometer

CONTINUED

Preheat the oven to 350°F. Line a rimmed baking sheet with aluminum foil or parchment paper.

In a food processor, combine the onion, carrot, celery, mushrooms, anchovy fillets, garlic, and parsley. Pulse until the vegetables are finely chopped; there should be no pieces bigger than the circumference of a pencil eraser.

In a large skillet, heat the butter and canola oil over medium-low heat. When the butter has melted, add the ground vegetable mixture and cook, stirring, until fragrant and the onion pieces are becoming translucent, about 5 minutes. Add the paprika and cook, stirring, for 1 minute more.

Add the stock, cream, soy sauce, and Worcestershire, increase the heat so the liquid is simmering, and simmer until most of the liquid has evaporated, about 10 minutes. Remove from the heat and let cool.

In a large bowl, combine the beef, pork, eggs, cheese, and bread cubes. Mix with your hands to combine, then add the cooled vegetable mixture, rosemary, thyme, mustard, salt, and pepper and mix until just incorporated.

Transfer the meat mixture to the prepared baking sheet and, with your hands, shape the meat into an elongated oval (or, if you prefer, divide the meat mixture in half and shape into two equal-size loaves). Bake for 1 hour, until the internal temperature registers 155°F on an instant-read thermometer.

While the meat loaf bakes, make the glaze: In a small bowl, whisk together the ketchup, vinegar, brown sugar, and pepper. When the meat loaf has baked for 30 minutes, remove it from the oven and spoon half the glaze over the surface. Return it to the oven and bake for the remaining 30 minutes. Remove it from the oven and let cool slightly before slicing. Serve the meat loaf warm, accompanied by onion rings, with the remaining glaze alongside.

The meat loaf can be eaten warm or cooled completely, wrapped in aluminum foil, and refrigerated for up to 2 days. If making sandwiches, let the meat loaf cool completely, then thinly slice.

To make a meat loaf sandwich, lightly toast bread slices. Slather each piece on one side with mayonnaise. Top with several thin slices of meat loaf, pickles, and onion rings. Serve immediately.

CRISPY ONION RINGS
SERVES 6

2 cups all-purpose flour
1 teaspoon kosher salt, plus more as needed
1 teaspoon freshly ground black pepper
1½ cups buttermilk
2 Spanish onions, sliced into ½-inch-thick rounds, "rings" separated
4 cups canola oil, for frying

SPECIAL EQUIPMENT: Deep-fry thermometer

Put a wire rack over a rimmed baking sheet, line the rack with a double thickness of paper towels, and set it nearby.

In a medium bowl, whisk together the flour, salt, and pepper. Pour the buttermilk into a second medium bowl. Dredge the onion rings in the seasoned flour, then dip each ring in the buttermilk, letting the excess drip off, and return it to the flour to coat. Transfer the onion rings to the wire rack and discard any remaining buttermilk and flour.

In a large heavy-bottomed saucepan, heat the canola oil over medium-high heat until it registers 375°F on a deep-fry thermometer. When the oil is hot, fry the onion rings in batches until golden brown, 3 to 4 minutes per batch, letting the oil return to temperature between each batch.

Use a spider to transfer the rings to the paper towel–lined rack. Season with salt and serve hot, alongside the meat loaf or piled onto a meat loaf sandwich.

BRINED PORK CHOPS
WITH APPLES AND CIPOLLINI ONIONS

My wife, Kate, and I try to choose a perfect fall day, when the air is crisp but the sun is still bright and the leaves have just started to change color, for our annual apple-picking outing with our boys. We can't help but pick too many (and eat more than our fair share while we're still at the orchard), and often this recipe is one of the first I make with our haul.

In fall, there's still time for a few more dinners cooked on the grill, so I brine the pork chops to keep them juicy and then cook them over hot coals until they're deeply browned and medium within. Pairing pork with *agrodolce* onions and apples is a sweet-tart mixture that's similar in spirit to the pork chops with applesauce you're already familiar with.

If I play it just right, I can convince Kate, a trained pastry chef, to make a pie for dessert to use up the rest of our apples. | SERVES 6

FOR THE BRINE		
½ cup kosher salt	2 pounds bone-in pork chops	2 tablespoons fresh lemon juice
½ cup packed dark brown sugar	2 tablespoons extra-virgin olive oil	1 tablespoon honey
1 tablespoon coriander seeds, toasted	12 cipollini onions (about 1 pound)	Leaves from 1 sprig rosemary, coarsely chopped
2 teaspoons caraway seeds, toasted	2 firm-sweet apples, such as Fuji, cored and cut into ½-inch cubes	2 tablespoons canola oil
2 star anise pods	4 garlic cloves	1 tablespoon unsalted butter
	½ cup oloroso sherry	1 tablespoon minced fresh chives
	½ cup chicken or pork stock	
		SPECIAL EQUIPMENT: Instant-read thermometer

Make the brine: In a large saucepan, combine the salt, brown sugar, coriander seeds, caraway seeds, star anise, and 4 cups water. Bring to a boil over high heat, then remove from the heat. Stir to dissolve the salt and sugar. Let cool to room temperature, then transfer to the refrigerator and cool completely. The brine can be made up to 2 days ahead; refrigerate until ready to use.

Put the pork chops in a bowl and pour the cooled brine over. Make sure the chops are completely submerged; if necessary, weigh them down with a small plate. Refrigerate the chops in the brine for at least 6 hours but no more than 12 hours; the longer the chops sit in the brine, the saltier they become.

CONTINUED

In a 12-inch skillet, heat the olive oil over medium heat. When the oil is hot, add the onions and cook, turning occasionally, until golden brown on all sides, about 10 minutes. Add the apples and cook, stirring occasionally, until the apples are caramelized and beginning to soften, 6 minutes more.

Add the garlic and cook until light brown, then pour in the sherry and reduce the heat to medium-low. Add the stock, lemon juice, honey, and rosemary and cook until the liquid has reduced by half, about 8 minutes. Remove the pan from the heat.

Prepare a gas or charcoal grill for direct, medium-high-heat grilling. Remove the pork chops from the brine, rinse with cold water, and pat dry with paper towels. Discard the brine. Drizzle the chops on both sides with the canola oil and grill, turning once, until browned on both sides and an instant-read thermometer inserted into the thickest part of the chop registers 155°F, about 10 minutes total. Transfer the chops to a rimmed platter and tent with aluminum foil; let rest 10 minutes.

Return the onion-apple mixture to medium heat. Cook, stirring, until heated through, then reduce the heat to low and stir in the butter and chives. Serve alongside the pork chops.

DUCK EGG SABAYON
WITH STRAWBERRIES AND CANDIED PISTACHIOS

This frothy dessert (known in Italian as *zabaglione*) is made by whisking together eggs, sugar, and wine over simmering water until the mixture has a mousselike consistency. Using duck eggs makes the dessert especially rich and luscious, though chicken eggs are a fine substitute. I love the combination of prosecco and strawberries, though you could substitute muscat or Madeira. | SERVES 6

FOR THE CANDIED PISTACHIOS	FOR THE STRAWBERRIES	FOR THE SABAYON
¼ cup sugar	1½ pounds strawberries, halved (or quartered, if large)	2 duck egg yolks, or 6 chicken egg yolks
1 cup shelled raw pistachios	¼ cup sugar	½ cup prosecco or Champagne
¼ teaspoon fine sea salt	Juice of ½ lemon	6 tablespoons sugar
		Pinch of kosher salt
		Crumbled meringue, for garnish (see page 95; optional)

Preheat the oven to 325°F.

Make the candied pistachios: In a small saucepan, combine the sugar and ¼ cup water. Cook over medium heat, stirring, until the sugar has dissolved. Remove from the heat and let the syrup cool to room temperature.

Put the pistachios in a bowl and toss with 4 teaspoons of the cooled syrup. Transfer to a rimmed baking sheet, spreading in a single layer, and sprinkle with the salt. Bake until light golden brown, 7 to 10 minutes. Remove from the oven and let cool. Save any remaining syrup; it can be used for cocktails or to sweeten iced tea or lemonade and will keep in the refrigerator for many months.

Prepare the strawberries: In a medium bowl, combine the strawberries, sugar, and lemon juice and toss to coat. Set aside.

Make the sabayon: Fill a saucepan with water to a depth of 1 inch and bring to a simmer over medium-high heat. In a large heatproof bowl, whisk together the egg yolks, prosecco, sugar, and salt. Set the bowl over the simmering water and reduce the heat to low; be sure the bottom of the bowl does not touch the water.

Whisk the egg yolk mixture vigorously and continuously until the egg yolks begin to thicken and have a beautiful pale yellow color, about 10 minutes. When you lift the whisk, the mixture should trail from it in a thick ribbon.

Divide the strawberries among six glasses. Top with a generous spoonful of the sabayon and garnish with some of the candied pistachios and crumbled meringue (if using). Serve immediately.

RHUBARB AND STRAWBERRY CRISP
WITH PORK FAT CRUMBLE

Who can resist a still-warm fruit crisp? The topping on this one may throw you for a curve: it's a combination of butter and rendered leaf lard. Yes! Rendered pork fat makes the topping especially lacy and delicate, with a hint of meaty savor. You'll note that I give a range for the sugar measurement; fruit can vary in sweetness, so add the minimum amount of sugar and taste the fruit, then add more as needed. This is a flexible recipe—you can substitute an equal amount of another type of fruit; peaches are an especially good stand-in if you're making this in late summer. | **MAKES ONE 9 X 13-INCH CRISP; SERVES 8 TO 10**

FOR THE OAT TOPPING

1½ cups plus 2 tablespoons all-purpose flour

½ cup plus 2 tablespoons old-fashioned rolled oats

½ cup packed light brown sugar

6 tablespoons granulated sugar

½ teaspoon ground cinnamon

¾ teaspoon kosher salt

4 tablespoons (½ stick) unsalted butter, melted

2 ounces leaf lard (or substitute unsalted butter), melted

FOR THE FILLING

Unsalted butter, for greasing

3 pounds rhubarb, preferably thinner, deep red stalks, trimmed and cut into 1-inch pieces

2 pounds strawberries, hulled and halved, or quartered if large

2 to 3 cups granulated sugar (see headnote)

¼ cup cornstarch

1 tablespoon kosher salt

¼ cup fresh lemon juice

¼ cup fresh orange juice

1 tablespoon grated fresh ginger

FOR THE LEMON-MASCARPONE CREAM

2 cups mascarpone cheese

Zest and juice of 1 lemon

½ cup confectioners' sugar

¼ teaspoon kosher salt

Confectioners' sugar, for dusting

Preheat the oven to 350°F. Lightly butter a 9 x 13-inch glass or ceramic baking dish.

Make the oat topping: In a large bowl, stir together the flour, oats, brown sugar, granulated sugar, cinnamon, and salt. Drizzle in the melted butter and lard and stir with a fork until the mixture clumps, breaking up any clumps larger than ½ inch. Transfer to the refrigerator while you prepare the filling.

Make the filling: In a large bowl, combine the rhubarb, strawberries, 2 cups of the granulated sugar, the cornstarch, salt, lemon juice, orange juice, and ginger. Mix well to combine and let macerate at room temperature for 20 minutes. Taste the fruit and add ½ to 1 cup additional sugar, depending on the tartness of the fruit. Transfer the fruit to the prepared baking dish and set the dish on a rimmed baking sheet. Use your fingers to crumble the oat topping over the fruit, blanketing it in a thick layer.

Bake until the oat topping is golden brown and the filling is bubbling at the edges, 45 minutes to 1 hour. If the topping is browning too quickly, cover the baking dish with aluminum foil. Remove from the oven and let cool to room temperature.

While the crisp is cooling, make the lemon-mascarpone cream: In the bowl of a stand mixer fitted with the paddle attachment (or in a large bowl using a handheld mixer), combine the mascarpone, lemon zest, confectioners' sugar, and salt. Slowly drizzle in the lemon juice and mix until creamy and well combined.

To serve, spoon the crisp into bowls, top with a spoonful of the mascarpone, and dust with confectioners' sugar.

CRANBERRY-GINGER HAND PIES
WITH CREAM CHEESE GLAZE

We tend to only think of cranberries around Thanksgiving, but these tart jewels are the MVP of the winter pantry, especially welcome when few other fruits are in season. These tender hand pies are made with a super-flaky lard crust and filled with a spiced cranberry mixture. A final drizzle of tangy cream cheese icing transforms them into what Pop-Tarts wish they were. | **MAKES 12**

FOR THE DOUGH

3 cups all-purpose flour, plus more for dusting

1 tablespoon granulated sugar

1 teaspoon kosher salt

5 ounces (1¼ sticks) cold unsalted butter, cut into ½-inch cubes

4 ounces chilled lard or butter, cut into ½-inch cubes

¼ to ½ cup ice water

FOR THE FILLING

1 (12-ounce) package fresh cranberries

1 cup granulated sugar

½ cup packed light brown sugar

¼ cup cornstarch

2 tablespoons fresh lemon juice

1½ teaspoons grated fresh ginger

½ teaspoon kosher salt

½ teaspoon ground ginger

¼ teaspoon ground cinnamon

Pinch of ground allspice

1 egg yolk

Sanding sugar, for topping

FOR THE CREAM CHEESE ICING

4 ounces cream cheese, at room temperature

¾ cup confectioners' sugar

½ teaspoon pure vanilla extract

⅛ teaspoon kosher salt

¼ cup whole milk, plus more as needed

Make the dough: In the bowl of a stand mixer fitted with the paddle attachment, combine the flour, granulated sugar, and salt. Add the butter and lard and mix on medium speed until the mixture is crumbly and resembles wet sand. Very gradually drizzle in half the ice water, then stop the mixer. Take a small handful of the mixture and gently squeeze it; if it forms a ball, you have added enough liquid. If not, gradually add more ice water until it holds together in a ball when squeezed. Transfer the dough to a sheet of plastic wrap (it may be crumbly, which is okay) and use the plastic wrap to form the dough into a ball. Wrap it tightly and refrigerate for a few hours or overnight. The

dough can also be frozen for up to 3 months; let thaw overnight in the refrigerator before using.

Make the filling: In a large heavy-bottomed pot, combine the cranberries, granulated sugar, brown sugar, cornstarch, lemon juice, fresh ginger, salt, ground ginger, cinnamon, allspice, and ½ cup water. Stir together and let sit for 10 minutes, then set the pot over medium heat and cook, stirring continuously, until the sugar has dissolved, the berries are tender, and the mixture is hot and slightly thickened, about 20 minutes.

Remove from the heat, transfer to a bowl, and let cool to room temperature. The filling can be made up to 2 days ahead of time; let cool to room temperature, then cover and refrigerate.

Line two rimmed baking sheets with silicone baking mats or parchment paper.

On a lightly floured surface, divide the dough into two pieces. Roll one half to a thickness of ⅛ inch. With a 5-inch round cutter, stamp out as many circles as you can, reserving the scraps. Transfer to the prepared baking sheets. Repeat with the second piece of dough, then gather and reroll the scraps and cut as many circles as you can; you'll want about 12 circles in total. Discard the scraps. Transfer the dough circles to the refrigerator and refrigerate for 30 minutes.

Preheat the oven to 375°F.

Remove the dough circles from the refrigerator. In a small bowl, whisk together the egg yolk and 1 tablespoon water. Place about 3 tablespoons of filling in the center of each chilled dough circle, then use a fingertip or pastry brush to brush the egg wash on the edge of half of each circle. Fold into half-moons and crimp the edges with a fork to seal. Place on the lined baking sheets, spacing them about 1 inch apart.

Place the pies in the freezer for 5 minutes, then cut three small slits in the top of each pie, brush each one lightly with the egg wash, and sprinkle with sanding sugar. The pies may be prepared to this point and frozen for up to 2 weeks; once they are completely frozen on the baking sheet, transfer to a plastic freezer storage bag. They can be baked when frozen.

Bake for 10 minutes, then rotate the pans and bake for 10 minutes more, until the pastry is golden brown and the fruit is bubbling from the cut vents (if you are baking the frozen hand pies, add 5 to 10 minutes to the baking time). Transfer to a wire rack and let cool.

While the hand pies cool, make the cream cheese icing: In the bowl of a stand mixer fitted with the paddle attachment (or in a large bowl using a handheld mixer), beat the cream cheese, confectioners' sugar, vanilla, and salt on medium-high speed until smooth. Reduce the speed to low and slowly pour in the milk to thin the icing. Dip a teaspoon into the icing to check the consistency: it should coat the back of the spoon but be thin enough to drizzle over the tops of the hand pies; add additional milk if needed.

When the pies are completely cool, drizzle the icing over each one and let stand until set, about 30 minutes.

FEAST | PORK AND BEANS

Pork and beans is an American classic that takes many forms—there's the canned version, first introduced in the 1880s, which was mostly beans with a small amount of pork; the time-honored combination of sausage and beans (or, in my childhood, hot dogs and beans); and myriad other dishes from all cultures that combine the two ingredients.

A whole boneless pork shoulder roast is a magnificent thing to cook—it's simple to prepare and, carved into thick slices, will feed many people. As Yankee tradition dictates, I like to serve it with my version of Boston baked beans and brown bread, with a sprightly Swiss chard salad to cut through the richness of the other dishes. Note that the beans must be soaked overnight (and, I think, they improve in flavor if cooked the day before you plan to eat them), and the meat should be seasoned at least a day in advance.

DRY-BRINED ROAST PORK SHOULDER

BOSTON BAKED BEANS

SWISS CHARD, ENDIVE, AND RADICCHIO SALAD

BROWN BREAD

DRY-BRINED ROAST PORK SHOULDER

SERVES 10 TO 12

1 tablespoon fennel seeds

1 tablespoon cumin seeds

1 tablespoon whole black peppercorns

1 tablespoon coriander seeds

1 teaspoon caraway seeds

¼ cup muscovado sugar

1 tablespoon sweet Spanish paprika

1 teaspoon dry mustard

4 teaspoons kosher salt, plus more as needed

1 whole pork shoulder (about 8 pounds)

¼ cup canola oil

1 medium yellow onion, cut into sixths

3 carrots, cut into 3-inch pieces

1 navel orange, quartered

1 apple, cored and quartered

2 bay leaves

Few sprigs thyme

1 (750-ml) bottle hard cider (pear or apple)

2 cups chicken stock

Freshly ground black pepper

1 In a small skillet over medium heat, combine the fennel seeds, cumin seeds, peppercorns, coriander seeds, and caraway seeds. Toast, shaking the pan, until fragrant and a wisp of smoke rises from the pan, 1 minute. Let cool, then transfer to a spice grinder and finely grind. Transfer to a bowl and stir in the sugar, paprika, mustard, and salt.

2 Place the pork in a large roasting pan and rub the spices all over the pork. Cover the shoulder loosely with plastic wrap and let it sit in the refrigerator overnight.

3 The next day, remove the roasting pan from the refrigerator. Rinse the pork with cold water and pat dry with paper towels. Set it on a rimmed baking sheet.

4 Preheat the oven to 325°F.

5 Wipe the roasting pan clean and set it on the stovetop, spanning two burners, over high heat. Heat the oil in the roasting pan. When the oil is hot, add the pork and sear, turning with tongs, until well browned on all sides, about 20 minutes.

6 Transfer to a rimmed baking sheet. Add the onion, carrots, orange, apple, bay leaves, and thyme to the roasting pan. Pour in the cider and stock. Put the pork on top of the vegetable nest and cover the pan tightly with aluminum foil. Roast the pork until the juices run clear and an instant-read thermometer inserted into the thickest part of the roast registers 145°F, about 3 hours.

7 Transfer the pork to a cutting board and tent with foil; let rest for 30 minutes.

8 Meanwhile, pour the braising liquid through a fine-mesh sieve into a saucepan. Discard the orange wedges, apple, bay leaves, and thyme; reserve the onions and carrots on a separate plate.

9 Skim the fat from the braising liquid and bring to a boil over high heat. Boil until reduced by three-quarters, about 15 minutes, then season with salt and pepper.

10 Slice the pork into thick slices and transfer to a platter. Surround the meat with the carrots and onions and serve the braising liquid alongside.

BOSTON BAKED BEANS

MAKES ABOUT 2 QUARTS; SERVES 8

1 pound (2 cups) dried Marfax, Jacob's Cattle, Yellow Eye, great northern, or navy beans

2 teaspoons kosher salt, plus more as needed

1 tablespoon canola oil

½ pound salt pork or bacon, diced

1 small yellow onion, diced

⅓ cup pure maple syrup

¼ cup plus 2 tablespoons blackstrap molasses

2 teaspoons dry mustard

1 teaspoon sweet Spanish paprika

¼ cup red wine vinegar

Boiling water

Freshly ground black pepper

1 Put the beans in a bowl and add cold water to cover. Let soak at room temperature overnight.

2 Preheat the oven to 250°F.

3 Drain the beans, transfer to a large saucepan, and add fresh water to cover. Add the salt, bring to a boil, reduce the heat so the liquid is simmering, and simmer until just tender. Drain and set aside.

4 In a Dutch oven with a lid, heat the canola oil over medium heat. When the oil is hot, add the salt pork and onion and cook until the onion is soft and some of the fat has rendered from the pork, about 8 minutes. Add the maple syrup, ¼ cup of the molasses, the mustard, and the paprika and stir to combine, then add the vinegar and

cook, stirring, for 2 minutes more. Add the beans and stir to coat.

5 Pour in enough boiling water to nearly submerge the beans. Cover and transfer to the oven. Bake for 2 hours, then uncover and stir in the remaining 2 tablespoons molasses. Season with salt and pepper. Increase the oven temperature to 350°F and return the beans (uncovered) to the oven. Cook until a crust forms on top of the beans, about 20 minutes. Serve.

Note: The baked beans can be made up to 2 days ahead; let cool to room temperature, then cover and refrigerate. Reheat in a low oven until warmed through.

SWISS CHARD, ENDIVE, AND RADICCHIO SALAD

SERVES 8

FOR THE DRESSING

½ cup sour cream

⅓ cup apple cider vinegar

Juice of 1 lemon

Juice of ½ lime

1 tablespoon Dijon mustard

1 tablespoon honey

¼ cup extra-virgin olive oil

1 teaspoon finely chopped fresh thyme leaves

Kosher salt and freshly ground black pepper

½ cup raisins

Boiling water

1 bunch Swiss chard, stemmed and thinly sliced into ribbons

1 head endive, halved lengthwise, cored, and cut lengthwise into batons

½ head radicchio, torn into bite-size pieces

1 sweet-tart apple, such as Pink Lady or Honeycrisp, cored and thinly sliced

¼ cup packed dill fronds

½ cup roasted salted cashews, finely chopped

1 Make the dressing: In a medium bowl, whisk together the sour cream, vinegar, lemon juice, lime juice, mustard, and honey. Whisking continuously, add the olive oil in a thin stream and whisk until the dressing is emulsified and frothy. Whisk in the thyme and season to taste with salt and pepper.

2 Put the raisins in a small bowl and add boiling water to cover. Let stand for 10 minutes, then drain and transfer to a paper towel–lined plate. Set aside.

3 In a large bowl, combine the chard, endive, radicchio, apple slices, and dill. Add ½ cup of the dressing (save the rest for another salad; it will keep in an airtight container in the refrigerator for up to 1 week) and toss to coat. Garnish with the raisins and cashews. Serve immediately.

BROWN BREAD

MAKES TWO 10-OUNCE LOAVES OR ONE 9 X 5 X 3-INCH LOAF

Nonstick cooking spray

½ cup plus 3 tablespoons white rye flour (dark rye flour can be substituted)

1 cup plus 2 tablespoons stone-ground whole wheat flour

1 cup fine yellow cornmeal

½ cup plus 3 tablespoons dark rye flour

2 teaspoons baking soda

½ teaspoon baking powder

½ teaspoon kosher salt

2 cups buttermilk

1 cup lightly packed dark brown sugar

1 tablespoon doenjang (Korean soybean paste; see Resources, page 331)

Scant ¾ cup blackstrap molasses

½ cup egg whites (from 4 or 5 large eggs)

Whipped butter, for serving

SPECIAL EQUIPMENT: Two 10-ounce steel coffee cans (optional)

1 Preheat the oven to 350°F. Generously coat the insides of two 10-ounce unlined tin coffee cans or a 9 x 5 x 3-inch loaf pan with nonstick cooking spray.

2 In a large skillet, toast the white rye flour over medium heat, whisking continuously, until the flour darkens slightly and smells nutty, about 7 minutes.

3 Transfer to a large bowl, add the whole wheat flour, cornmeal, dark rye flour, baking soda, baking powder, and salt and whisk to combine. In a separate bowl, whisk together the buttermilk, brown sugar, doenjang, and all but 1 tablespoon of the molasses until combined. Set aside.

4 In the bowl of a stand mixer fitted with the whisk attachment (or in a large bowl using a handheld mixer), whip the egg whites with the remaining 1 tablespoon molasses until they hold stiff peaks, about 5 minutes.

5 Stir the buttermilk mixture into the dry ingredients until combined. Using a rubber spatula, fold in the whipped egg whites in two additions.

6 Pour the batter into the prepared cans or loaf pan. Coat pieces of foil with cooking spray, then cover the tops of the cans or loaf pan securely. Set the cans or loaf pan in a baking dish and add enough hot water to come about ¼ inch up the sides of the cans or loaf pan. Transfer to the oven and bake until the top springs back when lightly touched and a toothpick inserted into the center of the bread comes out clean, about 1 hour 40 minutes for cans or 2 hours for a loaf pan. Let cool for 20 minutes on a wire rack, then invert onto a cutting board. Let cool completely before slicing. Serve with the whipped butter.

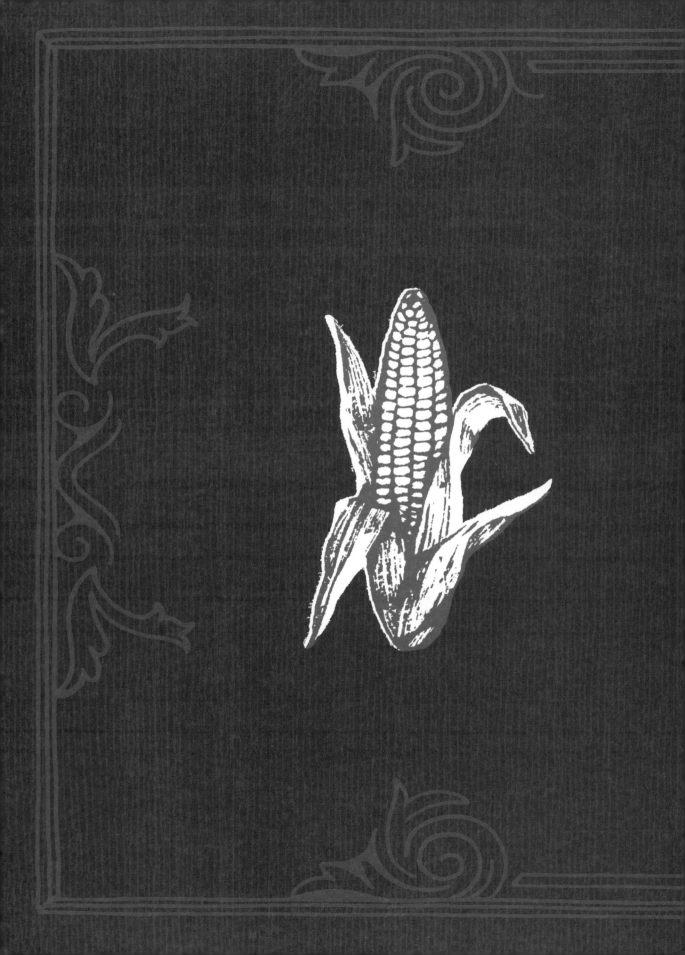

GARDEN AND ORCHARD

No ray of sunlight is ever lost, but the green which it awakes into existence needs time to sprout, and it is not always granted to the sower to see the harvest. All work that is worth anything is done in faith.

—Albert Schweitzer

When outsiders think of New England, it's often the bucolic countryside they imagine: the rolling green hills of Vermont, the dense pine forests of Maine. The physical landscape of this region and its seasons define what grows and thrives here and shape how and what we cook.

Our long, cold winters give way to warm spring days, when the maple sap starts to flow and farmers tap their trees for their annual syrup crop. Summer, longed for and anticipated through the dark days of February, is insistent when it arrives, and the bounty that appears in those vivid months is a boon for cooks, who try to serve and preserve as much as we can. Fall brings apples, sugar pumpkins, fat squash; each season has its culinary touchstones.

When I was growing up in New England, those touchstones provided a rhythm and routine to my young life. We'd go to Wilson Farm in Lexington, Massachusetts, for our pumpkins and Christmas trees, stain our fingers and mouths red with the first summer strawberries, hit up a roadside stand for a dozen ears of corn in August, buy bags of cranberries grown in Cape Cod bogs at Thanksgiving. Even living in metropolitan Boston, where I spent my childhood, we were surrounded by agriculture, and needed to drive only twenty minutes outside the city limits to hit farmland.

This proximity to the gardens and orchards of New England works in my favor as a chef. In spring, we receive deliveries of the first asparagus within hours of their stalks being cut. I can make a detour on my way to work to pick up flats of pristine raspberries, so recently harvested that there's still dew clinging to the fruit. In the fullness of summer, most of what we eat at home and what I serve at the restaurant comes from farms within a hundred-mile radius of Boston—the abundance is overwhelming, in the best possible way. Sometime each October, I always get an e-mail from Dan Geer, telling me the eggplants and peppers are ready. On Sunday, my day off, I'll load my two boys into the car and we'll drive the hour from Boston to North Smithfield, Rhode Island, to pay Dan a visit at Phoenix Rising Horse Farm.

Dan looks a little like Neil Young, with the same crazy, fluffy sideburns. Horses are his principal business now—boarding, lessons, horse shows—but he also keeps a three-acre vegetable farm and grows some of the best stuff around, including heirloom corn that he grinds into cornmeal using an old stone mill. And his tomatoes, eggplants, and peppers are good enough to pull a weary chef out of bed and onto the road after a ninety-hour week, because Dan doesn't deliver.

Dan's a unique guy, but the relationship we have isn't. In the fifteen years that I've cooked professionally, I've forged bonds with lots of farmers up and down the coast. After all, farmers are the lifeblood of cooking in New England.

My visits to the farm and farmstand are in some ways nothing exceptional, just an errand like any other, but it's something all home cooks would benefit from doing. Through those frequent visits you get to know the farmers and their crops, and build relationships that are similar to the ones I have with all my purveyors. Explore your area and find out where to go for the sweetest peas, for corn picked so recently the sugar in the kernels hasn't had time to turn to starch, for tomatoes with the deep, lasting flavor you'll reminisce about when the temperature dips below zero; seek out the best stuff, not only because your dinner will taste better, but because you'll be directly supporting a grower, a friend.

New England may have one of the shortest growing seasons in the country, but that only makes us embrace it harder. This chapter is filled with recipes that take advantage of the bounty of vegetables and fruit grown in the region. There's a stone fruit salad to make in deep summer (page 222), my version of a steakhouse wedge salad, with cabbage taking the place of iceberg lettuce (page 224), and a spring vegetable fricassee, lush with cream, to serve with tender biscuits (page 210). A roast chicken with Asian pears and winter greens, enhanced with mustard compound butter (page 236), is a cozy way to endure the winter months; and of course, there's dessert: a crostata enriched with almond cream that you can make with a variety of different fruits (page 247), blueberry cobbler bars (page 257), and sweet potato cupcakes crowned with a cloud of marshmallow (page 259).

FAVA BEAN AND STRACCIATELLA SPREAD

After a frigid winter, New England cooks clamor for the first radishes, ramps, peas, and fava beans, the harbingers of spring.

Though I call this recipe a spread, it's more like a coarsely chopped fava salad, with stracciatella added for creaminess. This Italian stretched-curd fresh cow's-milk cheese is milky, sweet, and mild. It's worth seeking out, but if you can't find it, you can substitute an equal amount of coarsely chopped burrata or buffalo milk mozzarella. | SERVES 6 AS A SNACK

5 pounds fresh fava bean pods	Zest and juice of 1 Meyer lemon	1 small bunch chives, thinly sliced
2 pounds English peas in the pod (2 cups shelled)	½ cup walnuts, toasted and coarsely chopped	¼ cup extra-virgin olive oil
½ cup stracciatella cheese, drained (burrata or buffalo milk mozzarella can be substituted)	1 tablespoon fresh thyme leaves, chopped	Kosher salt and freshly ground black pepper
2 tablespoons walnut oil	1 tablespoon finely chopped fresh flat-leaf parsley	Toasted bread or crackers, for serving

Bring a large pot of salted water to a boil. In a large bowl, make an ice bath by combining ice and water and set nearby. Shell the fava beans and place them in a bowl. Shell the peas and put in a separate bowl.

Add the fava beans to the boiling water and blanch for 1 minute, then use a spider or slotted spoon to transfer the beans from the boiling water to the ice water bath. Let cool completely, then transfer to a paper towel–lined plate. Refresh the ice water bath with additional ice as needed. Add the peas to the boiling water and blanch for 1 minute, then use a spider or slotted spoon to transfer them to the ice water bath; let cool completely, then drain and transfer to a bowl.

Peel each fava bean, exposing the brilliant green bean within. You should have 2 cups shelled fava beans.

In a food processor, combine the peeled fava beans, peas, stracciatella, walnut oil, lemon zest, and lemon juice. Pulse until coarsely pureed, then transfer to a bowl. Fold in the walnuts and herbs, reserving some of both for garnish, then add the olive oil and mix to combine. Season to taste with salt and pepper. Serve with toasted bread or crackers. The spread can be made several hours ahead; cover and refrigerate. Bring to room temperature before serving.

SPRING VEGETABLE FRICASSEE
WITH DROP BISCUITS

Fricassee is a vegetarian main course that feels generous and rich, the kind of thing you might make on that rogue New England April day when the first tender vegetables have arrived and then *bam!*—we receive one last dusting of surprise snow. You can serve the biscuits alongside or crumble them on top for a more rustic presentation. | SERVES 6 AS A MAIN COURSE

FOR THE BISCUITS

1½ cups all-purpose flour

2 teaspoons baking powder

1 teaspoon kosher salt

½ cup (1 stick) cold unsalted butter, cut into cubes

¾ cup whole milk

FOR THE VEGETABLES

3 bunches baby carrots, tops trimmed but left on, cleaned

2 cups shelled English peas

1 cup fiddlehead ferns

10 French breakfast or Easter Egg radishes, tops trimmed but left on, cleaned

6 artichoke hearts

½ pound asparagus, cut into 1-inch pieces

3 tablespoons extra-virgin olive oil

1 small onion, julienned

2 shallots, julienned

2 garlic cloves, thinly sliced

1 large leek, white and light green parts only, julienned

15 fresh morel mushrooms, halved lengthwise (or substitute cremini)

1 cup black trumpet mushrooms

Kosher salt and freshly ground black pepper

½ cup white wine

¾ cup vegetable or chicken stock

1½ cups heavy cream

½ cup grated Parmigiano-Reggiano cheese

1 tablespoon lemon zest

Pinch of freshly grated nutmeg

1 cup nettles (or substitute spinach)

1 teaspoon fresh thyme leaves

Make the biscuits: Preheat the oven to 400°F. Position a rack in the center of the oven. Line a rimmed baking sheet with parchment paper or a silicone baking mat.

In a large bowl, whisk together the flour, baking powder, and salt. With a pastry cutter or two butter knives, cut the butter into the dry ingredients until the butter is in pea-size pieces. Add the milk and stir with a fork until the mixture comes together; the dough will be sticky.

Use a serving spoon to spoon the dough onto the prepared baking sheet in eight plum-size mounds, spacing them about 2 inches apart. Bake until golden, 15 to 20 minutes. Remove from the oven and use a spatula to transfer the biscuits to a wire rack to cool completely.

Make the vegetables: Bring a large pot of salted water to a gentle simmer. Fill a large bowl with ice and water and set it nearby. Line a rimmed baking sheet with paper towels.

Blanch the carrots in the boiling water until just tender, about 5 minutes, then use a spider or slotted spoon to transfer them to the ice water bath. Let cool completely, then transfer to the prepared baking sheet to drain. Blanch the peas, fiddleheads, radishes, artichokes, and asparagus one at a time using the same method, replenishing the ice in the ice water bath as necessary. When all the vegetables have been blanched, discard the blanching water and ice water bath.

In a large saucepan, heat the olive oil over medium heat. Add the onion, shallots, and garlic and sauté until translucent, about 2 minutes. Add the leek and sauté until the leek is softened; do not let the mixture take on any color. Add the morels and black trumpet mushrooms, season with salt and pepper, and cook, stirring, until wilted, 5 minutes.

Pour in the wine and simmer until almost all the wine has evaporated. Pour in the stock and simmer for 2 to 3 minutes more. Add the cream and return to a simmer, then stir in the Parmigiano-Reggiano, lemon zest, and nutmeg and simmer until the cream sauce has thickened and reduced slightly, about 5 minutes. Add the blanched vegetables, turn to coat in the cream sauce, and cook until warmed through, about 3 minutes.

Carefully, using tongs and making sure not to touch the nettles with your bare hands (they sting!), add the nettles and thyme and remove the pan from the heat. Stir until the nettles wilt, then season with salt and pepper. Spoon the fricassee into warmed bowls and serve the biscuits on top or alongside.

FARM VEGETABLE FRITTO MISTO
WITH MAPLE-MISO AIOLI

One day on my drive back to the city after visiting a farmer, I passed by a small clam shack on the water. I thought about how much I loved fried clams. Then I thought how amazing it would be if one could purchase little fried vegetables—like fried clams—in a paper container, with sauces for dipping.

When I got back to the kitchen that day, I started working on the recipe. Seek out the smallest, most beautiful little baby vegetables for the fritto misto. The younger and more delicate the vegetables, the better this dish will be. A good mixture could include pattypan squash, baby carrots, radishes with their greens still attached, spring onions, and squash blossoms, but you could vary it to include tender baby fennel or asparagus or snap peas—anything tender and sweet. The trick to ensuring that the fried vegetables are crispy, not greasy, is cold batter. Add a couple of ice cubes to the batter; as they melt, they will thin and chill it. | **SERVES 6 AS A SNACK OR FIRST COURSE**

4 cups canola oil, for frying	6 baby yellow squash or zucchini (each about the length of your index finger), halved lengthwise	1 small bunch French breakfast radishes (about 6), tops trimmed but left on, cleaned
2½ cups rice flour		8 squash blossoms
1 cup ice-cold seltzer	1 small bunch small carrots (about 6), tops trimmed but left on, cleaned	Maple-Miso Aioli (recipe follows), for serving
2 egg yolks, beaten		
Kosher salt and freshly ground black pepper	3 spring onions, halved	**SPECIAL EQUIPMENT:** Deep-fry thermometer

In a high-sided heavy pot or Dutch oven, heat the canola oil over medium-high heat until it registers 375°F on a deep-fry thermometer. Preheat the oven to 200°F. Line a baking sheet with paper towels.

While the oil is heating, in a large bowl, whisk together 2 cups of the rice flour, the seltzer, and the egg yolks until well combined and smooth. Season the batter with a pinch of salt and pepper. Add a few ice cubes to the batter and let them melt, then whisk (this will simultaneously chill and thin the batter, which should have the consistency of pancake batter).

CONTINUED

Pour the remaining ½ cup rice flour into a cake pan or rimmed plate. Working in batches, dredge the vegetables in the rice flour, ensuring they are all evenly coated in a thin layer of the flour. Using chopsticks, pick up individual vegetables and gently plunge them into the batter, shake off the excess, and carefully deposit the pieces into the hot oil, taking care not to overcrowd. For the radishes, hold by the tops and dip only the radishes in the batter.

Fry until the vegetables are cooked through and the batter is golden, about 4 minutes. Remove the vegetables from the hot oil with chopsticks or a spider and transfer them to the prepared pan to drain. Season with salt and pepper and transfer to the oven to keep warm while you fry the remaining vegetables in batches, allowing the oil to return to temperature between each batch.

Transfer the fried vegetables to a plate and serve with the aioli alongside.

MAPLE-MISO AIOLI
MAKES ABOUT 1½ CUPS

2 egg yolks
1 teaspoon Dijon mustard
1 teaspoon red miso
Pinch of cayenne pepper
1½ cups canola oil
⅓ cup pure maple syrup
1 to 2 tablespoons warm water, as necessary
Kosher salt and freshly ground black pepper

In a food processor, combine the egg yolks, mustard, miso, and cayenne and process until combined. With the motor running, very slowly drizzle in the canola oil, drop by drop at first until the mixture thickens and emulsifies, then in a steady, thin stream until all the oil has been incorporated and the mixture is thick. Drizzle in the maple syrup. When all the maple syrup has been added, stop the food processor. Transfer to a bowl; the aioli should be smooth and thick, but if it looks stiff, whisk in some of the water, a tablespoon at a time. Season with salt and pepper.

CHARRED BRUSSELS SPROUTS
WITH LARDO, FIORE SARDO, AND PIQUILLO PEPPERS

When fall arrives and the leaves begin to turn, I start to get excited—yes, really, excited!—for brassicas and crucifers. Brussels sprouts have gotten such a bad rap because they're too often overcooked until army green and mushy—they actually taste best when they are a tad *undercooked*.

In this recipe, the Brussels sprouts are blanched, then pan-seared until nicely caramelized and crispy, then tossed with a zippy combination of lardo, peppers, and vinegar. If you can't find lardo, substitute pancetta or bacon. If Fiore Sardo cheese is hard to come by, swap in Pecorino Romano. In addition to its great flavor, this is also a beautiful dish, all green and red, and would be terrific alongside a steak or pork roast. Or try it this year as a Thanksgiving side dish. | **SERVES 6 AS A FIRST COURSE OR SIDE DISH**

4 cups whole Brussels sprouts, trimmed and halved	2 garlic cloves, thinly sliced	¼ teaspoon lemon zest
2 tablespoons extra-virgin olive oil, plus more as needed	½ cup diced piquillo peppers (or substitute roasted red peppers)	1½ teaspoons fresh lemon juice
½ cup ¼-inch-diced lardo (or substitute pancetta or bacon)	2 tablespoons sherry vinegar	Kosher salt and freshly ground black pepper
1 shallot, thinly sliced	½ teaspoon sweet Spanish paprika	2 teaspoons chopped fresh oregano
	1 tablespoon unsalted butter	2 teaspoons thinly sliced fresh chives

Bring a large pot of water to a boil and add salt. Line a rimmed baking sheet with paper towels. Fill a large bowl with ice and water and set it nearby.

Add the Brussels sprouts to the boiling water and cook until crisp-tender, about 4 minutes. Remove from the boiling water with a spider or slotted spoon and immediately transfer to the ice water bath. Once cool, transfer to the prepared baking sheet.

In a large cast-iron skillet, heat the olive oil over medium-high heat. When the oil is hot, add as many Brussels sprouts as will fit in a single layer, facedown, and sear until the sprouts are nicely browned on one side and warmed through, about 4 minutes. Repeat with the remaining Brussels sprouts, adding more oil to the pan as necessary.

When all the sprouts have been browned, reduce the heat to medium. Add the lardo to the pan and gently sauté, stirring occasionally, until some of the fat begins to render. Add the shallot and cook, stirring, until the shallot is translucent and the pieces of lardo are golden, about 4 minutes. Add the garlic and cook for 1 minute more. Stir in the piquillo peppers and cook, stirring, for

3 minutes more, then add the vinegar, paprika, butter, lemon zest, and lemon juice and cook, stirring occasionally, until most of the liquid has reduced, about 5 minutes. Season with salt and black pepper.

Transfer the piquillo pepper mixture to the bowl with the Brussels sprouts and toss to coat. Stir in the oregano and chives and season with salt and black pepper. Transfer the sprouts to a platter or plates and serve immediately.

MARINATED MELON AND HEARTS OF PALM
WITH COPPA AND BASIL CREMA

This beautiful summer salad showcases two types of melon, paired with rich slices of porky coppa. The coppa should be so thinly shaved that you can read a book through it, even if that means you have to be a squeaky wheel at the deli counter to get it sliced properly. If you want to make this salad vegetarian, substitute a handful of chopped Marcona almonds for the coppa. Palm hearts aren't native to New England, of course, but this salad benefits tremendously from their vegetal flavor and crunchy texture. | **SERVES 6 AS A STARTER**

⅓ cup apple cider vinegar	½ small cantaloupe, peeled, seeded, and very thinly sliced	12 slices coppa
1 tablespoon fresh lime juice	½ cup packed fresh basil leaves, plus a few more for garnish	1 (14-ounce) can hearts of palm, drained, rinsed, and cut into ½-inch rings
2 teaspoons sugar	⅓ cup cream cheese, plus more as needed	Kosher salt and freshly ground black pepper
1 tablespoon finely chopped fresh mint	½ cup sour cream	Lemon verbena, borage flowers, and nasturtium leaves, for garnish (optional)
½ cup extra-virgin olive oil	¼ cup heavy cream	
½ small honeydew melon, peeled, seeded, and very thinly sliced		

In a large bowl, whisk together the vinegar, lime juice, sugar, mint, and olive oil. Add the sliced melon and toss to coat. Let stand at room temperature for 10 to 30 minutes.

Bring a small saucepan of water to a boil. Fill a medium bowl with ice and water and set it nearby. Line a plate with paper towels.

Add the basil leaves to the boiling water and blanch for 10 seconds. Remove from the water with a slotted spoon and transfer to the ice water bath. Once cool, transfer to a paper towel–lined plate to drain. In a blender, combine the blanched basil, cream cheese, sour cream, and heavy cream. Blend on high speed until smooth; it should be thick and creamy. If it's too thin, blend in another spoonful of cream cheese. If it's too thick, blend in a couple tablespoons of water. Set aside.

Spoon out about a tablespoon of crema on each plate. Drain the marinated melon and discard the marinade. Roll the slices of melon into loose pinwheels and divide among the plates. Roll the coppa into "cigars" and add them to the plate, along with the hearts of palm. Garnish each plate with a few basil leaves and lemon verbena, borage flowers, and nasturtium leaves (if using).

STONE FRUIT SALAD
WITH GOAT CURD AND ALMOND VINAIGRETTE

Stone fruit are such long-awaited jewels of the orchard. In New England, the best stone fruit don't ripen until late August or early September—we wait a long time for a few weeks of perfect peaches! But they sure are worth waiting for.

As with everything you cook, the end result can only be as good as the ingredients you begin with. To make this salad, seek out perfectly ripe stone fruit. The exact varieties aren't as important as the fruit's ripeness; aim for a mixture of fruits to get the most beautiful and delicious salad. Goat curd adds a beautiful, tangy flavor and creamy texture to the salad. It can be difficult to find (you might check with a vendor of goat cheese at your farmers' market), so you can certainly substitute a fresh goat's-milk cheese or feta. The arugula adds a peppery flavor that complements the fruit and cheese, and a final showering of toasted almonds adds some nice crunch to the salad. | SERVES 6 AS A FIRST COURSE

2 tablespoons Champagne vinegar	¾ cup slivered almonds, lightly toasted	¼ of an English cucumber, thinly sliced
1 tablespoon fresh lemon juice	3 pounds assorted stone fruit (such as peaches, nectarines, plums, apricots, and cherries); peaches and nectarines pitted and sliced into sixths, plums and apricots pitted and quartered; cherries halved and pitted	4 ounces arugula (4 loosely packed cups)
1½ teaspoons honey		⅓ cup fresh mint leaves
2 teaspoons fresh thyme leaves, finely chopped		⅓ cup fresh basil leaves
¼ cup canola oil		⅓ cup fresh tarragon leaves
¼ cup extra-virgin olive oil		⅓ cup fennel fronds (optional)
Kosher salt and freshly ground black pepper		1 cup goat curd (or substitute fresh goat's-milk cheese or feta)

In a medium bowl, whisk together the vinegar, lemon juice, honey, and thyme. While whisking continuously, drizzle in the canola and olive oils until combined. Season with salt and pepper. Stir in ½ cup of the almonds.

In a large bowl, gently fold together the fruit, cucumber, arugula, herb leaves, and fennel fronds, if using. Drizzle in the almond vinaigrette and mix gently to combine. Transfer the salad to a platter and crumble the goat curd over the top. Garnish with the remaining ¼ cup almonds and serve immediately.

RED CABBAGE WEDGE SALAD

Celebrating humble ingredients is a cornerstone of New England cooking, and cabbage is perhaps one of the humblest of all. But it's a surprisingly versatile ingredient: crunchy, peppery, and slightly bitter when raw, it becomes luscious and sweet when cooked.

This recipe is a riff on a classic wedge salad, with pan-roasted red cabbage standing in for the traditional iceberg. Some razor-thin slices of Asian pear and apple and a sprinkling of pumpkin seeds and bacon complete this wintry composed salad. | SERVES 6

FOR THE DRESSING
½ cup whole-grain mustard
¼ cup pure maple syrup
¼ cup apple cider vinegar
1 teaspoon fennel seeds, toasted
¼ cup canola oil
¼ cup extra-virgin olive oil
Kosher salt and freshly ground
    black pepper

FOR THE SALAD
2 thick-cut bacon slices (about
    ¼ pound), cut crosswise into
    ¼-inch pieces
2 tablespoons canola oil
1 medium head red cabbage, cut
    into sixths, loose outer leaves
    removed but core intact
2 tablespoons unsalted butter
Kosher salt and freshly ground
    black pepper

½ tart apple, such as Gala
    or Honeycrisp, cored and sliced
    into thin wedges
½ Asian pear, cored and sliced into
    thin wedges
Handful of frisée leaves
4 roasted shallots (see page 30),
    peeled and coarsely chopped
½ cup raw pumpkin seeds, toasted

Make the dressing: In a small bowl, whisk together the mustard, maple syrup, vinegar, and fennel seeds. Whisk in the canola and olive oils; season to taste with salt and pepper.

Make the salad: Heat a 12-inch cast-iron skillet over medium heat. Add the bacon and cook, stirring, until golden brown. Use a slotted spoon to transfer to a paper towel–lined plate and set aside.

Add the canola oil to the bacon fat in the pan. Set the wedges of cabbage in the pan, cut-side down. Add the butter and sear the cabbage, turning once, until each wedge is browned on both sides and tender, about 10 minutes. Transfer the cabbage to a plate, season to taste with salt and pepper, and let cool slightly.

Arrange the wedges of cabbage cut-side up on a platter or individual plates. Top each wedge with some of the apple and pear slices and a few leaves of frisée, tucking them into the layers of cabbage. Drizzle with the dressing and top with some of the bacon, roasted shallots, and pumpkin seeds. Serve immediately, with the remaining dressing alongside.

ROASTED SQUASH SALAD
WITH GOUDA AND APPLE BUTTER

The change of season happens suddenly in New England, or so it always seems. One week you're walking past farmers' market tables heaped with tomatoes and peppers, and by the next week, it's piled with winter squash as far as the eye can see. Winter squash grows particularly well in our cold-weather climate. The plant's ability to fight the elements actually makes the squash sweeter, as the plant and fruit generate extra natural sugars to adapt to the changing environment and keep its nutrients circulating.

In this salad, roasted squash, caramelized and sweet, is offset by nutty, salty, aged Gouda. When building the salad, make a swipe of spiced apple butter the base, then layer on the squash and lettuce and finish with a snowdrift of grated cheese. I've given a recipe for homemade apple butter, though you can substitute store-bought. | SERVES 6 AS A FIRST COURSE

---

2 delicata squash, halved lengthwise, seeded, and sliced into ½-inch-thick half-moons

1 medium acorn squash, peeled, halved, seeded, and cut into ½-inch-thick wedges

2 tablespoons canola oil

Kosher salt and freshly ground black pepper

3 tablespoons apple cider vinegar

5 tablespoons extra-virgin olive oil

1 sweet-tart apple, such as Honeycrisp, cored, halved, and cut into ¼-inch-thick slices

1 head butter or Bibb lettuce, washed, outer leaves removed and discarded

6 tablespoons apple butter, homemade (recipe follows) or store-bought

2 ounces aged Gouda cheese

Flaky salt, such as Maldon, for garnish

Leaves from 2 sprigs tarragon, for garnish

Preheat the oven to 350°F.

Put the delicata and acorn squash pieces in a bowl and add the canola oil. Season with kosher salt and pepper and toss so the squash pieces are coated in the oil. Transfer to a rimmed baking sheet and bake until tender and light golden brown, about 30 minutes. Remove from the oven and let cool.

Meanwhile, put the vinegar in a medium bowl. Whisk in the olive oil. Season with salt and pepper.

Put the apple and lettuce in a large salad bowl. Add a few tablespoons of the dressing (save the rest for another salad; it will keep in an airtight container in the refrigerator for up to 1 week) and toss with your hands to coat. Season with salt and pepper.

CONTINUED

To plate the salad, smear 1 tablespoon of the apple butter onto each of six salad plates. Top with a few leaves of lettuce and a few pieces of apple, alternating with a few pieces of the squash, making a loose stack. With a rasp-style grater, grate some of the aged Gouda over each salad. Garnish with a pinch of flaky salt and a sprinkling of tarragon leaves. Or serve it family-style, using the same approach in one big bowl. Serve immediately.

APPLE BUTTER

MAKES ABOUT 2 CUPS

3 pounds mixed sweet-tart red-skinned apples, such as Pink Lady and Honeycrisp, coarsely chopped (no need to core or peel)

3 cups apple cider

½ cup sugar

½ cinnamon stick

1 whole clove

½ teaspoon kosher salt

2 teaspoons apple cider vinegar

SPECIAL EQUIPMENT: Food mill

In a large, wide pot, combine the apples, cider, sugar, cinnamon stick, clove, and salt and bring to a boil over medium heat. Cook, stirring frequently with a wooden spoon, until most of the liquid has evaporated and the apples are very soft, 1 to 1½ hours. Remove and discard the cinnamon stick. Pass the apple mixture through the fine disk of a food mill, or strain through a coarse-mesh sieve, pressing on the solids with a rubber spatula. Discard the solids.

Preheat the oven to 350°F.

Transfer the apple mixture to a 9 x 13-inch baking pan and bake, stirring every 30 minutes, until reduced by half and very thick and dark amber in color, 1½ to 2 hours.

Remove from the oven and stir in the vinegar. Let cool to room temperature, then transfer to a lidded jar and refrigerate until ready to use. The apple butter will keep in the refrigerator for up to 2 weeks, or frozen for up to 2 months.

COOKING IN THE SHOULDER SEASON

The shoulder season is the time when one season is transitioning into the next, and for a few brief weeks the two seem to overlap. In New England, when the summer season is coming to an end and the first of the fall ingredients are beginning to trickle into the markets, it is undoubtedly the most rewarding time of year to be a chef.

By October, tomatoes are beginning to wane, but those that are still available are juicy and super-sweet. There's still corn and herbs and eggplants and peppers to be had. But the first autumn squash, orchard fruits, and root vegetables start to appear, too, and for a while there's an embarrassment of riches that prompts a flurry of activity in my kitchen, for we all know what comes next: a solid six months of winter.

In a region like New England, with its four distinct seasons, the challenge is learning how we can extend the seasons, and there are some tactical ways in which we approach this task that home cooks can use, too.

Tomatoes get canned, dried, or turned into sauce and frozen. Stone fruit is jammed and jarred for future use. I smoke and salt, dehydrate and dry and pickle—boy, do I pickle (see page 238). These are all tricks of the trade that I utilize to ensure the

bounty from the shoulder season is available during the months of frost and subzero temperatures. And speaking of subzero temperatures: freezing is also a method you can use to preserve the season. If you're averse to canning tomatoes, you can also halve them, roast them until the skins blister, peel them, and slip them into the freezer in plastic storage bags. Vegetables—including sweet corn, beans, and more—can be blanched and frozen, too. Yes, of course you can buy frozen corn and peas year-round in any supermarket. But when you process and freeze them yourself you can be sure you're freezing peak-season vegetables—the sweetest of the season.

The shoulder season is a New England cook's brightest, busiest moment—take solace in the fact that there are many of us in the same boat, frantically trying to make (and preserve) the most of this season, and buying up all the Ball jars we can find at the local hardware store. We are in this together!

And your industry will be rewarded; in the cold months, bust out those ingredients from seasons past and revel in how wholly they brighten up your cooking. A chunky ragout of canned vegetables makes winter pasta taste bright and fresh. Adorn a cheese board (see page 34) with pickled plums, or drizzle a wedge of chocolate cake with a cherry sauce made from canned fruit. Stack homemade pickles on sandwiches; add some pickled peppers for heat. Slather toast with peach jam. Think of the items you have put away—whether by freezing, drying, preserving, or pickling—as money in the bank, and take solace in the knowledge that spring will be here soon enough.

SUMMER TAGLIATELLE
WITH SWEET CORN, BLISTERED CHERRY TOMATOES, UNI, AND BACON

This simple pasta highlights three of my favorite summer ingredients: corn, tomato, and basil. Their sweetness is balanced by briny sea urchin roe (also called uni) and smoky bacon, though it's equally good even without the uni. It's fun to make your own tagliatelle, but store-bought fresh pasta is a perfectly acceptable substitute. | **SERVES 6 AS A MAIN COURSE**

⅓ pound bacon, cut crosswise into ¼-inch pieces

2 cups cherry tomatoes

⅓ cup extra-virgin olive oil

3 cups corn kernels (from about 4 large ears corn)

1 garlic clove, thinly sliced

½ cup plus 2 tablespoons freshly grated Parmigiano-Reggiano cheese

⅓ cup walnuts, toasted and coarsely chopped

1 pound fresh tagliatelle, homemade or store-bought

1 tablespoon unsalted butter

¼ cup fresh parsley leaves, finely chopped

Kosher salt and freshly ground black pepper

1 cup fresh basil leaves, hand torn into small pieces

2 lobes uni (sea urchin roe)

Bring a large pot of salted water to a boil over high heat.

In a large skillet, cook the bacon over medium heat, stirring, until crisp, about 6 minutes. With a slotted spoon, transfer the bacon to a paper towel–lined plate. Pour off all but 1 tablespoon of the fat from the skillet.

Add the cherry tomatoes and sauté until blistered but not popped, about 4 minutes. Add the olive oil, corn, and garlic and sauté until the corn is tender but not browned, about 4 minutes more. Reduce the heat to low and fold in ½ cup of the Parmigiano-Reggiano and the walnuts.

Add the pasta to the boiling water and cook until just tender, 3 to 5 minutes. Drain, reserving ½ cup of the pasta cooking water. Return the pasta pot to the stove over low heat and transfer the contents of the skillet to the pasta pot. Stir in the butter and reserved pasta water, then add the pasta and parsley and toss gently to combine. Season with salt and pepper. Transfer to a serving bowl and sprinkle with the remaining cheese, the bacon, basil, and fresh uni. Toss gently to combine.

MARINATED SUMMER VEGETABLES WITH FETA, BLACK OLIVES, AND ROASTED GARLIC

During the summer, make a big vegetable salad for dinner. It's often too hot to do much cooking, but that way you can also get your fill of veg while they're at their peak.

Caramelizing the vegetables in a hot pan gives the salad some dimension, but the key is not to overcook them; when combined, they should still retain some texture. The roasted garlic vinaigrette is a terrific staple to keep in the fridge all summer long; it's good with almost every summer vegetable. A big bowl of this salad and some bread is a filling summer dinner, but you could also round it out with some grilled chicken or fish. | SERVES 6 AS A MAIN COURSE

---

1 medium eggplant, sliced crosswise into 1½-inch rounds

Kosher salt

3 tablespoons extra-virgin olive oil

1 seedless cucumber, halved lengthwise, each half cut crosswise into 2-inch pieces

2 small zucchini, cut into 1-inch pieces

1 pound heirloom tomatoes, cored and quartered

8 radishes, quartered (or cut into sixths if large)

½ small red onion, cut into ½-inch-thick rings

1 cup oil-cured black olives, pitted and halved

FOR THE VINAIGRETTE

1 head Roasted Garlic (page 166), cloves peeled

3 tablespoons Champagne vinegar

1 tablespoon honey

½ cup crumbled feta cheese

½ cup feta brine

Zest and juice of 1 lemon

2 teaspoons fresh thyme leaves

1 tablespoon fresh oregano leaves

⅓ cup olive oil

Kosher salt and freshly ground black pepper

Place the eggplant slices on a rimmed baking sheet and liberally salt both sides. Set aside.

In a large cast-iron skillet, heat 1 tablespoon of the olive oil over medium heat. Add the cucumber pieces and sear until caramelized on one side, about 3 minutes. Transfer to a plate. Add the zucchini to the pan and cook until caramelized on one side and tender, about 3 minutes. Transfer to the plate with the cucumbers.

Add the remaining 2 tablespoons olive oil to the pan, then add the eggplant slices and cook, turning as needed, until the eggplant slices are nicely browned on both sides and the skin is beginning to color, about 7 minutes. Transfer to the plate with the other vegetables.

Cut the eggplant into 1-inch cubes. Transfer to a bowl and add the cucumber, zucchini, tomatoes, radishes, onion, and olives.

Make the vinaigrette: In a blender, combine the roasted garlic, vinegar, honey, ¼ cup of the feta, the feta brine, lemon zest, lemon juice, thyme, oregano, and 1 tablespoon water. Blend on high speed until smooth. With the blender running, pour in the olive oil in a slow, steady stream until the mixture emulsifies, scraping down the sides of the blender with a rubber spatula as needed. Season to taste with salt and pepper.

Pour the vinaigrette over the vegetables. With a slotted spoon, carefully toss the vegetable salad until combined. Let marinate at room temperature for about 10 minutes, then transfer to a serving dish and sprinkle the remaining ¼ cup feta over the top. Serve at room temperature.

BUTTER-ROASTED CHICKEN
WITH ASIAN PEARS AND WINTER GREENS

I'd be lying if I told you that the New England winter doesn't get to me. After months of darkness and cold, the bounty of summer seems impossibly far away, and if you're committed to eating as locally as possible, winter in New England presents a challenge. Thankfully, we have dark, leafy greens—nutritional powerhouses—to sustain us during the dark days, and we can always fall back on herbed butter when faced with another subzero day.

Spatchcocking—that is, cutting out the backbone and flattening the chicken—helps the chicken roast quickly and evenly. The bird is generously anointed with a mustard-and-sage butter, which drips off the chicken, basting the Asian pear halves tucked beneath. Serve the chicken pieces directly on top of the greens, so they're infused with the buttery juices. | **SERVES 4 TO 6 AS A MAIN COURSE**

FOR THE CHICKEN

1 (3½- to 4-pound) whole chicken
½ cup (1 stick) unsalted butter, at room temperature
2 garlic cloves, minced
4 sprigs flat-leaf parsley, finely chopped
3 fresh sage leaves, finely chopped
1 tablespoon whole-grain mustard
Kosher salt and freshly ground black pepper
3 Asian pears, cored and quartered

FOR THE GREENS

2 tablespoons extra-virgin olive oil
4 anchovy fillets, minced
2 garlic cloves, thinly sliced
Pinch of red pepper flakes
3 bunches lacinato kale, stemmed, leaves coarsely chopped
1 bunch escarole, cored and coarsely chopped
¾ cup chicken stock
Kosher salt and freshly ground black pepper

Flaky salt, such as Maldon, for sprinkling
1 tablespoon finely minced fresh chives, for garnish

SPECIAL EQUIPMENT: Instant-read thermometer

Preheat the oven to 375°F.

Remove the chicken from the refrigerator and let it come to room temperature. Put the chicken on a cutting board, breast-side down, and use a pair of kitchen shears (or a sharp knife) to cut along each side of the backbone. Remove and discard the backbone (or save it for stock). Flip the chicken breast-side up, opening it like an upside-down book, and with the heel of your hand, press down firmly on the breast bone, flattening the chicken. With your fingers, gently lift the chicken skin on the breasts, separating it from the meat.

In a medium bowl, combine the butter, garlic, parsley, sage, and mustard and mix with a rubber spatula or wooden spoon until well combined.

Use your fingertips to scoop out about half the compound butter and stuff it under the skin over the chicken breasts. Make sure you get this compound butter all the way under the breast skin. Smear the remaining butter all over the outside of the chicken and season all over with kosher salt and black pepper. Put the pear quarters in the center of a rimmed baking sheet and set a wire rack over the pears. Set the chicken, skin-side up, on the wire rack (the pears should be beneath the chicken). Transfer to the oven and roast, basting occasionally with the pan juices, until the chicken is golden brown and an instant-read thermometer inserted into the thigh near the bone registers

165°F, about 1 hour 15 minutes. Remove from the oven and let rest for 15 minutes.

While the chicken roasts, make the greens: In a large skillet over medium-high heat, combine the olive oil, anchovy fillets, garlic, and red pepper flakes. Cook, stirring, for 30 seconds, then add the greens in large handfuls (the greens will not all fit into the pan at first, but as they cook and wilt, you'll be able to add more). Once all the greens have been added to the pan, pour in the stock, cover, and reduce the heat to medium-low. Cook, stirring occasionally, until the greens are tender, about 10 minutes. Uncover, increase the heat to medium, and cook off any remaining liquid; season the greens with kosher salt and black pepper.

Transfer the greens to a platter. Carve the chicken into eight pieces and set the pieces on top of the greens, with the roasted pears alongside. Sprinkle with flaky salt and chives and serve.

PICKLES AT HOME

Homemade pickles are an easy way both to save the season and to introduce an acidic element to dishes. In particular, pickled vegetables are excellent companions to richer meat- and dairy-based recipes, from molten wheels of baked cheese (page 29) to lamb meatballs in yogurt sauce (page 43) and rabbit rillettes (page 290). Of course, pickles also have more-pedestrian uses; some bread-and-butter cucumber pickles are particularly nice stacked on a meat loaf sandwich (see page 185).

Quick pickles, as the name suggests, are simple to make. Because they are not processed in a pressure canner or hot water bath, they must be refrigerated and eaten within a few weeks. But any of the recipes here can be made in a larger batch and processed to keep for longer in your pantry. To do so, pack the pickles into clean, sterilized canning jars, seal each jar with a new lid, and process in a boiling water bath. For longer storage instructions, see Note on page 242. Pickles processed this way are shelf-stable and will keep for a long time—ideally until the next harvest. Make enough to get yourself through the winter, when their bright flavor is particularly welcome.

GIARDINIERA

| MAKES ABOUT 1 QUART

3 cups warm water	1 cup diced or sliced red bell pepper	½ teaspoon coriander seeds
3 tablespoons sea salt, pickling salt, or kosher salt	1 celery stalk, sliced	¼ teaspoon whole black peppercorns
1 cup small cauliflower florets	1 garlic clove, smashed	1 or 2 jarred grape leaves (optional, to help keep the pickles crisp)
1 cup sliced carrot, cut about ½-inch thick	1 bay leaf	

Put the water in a large measuring cup, add the salt, and stir until the salt has dissolved.

In a medium bowl, combine the cauliflower, carrot, bell pepper, celery, garlic, bay leaf, coriander seeds, and peppercorns and stir to mix. Transfer to a clean quart-size mason jar and add the grape leaves, if using. Pour the salt water over the vegetables, leaving at least 1 inch of headspace at the top of the jar.

Cover the jar tightly and let it stand at room temperature. Once a day, open the jar to taste the pickles and release the gases produced during fermentation. If any mold or scum has formed on the top, simply skim it off. Taste the pickles after 2 weeks; they should be tangy and fermented, but still crisp. Transfer the jar to the refrigerator. The pickles will continue to ferment very slowly, but cold storage will largely halt fermentation. They will keep in the refrigerator for at least 1 month.

PRESERVED MEYER LEMONS

| MAKES 10 |

| 10 small Meyer lemons (Eureka lemons can be substituted) | 1 cup kosher salt
1 cup fresh lemon juice | |

Scrub and rinse the lemons. With a paring knife, cut off and remove any stems. Cut a ¼-inch slice from both ends of each lemon. Cut into each lemon lengthwise, in quarters, but keep the lemon attached at the base, making sure not to cut all the way through the fruit.

Working over a bowl, gently pull the lemons open and liberally sprinkle with the kosher salt inside and out. Put the lemons in a large mason jar or other glass storage container, pressing them down so the juice comes out and rises toward the level of the fruit. Top with any salt that has collected in the bowl. Add the fresh lemon juice; the lemons should be almost completely submerged.

Seal the jar with the lid. Let it sit at room temperature for at least 3 days and up to 1 week. Turn the jar upside down every couple of days to redistribute the liquids and salt inside. After 3 days, place the jar in the refrigerator for at least 3 weeks or up to 6 months, rotating the jar every week or so. The rinds of the lemons will soften during this time.

To use, remove a lemon from the jar and rinse with cold water. Remove and discard the pulp and use the rind as directed in the recipe.

PICKLED FRESNO CHILES

| MAKES ABOUT 2 CUPS

½ pound red Fresno chiles (about 10 medium) 2 garlic cloves, smashed 1 red bell pepper, julienned	1 cup apple cider vinegar 2 tablespoons honey 1 teaspoon kosher salt	SPECIAL EQUIPMENT: One pair latex gloves

Put on a pair of latex gloves and, with a sharp knife or mandoline, thinly slice the chiles into rounds. For less spicy pickles, use a paring knife to remove the chile membranes and seeds before slicing.

Combine the chiles, garlic, and bell pepper in a quart-size mason jar. In a small saucepan, combine the vinegar, honey, salt, and 1 cup water. Bring the mixture close to a boil on the stove, stirring to dissolve the honey. Remove from the heat and carefully pour the liquid over the peppers. Use a spoon to poke down the peppers so they're submerged beneath the pickling liquid and there aren't any hidden air pockets.

Let the pickles cool to room temperature in the jar. The pickles can be used right away, or covered and refrigerated for up to 3 days. For longer storage instructions, see Note, page 242.

PICKLED SHALLOTS

| MAKES ABOUT 1¼ CUPS

⅔ cup red wine vinegar 1 tablespoon sugar ½ teaspoon kosher salt	10 small shallots, sliced into ¼-inch-thick rounds with a mandoline or sharp knife	

In a small saucepan, combine the vinegar, sugar, and salt and bring to a boil, stirring, until the sugar and salt have dissolved. Put the sliced shallots into a bowl or glass jar and pour the pickling liquid over them. Let cool to room temperature, then transfer to a lidded jar and refrigerate for at least 6 hours. The pickled shallots will keep, refrigerated in the vinegar mixture, for up to 1 month. Drain before using. For longer storage instructions, see Note, page 242.

SIMPLE BREAD AND BUTTER PICKLES

| MAKES 3 PINTS

---

2 pounds pickling cucumbers

1 pound yellow or sweet white onions, peeled and julienned

⅓ cup kosher salt

3 cups distilled white vinegar

2 cups sugar

2 tablespoons whole yellow mustard seeds

2 teaspoons ground turmeric

2 teaspoons celery seed

1 teaspoon whole black peppercorns

1 teaspoon ground ginger

SPECIAL EQUIPMENT: Three pint-size canning jars; clean unused lids; metal screw bands for the lids

---

Wash the cucumbers and thinly slice with a sharp knife or mandoline into ¼-inch slices. Place the cucumbers and onions in a large, nonreactive bowl and sprinkle with the salt. Cover with ice and let sit at room temperature for 1 to 2 hours.

In a large saucepan, combine the vinegar, sugar, mustard seeds, turmeric, celery seed, peppercorns, and ginger. Bring to a boil over high heat, then turn the heat off. Drain the cucumbers and onions and rinse with cold water. Add them to the vinegar mixture and return to a boil. Remove from the heat.

With a slotted spoon, divide the cucumbers and onions among the jars. Add the vinegar mixture to cover, leaving ¼ inch of headspace at the top of each jar. Use a chopstick to remove any air bubbles in the jars, then wipe the rim of each jar and place a sterilized lid on each. Secure with a metal screw band. The pickles are ready to eat after 24 hours. They can be stored in the refrigerator.

NOTE: For longer storage, process in a hot water bath. Set the jars in a stockpot and add water to cover by 1 inch. Bring to a boil and boil hard for 15 minutes. Remove from the heat and, with tongs, carefully remove from the water. Hot water–processed pickles will keep at room temperature indefinitely.

SPICY PICKLED RAMPS

| MAKES 2 PINTS

---

1 pound fresh ramps, cleaned
¼ cup red pepper flakes
3 fresh bay leaves
4 teaspoons fennel seeds

2 teaspoons whole black
    peppercorns
2 cups white wine vinegar
1 cup sugar

2 tablespoons kosher salt

SPECIAL EQUIPMENT: Two pint-size canning jars; clean unused lids; metal screw bands for the lids

---

Trim the root end off of each ramp and discard. Cut the leafy green tops from each ramp and reserve for another use (I like to sauté them and fold into pasta). Divide the ramp bulbs between the jars and add half of the red pepper flakes, the bay leaves, fennel seeds, and peppercorns to each jar.

In a medium saucepan, combine the vinegar, 2 cups water, the sugar, and salt. Bring to a boil over high heat, stirring to dissolve the sugar and salt. Pour the liquid over the ramps, leaving about ¼ inch of headspace at the top of each jar. Use a chopstick to remove any air bubbles in the jars, then wipe the rim of each jar and place a sterilized lid on each. Secure with a metal screw band.

The pickled ramps are ready to eat after 24 hours. They can be stored in the refrigerator for up to 3 weeks; for longer storage, see Note, opposite.

CREAM CHEESE ICE CREAM
WITH CHERRY TOMATO–PEPPER JELLY

This recipe, which features a sweet-savory jelly made from tomatoes and peppers, comes from former Townsman pastry chef Meghan Thompson. She spoons it over tart cream cheese ice cream, and says she owes this recipe to her aunt Judy, whose signature snack, served at all family gatherings, was red pepper jelly whipped together with cream cheese and served with crackers. It's a surprising summer dessert. | SERVES 6

---

1 pound cherry tomatoes
1 large red bell pepper, stemmed, seeded, and cut into medium dice
1 small yellow banana pepper, stemmed, seeded, and finely diced

1¼ cups apple cider vinegar
2 teaspoons ground ginger
1¼ cups packed light brown sugar
2 teaspoons pectin
1 tablespoon blackstrap molasses
2 tablespoons bourbon (optional)

Kosher salt
1 quart Cream Cheese Ice Cream (recipe follows)
Balsamic vinegar, for garnish
12 fresh basil leaves, for garnish

In a large pot, combine all but 10 of the cherry tomatoes, the bell pepper, banana pepper, apple cider vinegar, and ginger. Bring to a boil over medium-high heat, then reduce the heat so the mixture is simmering. Simmer, stirring occasionally, until the mixture thickens and reduces slightly, about 30 minutes. Whisk in the brown sugar and pectin and return to a simmer. Simmer for 5 minutes, then whisk in the molasses and bourbon (if using) and season to taste with salt; the mixture should have the consistency of grape jelly. Pour into a heatproof container and let cool to room temperature, then cover and refrigerate until cold. This recipe makes more of the tomato-pepper jelly than you'll need to top the ice cream. Leftover jelly will keep, refrigerated, for up to 3 weeks. Use the surplus on cheese boards (see page 34) or spread on sandwiches.

Scoop the ice cream into six bowls. Thinly slice the reserved cherry tomatoes. Top each scoop of ice cream with a spoonful of the cooled cherry tomato–pepper jelly and a few drops of balsamic vinegar. Garnish each serving with a few torn basil leaves and some of the sliced cherry tomatoes. Serve immediately.

CONTINUED

CREAM CHEESE ICE CREAM

MAKES 1 QUART

2½ cups half-and-half

8 whole green cardamom pods, lightly crushed

1⅓ cups confectioners' sugar

2 egg yolks

1 (8-ounce) package cream cheese, at room temperature

1 teaspoon pure vanilla extract

¼ teaspoon kosher salt

SPECIAL EQUIPMENT: Ice cream maker; instant-read thermometer

Fill a large bowl with ice and water and set it nearby.

In a large heavy-bottomed saucepan, heat the half-and-half and cardamom over medium heat until bubbles form around the edges of the pan. In a medium bowl, whisk together the confectioners' sugar and egg yolks until well combined; it may look for a moment like the yolks and sugar will not combine, but continue whisking until they do.

While whisking continuously, slowly add about 1 cup of the hot cream mixture to the egg yolks, then pour the egg mixture into the saucepan with the remaining cream. Heat over medium-low heat, stirring continuously, until the mixture thickens and coats the back of the spoon (if you draw your finger through it, it should leave a trail) and an instant-read thermometer registers 160°F.

Pour the custard through a fine-mesh sieve into a medium clean bowl and set the bowl in the ice water bath. Let cool, stirring occasionally, until the custard is room temperature, then blend in the cream cheese with an immersion blender until smooth (alternatively, you can transfer the custard to a blender, add the cream cheese, and blend until smooth). Stir in the vanilla and salt, then cover with plastic wrap and refrigerate overnight.

Transfer the chilled custard to an ice cream machine and freeze according to the manufacturer's instructions. Transfer to a freezer-proof container and freeze until solid, at least 2 hours.

PEACH CROSTATA
WITH ALMOND CREAM

Originally hailing from Italy, a crostata is a rustic, free-form fruit tart, one that's forgiving and by definition imperfect. When peaches are in season, you can't do better than the combination of peaches and almond-rum cream, but you can substitute other fruit at other times of year. | **MAKES 1 LARGE CROSTATA; SERVES 10 TO 12**

FOR THE ALMOND CREAM	1 egg	¼ to ½ cup granulated sugar
1 cup almond flour	1 tablespoon dark rum	4 teaspoons cornstarch
2 tablespoons all-purpose flour, plus more for dusting	2 pounds peaches (or substitute nectarines, plums, apricots, blueberries, cherries, or a mixture), pitted and cut into ½-inch wedges	1 to 2 teaspoons fresh lemon juice
½ cup (1 stick) unsalted butter, at room temperature		½ teaspoon kosher salt
1 cup confectioners' sugar		1 recipe Pâte Brisée (page 54)
		1 egg yolk
		1 tablespoon sanding sugar

Make the almond cream: In a medium bowl, whisk together the almond flour and all-purpose flour. In the bowl of a stand mixer fitted with the paddle attachment, beat the butter on high speed until creamy, then add the confectioners' sugar and beat until fluffy. Scrape down the sides of the bowl, reduce the speed to low, and add the flour mixture, then add the egg and rum and mix until smooth.

In a large bowl, combine the fruit, half the granulated sugar, the cornstarch, half the lemon juice, and the salt. Mix to combine, then taste a piece of the fruit and add more sugar or lemon juice as needed.

Put the pâte brisée on a lightly floured work surface and let stand for 10 minutes; it's easier to roll this dough if it's slightly cold, but it's difficult to roll straight from the refrigerator.

With a lightly floured rolling pin, roll the dough into a round about 14 inches in diameter and ¼ inch thick, trimming the edges. Transfer to a silicone baking mat or piece of parchment paper. Spread the almond cream on the dough, starting in the center and working your way outward, leaving a 2-inch border uncovered all the way around. Arrange the fruit slices in a decorative pattern on top of the almond cream, then gently fold the border over the filling, folding and pinching the dough (the fruit at the center will be exposed).

In a small bowl, whisk the egg yolk with 1 teaspoon water. With a pastry brush, brush the crust with the egg wash and sprinkle with sanding sugar. Transfer the crostata (still on the silicone baking mat or parchment) to a rimmed baking sheet and refrigerate (or freeze, if you have space in your freezer) for 20 minutes.

CONTINUED

Preheat the oven to 375°F.

Bake on the center rack for 15 minutes, then rotate the pan and bake for 10 minutes more, or until the crostata is golden brown and the fruit is bubbling. Remove from the oven and transfer to a wire rack. Let cool completely before cutting into wedges and serving.

APPLE FRITTERS WITH CARAMEL SAUCE

One has not truly experienced fall in New England until one has eaten a freshly fried apple-cider doughnut. The doughnuts, made with a bit of cider in the batter and fragrant with nutmeg, are sugar-dusted, crunchy, craggy paradigms of the doughnut form. And a sweet-tart cup of cider direct from the press is the perfect companion.

My young boys love heading out to orchards in western Massachusetts or southern Vermont to go apple-picking with us—they act like they own the place. Sawyer, who is eight, and Coleman, who is five, run through the orchard rows, throwing fallen apples at each other, climbing in the branches of sturdy trees, and stuffing their pockets (and mouths) with fruit. The promise of doughnuts and cider is often the only thing that will lure them out of the trees. These fritters, studded with bits of apple and rolled in cinnamon-sugar, are directly inspired by those doughnuts and special autumn days. | MAKES ABOUT 24 FRITTERS

FOR THE FRITTERS
1 cup cake flour
½ cup Wondra flour (see Note)
1 tablespoon packed dark brown sugar
2 teaspoons baking powder
½ teaspoon kosher salt
⅔ cup buttermilk
2 eggs

1 tablespoon olive oil
3 cups finely diced peeled sweet-tart apples, such as Pink Lady or Honeycrisp
2 quarts canola oil, for frying

FOR THE CINNAMON-SUGAR
1½ cups granulated sugar
1 teaspoon ground cinnamon

½ teaspoon ground ginger
¼ teaspoon freshly grated nutmeg
¼ teaspoon kosher salt

Caramel Sauce (page 73) or Vanilla Ice Cream (page 70), for serving

SPECIAL EQUIPMENT: Deep-fry thermometer

Make the fritters: In a large bowl, stir together the cake flour, Wondra flour, brown sugar, baking powder, and salt. In a separate bowl, whisk together the buttermilk, eggs, and olive oil until well combined. With a rubber spatula, stir the wet ingredients into the dry, stirring until combined, then stir in the apples.

In a large heavy pot or Dutch oven, heat the canola oil over high heat until it registers 350°F on a deep-fry thermometer. Line a rimmed baking sheet with paper towels and set it nearby.

While the oil heats, make the cinnamon-sugar: In a large bowl, stir together the sugar, cinnamon, ginger, nutmeg, and salt until well combined. Set aside.

CONTINUED

When the oil is hot, carefully drop, in batches, golf ball–size spoonfuls of the batter into the hot oil and fry until golden brown, about 5 minutes. Use a spider or slotted spoon to gently turn the fritters in the oil so they brown evenly. Transfer to the paper towel–lined pan to drain. Between batches, let the oil return to temperature and stir the batter well, as the apples will sink.

While the fritters are still warm, toss them in the cinnamon-sugar to coat. Serve warm, accompanied by caramel sauce for dipping or vanilla ice cream.

NOTE: Wondra is the most readily available brand of instant flour. Instant flour is a low-protein, finely ground flour that's designed to dissolve instantly in liquid. It's used in baked goods (often in place of pastry flour), contributing to a tender crumb. It's also great for thickening gravy (because it dissolves instantly, it doesn't become lumpy), dusting baking pans, and coating food for frying. It's available at most supermarkets.

MOLASSES SHORTCAKES
WITH PERNOD PLUMS AND CREAM

Molasses is a New England staple, and in Boston the ingredient has some lore attached to it: In January 1919, a molasses storage tank on the city's waterfront burst, releasing two million gallons of the sticky sweetener into the streets of the North End, a fifteen-foot wave that destroyed everything in its path and killed twenty-one people. As the story goes, if you're in the neighborhood on a hot summer day, you may still catch a whiff of molasses.

The beauty of these little shortcakes is that they are great for breakfast, spread with butter and jam, or can be dressed up for dessert with whipped cream and Pernod-spiked plums. If you'd like to make these shortcakes ahead, they can be formed, then frozen on a baking sheet. Once frozen, transfer them to a plastic freezer storage bag. They can be baked directly from frozen; add two minutes to the baking time.

| MAKES 12 SMALL SHORTCAKES; SERVES 6

FOR THE SHORTCAKES
2 cups all-purpose flour
½ cup granulated sugar
1½ teaspoons ground cinnamon
1 teaspoon baking soda
½ teaspoon kosher salt
½ cup (1 stick) cold unsalted
    butter, cut into cubes
½ cup blackstrap molasses

⅓ cup whole milk
2 tablespoons finely diced candied
    ginger (optional)
1 tablespoon sanding sugar,
    for topping

FOR THE PLUMS
3 small plums, pitted and cut into
    ¼-inch wedges

2 tablespoons Pernod
1 teaspoon granulated sugar
Pinch of kosher salt

FOR THE CREAM
1 cup heavy cream
2 tablespoons granulated sugar
½ teaspoon pure vanilla extract

Make the shortcakes: Preheat the oven to 350°F. Line a rimmed baking sheet with parchment paper.

In a large bowl, whisk together the flour, granulated sugar, cinnamon, baking soda, and salt. With your fingers or a pastry cutter, cut the butter into the dry ingredients until the butter forms pea-size pieces. Using a wooden spoon, stir in the molasses, milk, and candied ginger (if using) until just combined.

Using a small scoop or large spoon, scoop the dough onto the prepared pan, spacing the shortcakes 2 to 3 inches apart. Sprinkle each shortcake with sanding sugar and transfer to the oven. Bake for 10 minutes, then rotate the pan

and bake until golden brown and set in the middle, 10 minutes more. The shortcakes will feel soft, but shouldn't be gooey. Let cool on the pan for 10 minutes, then transfer to a wire rack and let cool completely.

Make the plums: In a small bowl, combine the plums, Pernod, granulated sugar, and salt and toss to combine.

Make the cream: In the bowl of a stand mixer fitted with the whisk attachment (or in a large mixing bowl using a whisk or handheld mixer), beat the cream, granulated sugar, and vanilla on high speed until the cream holds soft peaks.

Serve the shortcakes with the whipped cream and plums alongside.

BLUEBERRY COBBLER BARS
WITH GRILLED LEMON CURD

The recipe for these double-crusted fruit bars comes from the mother of Townsman's former pasty chef. She makes hers with canned cherry pie filling, but we rejiggered the recipe, swapping blueberries for cherries. These bars are great for potlucks and picnics, and they also freeze well. | **MAKES 12 BARS**

FOR THE FILLING
4 cups fresh or frozen blueberries
¾ cup sugar
2 tablespoons cornstarch
¼ teaspoon ground cinnamon
¼ teaspoon kosher salt
Zest and juice of ½ lemon

FOR THE BATTER
1 cup (2 sticks) unsalted butter, at room temperature, plus more for greasing
2 cups sugar
4 eggs
½ teaspoon pure vanilla extract

¼ teaspoon almond extract
2 cups all-purpose flour
1 cup almond flour

Grilled Lemon Curd (recipe follows), for serving

Make the filling: In a large saucepan, combine the blueberries, sugar, cornstarch, cinnamon, salt, lemon zest, and lemon juice. Cook over medium heat, stirring occasionally, until the sugar has dissolved, the blueberries begin to soften, and the juices have thickened slightly, about 6 minutes. Remove from the heat and let cool.

Make the batter: Preheat the oven to 325°F. Grease and flour a 9 x 13-inch pan. In the bowl of a stand mixer fitted with the paddle attachment (or in a large bowl using a handheld mixer), beat the butter and sugar on high speed until light and fluffy, 3 to 4 minutes. Reduce the speed to low and add the eggs one at a time, followed by the vanilla and almond extracts. Stop the mixer and scrape down the sides of the bowl with a rubber spatula. With the mixer on low, gradually add the all-purpose and almond flours and mix until combined.

With an offset spatula or the back of a spoon, spread about two-thirds of the batter into the prepared pan. Top with the cooled blueberry filling, spreading it in an even layer, then dollop spoonfuls

of the remaining batter over the top, spacing them evenly. Transfer to the oven and bake until the topping is light golden brown and the blueberry filling is thick and bubbling, 40 to 45 minutes. Remove from the oven and let cool on a wire rack. Cut into squares and transfer to plates. Spoon some of the lemon curd alongside and serve.

GRILLED LEMON CURD
MAKES ABOUT 2 CUPS

5 lemons, halved
4 eggs
1¼ cups sugar
6 ounces cold unsalted butter, cut into cubes, plus more for greasing
Pinch of kosher salt

Prepare a gas or charcoal grill for direct high-heat grilling (alternatively, heat a dry cast-iron pan over high heat).

When the grill or pan is hot, add the lemons, cut-side down, and cook without disturbing until caramelized, 3 to 5 minutes. Remove from the heat and let cool, then juice the lemons. Measure out ½ cup plus 2 tablespoons of the lemon juice.

Fill a medium saucepan with a few inches of water and bring to a simmer over medium-high heat. In a nonreactive bowl, whisk together the lemon juice, eggs, and sugar. Place the bowl on top of the saucepan; be sure the bottom of the bowl does not touch the water. Cook, whisking, until the mixture thickens. Remove from the heat and use an immersion blender to blend in the cold butter (alternatively, transfer the mixture to a blender and blend in the cold butter). Season with the salt and transfer to a bowl. Cover the bowl with a sheet of greased plastic wrap, pressing it directly against the surface of the curd to prevent a skin from forming, and refrigerate until completely cool. Once cool, transfer to a lidded jar; it will keep, refrigerated, for up to a week.

SWEET POTATO CUPCAKES
WITH MARSHMALLOW CRÈME AND POACHED CRANBERRIES

My grandparents had a beautiful sideboard in their dining room. It had all these drawers, large and small. Some had our family's best silver stored in them; another drawer held their matchbook collection; and one small drawer was filled with pie servers. The whole drawer. Full of pie servers.

At Christmas, my grandmother would make marshmallow-topped sweet potatoes and serve the messy, sticky side dish—masquerading-as-dessert with one of those pie servers. By the time everyone had gone through the buffet, the pie server would be coated with a layer of caramelized potatoes and marshmallow, which I'd scrape off and eat.

However, I think the combination of sweet potato and marshmallow is best at the conclusion of a meal, so I've reconfigured the side dish into a proper dessert: a tender-crumbed sweet potato cupcake with a crown of marshmallow crème. Marshmallow crème often goes by the brand name Fluff, and is a beloved New England ingredient (as well as a key ingredient in the Fluffernutter, a peanut butter–and-Fluff sandwich). It was invented in a suburb of Boston, and the white plastic tubs of the sticky stuff are a (somewhat questionable) source of regional pride. | **MAKES 12 CUPCAKES**

FOR THE CUPCAKES
¾ cup plus 2 tablespoons packed dark brown sugar
6 tablespoons canola oil
2 eggs
½ teaspoon pure vanilla extract
1 cup cooked mashed sweet potatoes (about 2 medium sweet potatoes; or substitute canned sweet potato puree)
¼ cup fresh orange juice
1 cup all-purpose flour
1½ teaspoons baking powder
1 teaspoon baking soda
½ teaspoon ground cinnamon
¼ teaspoon ground ginger
⅛ teaspoon kosher salt

FOR THE POACHED CRANBERRIES
½ cup light corn syrup
¼ cup granulated sugar
¾ cup fresh cranberries

FOR THE MARSHMALLOW CRÈME
½ cup light corn syrup
1 egg white
⅛ teaspoon kosher salt
½ cup confectioners' sugar, sifted
¼ teaspoon pure vanilla extract

CONTINUED

Make the cupcakes: Preheat the oven to 350°F. Line a 12-cup standard muffin tin with cupcake liners.

In a large bowl, whisk together the brown sugar, canola oil, eggs, and vanilla. Whisk in the sweet potatoes and orange juice. In a separate large bowl, sift together the flour, baking powder, baking soda, cinnamon, ginger, and salt, then add to the wet ingredients and stir until combined.

Divide the batter evenly among the prepared muffin cups. Bake until the cupcakes spring back lightly when touched and a tester inserted into the center comes out clean, 10 to 12 minutes, rotating the pan at the halfway mark. Transfer to a wire rack and let cool for 10 minutes, then turn out of the pan and let cool completely on the rack.

Meanwhile, make the poached cranberries: In a small saucepan, combine the corn syrup and granulated sugar and warm gently over medium-low heat until the sugar has dissolved. Add the cranberries and cook, stirring, until the berries are tender, about 5 minutes; a few may burst, but the majority of the berries should remain intact. Remove from the heat.

Make the marshmallow topping: In the bowl of a stand mixer fitted with the paddle attachment, beat the corn syrup, egg white, and salt on high speed until light, fluffy, and voluminous, about 8 minutes. Reduce the speed to medium and add the confectioners' sugar and vanilla, then raise the speed to high and beat for 2 minutes more.

Transfer the cupcakes to a baking sheet and spread some of the marshmallow topping onto each cupcake with an offset spatula. Preheat the broiler to high and set an oven rack 4 inches from the heating element. Put the cupcakes under the broiler and broil, paying close attention, until the marshmallow is golden brown (alternatively, if you have a kitchen torch you can use that to brown the marshmallow).

Just before serving, spoon a few of the poached cranberries on top of each cupcake (save any remaining cranberries and syrup; they're great in yogurt, over ice cream, or in a glass of Champagne).

CHOCOLATE BEET CAKE
WITH CHOCOLATE-ORANGE GLAZE

As family lore goes, canned beets were a beloved food of my childhood, when I'd happily eat them cold off the tray of my high chair. Beets are one of those ingredients that are perpetually in season in New England. We see them toward the end of summer, all through the fall, and into winter, with a spring variety poking through the cool earth in early April as well.

Chocolate and beets are a natural pair. The earthiness of the beets contrasts with the richness and sweetness of chocolate. The milk chocolate frosting on this cake is laced with orange zest—orange tastes great with both chocolate and beets. If you're doubtful, that's even more reason to try it out for yourself. I'm sure you'll come away with a new love for the beet. | **MAKES ONE 10½-INCH BUNDT CAKE; SERVES 12**

FOR THE CAKE
Unsalted butter, for greasing
1 pound red or golden beets, trimmed
1 tablespoon extra-virgin olive oil
Kosher salt
1¾ cups all-purpose flour, plus more for dusting
2 cups sugar
¾ cup unsweetened Dutch-process cocoa powder

2 teaspoons baking soda
1 teaspoon baking powder
1 cup buttermilk
2 eggs
½ cup canola oil
1 teaspoon pure vanilla extract

FOR THE GLAZE
6 ounces good-quality milk chocolate, chopped
½ cup heavy cream

Zest of 1 navel orange
1 tablespoon extra-virgin olive oil
Pinch of kosher salt

Flaky salt, such as Maldon, for garnish

SPECIAL EQUIPMENT: One 10½-inch Bundt pan or 10-inch angel food cake pan

Make the cake: Preheat the oven to 325°F. Grease with the butter and flour a 10½-inch Bundt or 10-inch angel food cake pan.

Put the beets in a baking dish, drizzle them with the olive oil, and sprinkle with some kosher salt. Cover the dish with aluminum foil and bake until the beets are tender when poked with the tip of a knife, 45 minutes to 1 hour, depending on their size. Remove from the oven and let cool. Increase the oven temperature to 350°F.

When cool enough to handle, peel the beets and put them in a food processor; process until smooth. Measure the beet puree and set aside 1¼ cups (10 ounces); reserve any remaining beet puree for another use (it can be combined with ricotta or goat cheese and used as a sandwich spread).

In a large bowl, sift together the flour, sugar, cocoa powder, baking soda, baking powder, and 1 teaspoon kosher salt. In a separate bowl, whisk together the buttermilk, eggs, canola oil, vanilla, and beet puree. Stir the wet ingredients into the dry ingredients and mix until well combined. Transfer the batter to the prepared cake pan and bake until a tester inserted into the center of the cake comes out clean, 55 to 60 minutes.

Transfer the cake to a wire rack and let cool in the pan for 15 minutes, then turn the cake out of the pan and let cool completely on the rack.

Make the glaze: Put the chocolate in a bowl. In a small saucepan, gently heat the cream to a bare simmer. Pour the cream over the chopped chocolate and add the orange zest. Let stand for 10 minutes, then gently whisk until smooth. Whisk in the olive oil and kosher salt.

Set the cake (still on the wire rack) over a rimmed baking sheet. Pour the glaze over the cake and use an offset spatula or a spoon to spread the glaze over the top and sides of the cake, letting the excess drip off. Garnish with a sprinkle of flaky salt.

FEAST | **GARDEN BRUNCH**

Most chefs hate brunch. The hatred stems from working insane hours, most of them at night. Come Sunday morning, it's tough to be motivated to cook eggs and make toast for an often hungover clientele. But I'm the odd chef out, I guess, because I love brunch—eating it, certainly, but also cooking it. Perhaps, like me, you may have gotten to the point in your life where you'd rather cook the meal at home than stand in line, undercaffeinated, only to pay $14 for a plate of pancakes and bacon. While there are hundreds of recipes in the brunch canon from which to choose, my favorite mix includes a rich egg-and-bread custard, shot through with bits of roasted tomato; a "red flannel" hash, a classic New England dish named for the color contributed by the addition of cooked red beets; simple zucchini dressed with mint and lime juice; and an unusual salad that combines plums and avocados with a cilantro vinaigrette. Serve it all with eggs cooked in your favorite style. This brunch is loaded with vegetables, but feel free to complete the feast with a platter of crisp bacon or pork sausage links if you can't resist.

**ROASTED TOMATO
BREAD CUSTARD**

RED FLANNEL HASH

**AVOCADO AND
GOLDEN PLUM SALAD**

**GRILLED ZUCCHINI
WITH MINT**

ROASTED TOMATO BREAD CUSTARD

SERVES 8 TO 10

9 roma tomatoes, cored and halved lengthwise

3 tablespoons canola oil

Kosher salt and freshly ground black pepper

3 cups whole milk

3 whole eggs

3 tablespoons unsalted butter, melted and cooled, plus more for greasing

1 loaf crusty bread, such as a baguette, cut into 1-inch cubes (about 9 cups cubed bread)

1½ cups grated sharp cheddar cheese

3 teaspoons sweet Spanish paprika

1 teaspoon red pepper flakes

1 Preheat the oven to 400°F. Put the halved tomatoes in a medium bowl and drizzle with the canola oil. Toss so the tomatoes are coated, then season with salt and black pepper. Lay the tomatoes on a rimmed baking sheet cut-side down in a single layer. Transfer to the oven and roast until the skins begin to separate from the flesh and the tomatoes begin to color slightly, 10 minutes. Remove the tomatoes from the oven and set aside to cool.

2 Reduce the oven temperature to 350°F. Lightly grease a 9 x 13-inch glass or ceramic baking dish with butter.

3 In a large bowl, whisk together the milk, eggs, and melted butter until well combined. Add the cubed bread and stir so the bread is well coated with the custard.

4 Once the tomatoes have cooled slightly, coarsely chop and add to the bowl with the bread and custard. Stir in the cheddar, paprika, and red pepper flakes until combined.

5 Pour the bread-custard mixture into the prepared baking dish. Cover the dish with aluminum foil, transfer to the oven, and bake for 25 minutes. Uncover, increase the oven temperature to 375°F, and continue baking until the top has browned slightly and appears crusty and a wooden skewer inserted in the center comes out clean, 8 to 10 minutes more.

6 Let cool to room temperature and serve.

RED FLANNEL HASH

SERVES 8 TO 10

5 medium red beets

Extra-virgin olive oil, for drizzling

Kosher salt and freshly ground black pepper

3 medium sweet potatoes (about 1 pound), peeled and cut into large dice

1½ pounds small red potatoes, quartered

12 ounces bacon, cut crosswise into ¼-inch pieces

1 large yellow onion, finely diced

1½ teaspoons fennel seeds, toasted and ground

1½ teaspoons cumin seeds, toasted and ground

1½ teaspoons mustard seeds, toasted and ground

2 tablespoons fresh thyme leaves, finely chopped

2 tablespoons minced fresh parsley

1 Preheat the oven to 400°F.

2 Cut the tops and roots off each beet and peel them. Cut into 1½-inch cubes and place on a rimmed baking sheet. Drizzle with olive oil and season with salt and pepper. Roast until tender and caramelized, stirring occasionally, about 40 minutes.

3 Bring a large saucepan of salted water to a boil over high heat. Add the sweet potatoes and cook until fork-tender, 7 to 9 minutes. Remove the sweet potatoes from the water with a slotted spoon and transfer to another rimmed baking sheet. Add the red potatoes to the simmering water and cook until fork-tender, about 8 minutes. Drain, then add to the pan with the sweet potatoes. Drizzle the sweet and red potatoes liberally with olive oil. Let cool.

4 In a large skillet or cast-iron pan over medium heat, add the bacon. Cook, stirring, until the bacon has rendered some of its fat but is not crisp, about 5 minutes. Add the onion and cook, stirring, for 3 minutes, until slightly translucent. Add the ground fennel, cumin, and mustard seeds, stir to combine, and cook 1 minute more.

5 Add the sweet and red potatoes to the skillet and continue to cook,

stirring, until the potatoes are golden brown, the onions are lightly caramelized, and the bacon is crisp, 8 to 10 minutes more. Stir in the beets and thyme and cook, stirring occasionally, for 5 minutes more. Remove from the heat and stir in the parsley. Season to taste with salt and pepper. Serve hot.

AVOCADO AND GOLDEN PLUM SALAD

SERVES 8 TO 10

15 ripe medium yellow plums (red plums can be substituted)

8 ripe medium avocados

2 medium red onions, julienned

Juice of 1 lemon

Kosher salt

3 garlic cloves

3 dried chipotle peppers, stemmed

6 to 8 tablespoons unseasoned rice wine vinegar

1½ cups coarsely chopped fresh cilantro

¾ cup extra-virgin olive oil

4 ounces Parmigiano-Reggiano cheese, shaved into long pieces with a vegetable peeler

½ cup finely sliced chives

1 Peel the plums, pit, and cut into ½-inch cubes. Transfer the plums to a medium bowl.

2 Peel and pit the avocados, cut them into ½-inch cubes, and add the avocado to the bowl with the plums. Add the onions, then pour the lemon juice over and gently toss with your hands to combine, taking care not to break up the pieces of avocado. Season with salt.

3 Using a mortar and pestle, pound the garlic with a pinch of salt. Add the chipotles and continue pounding into a coarse paste. Add 6 tablespoons of the vinegar, then add the cilantro and continue to pound until the cilantro is finely ground. Stir in the olive oil and season to taste with salt.

4 Drizzle the dressing over the plums and avocado and toss gently to coat. Let the salad sit for 10 minutes, then season to taste with salt. Transfer to a serving bowl or platter and garnish with the Parmigiano-Reggiano and chives. Serve immediately.

GRILLED ZUCCHINI WITH MINT

SERVES 8 TO 10

3 pounds zucchini (about 6 large), sliced lengthwise into ⅛-inch-thick slices

3 tablespoons extra-virgin olive oil

Kosher salt and freshly ground black pepper

1 teaspoon red pepper flakes

3 tablespoons julienned fresh mint

1 lime, halved

1 Prepare a gas or charcoal grill for medium-high-heat direct grilling. Place the zucchini on a rimmed baking sheet and drizzle with the olive oil, turning to coat on both sides. Season with salt and black pepper.

2 When the grill is hot, lay the slices of zucchini on the grill grate and grill, turning once, until tender and charred in spots, about 2 to 3 minutes per side. Transfer to a platter and sprinkle with the red pepper flakes and mint. Squeeze the lime halves over and season to taste with additional salt.

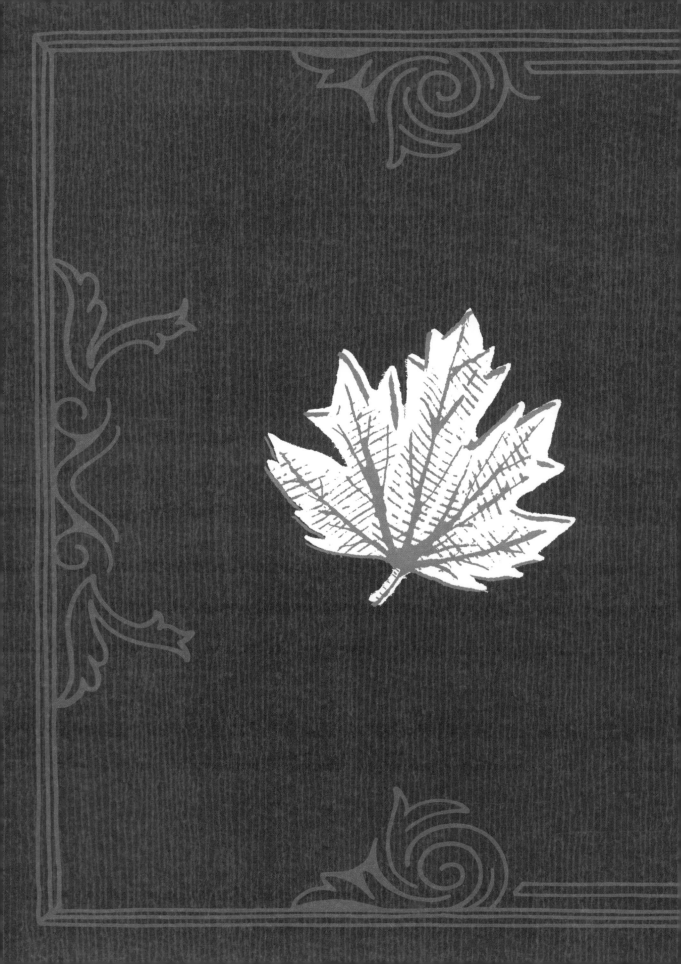

FOREST

I went to the woods because I wished to live
deliberately, to front only the essential facts of
life, and see if I could not learn what it had to
teach, and not, when I came to die, discover that
I had not lived.

—Henry David Thoreau

My childhood home in Milton, Massachusetts, was situated not far from a creek and small pond. Most days, when the weather cooperated, I would get out of school, pack a snack, and disappear into the woods for hours, returning home in time for dinner.

I still find a walk in the woods to be incredibly restorative. Getting lost in nature, alone with my own thoughts, is a respite from the frenzy of running a restaurant and raising two young boys. And the more time I spend in the forest, the more secrets it reveals: edible mushrooms springing forth from a tree stump, a covey of quail erupting from the hedgerow, tender watercress crowding a riverbank.

New England forests have had a comeback. In the mid-1800s, only 30 to 40 percent of New England was forested. The majority of the land had been cleared for agriculture, the logs harvested for paper and building. But as the population shifted and more people moved into cities, abandoning rural areas, the forest rebounded. Today, New England is the most heavily forested region in the United States—some 80 percent is covered by woods.

Beginning when I turned fourteen, my grandfather, an avid hunter, would take me on his hunting excursions in rural western Massachusetts. His preference was fowl, so we would flush grouse, quail, and duck from the brush with the help of his retriever.

At the end of the day, we'd carefully lay the duck and pheasant we shot in the trunk of his Lincoln sedan and head back to the suburbs.

Those trips with my grandfather were a way for us to bond, of course, but they also gave me the opportunity to connect in a tactile way to the landscape around me, and to the food available there.

After I opened Farmstead, my friend Beau Vestal asked me to accompany him on one of his foraging trips to the woods in nearby Tiverton and Little Compton, Rhode Island, where he'd been finding incredible local mushrooms. I accompanied him to the forest. Knee-deep in thick, wet brush, the fallen pine needles making a soft carpet beneath our feet, we looked for treasure.

"There's one," Beau said, pointing to a spot about fifteen feet away. I got closer and noticed a bright orange shelflike fungus growing from a crack in a rotting fallen log.

"Chickens!" Beau exclaimed, his enthusiasm contagious. My first introduction to foraging began with those neon-hued chicken of the woods mushrooms, which I learned to look for in stands of oak trees. Later, I focused my attention on finding *Grifola frondosa*—hen of the woods mushrooms, even more prized than the chickens—that would appear almost magically, seemingly overnight, their light gray, speckled flesh protruding from the damp leaves carpeting the forest floor.

I began taking field classes with experts, amassing a huge library of books on wild foods, consulting with nearby professors, enthusiasts, and other chefs. I learned to identify miner's lettuce and sorrel, wild herbs, edible roots, and tubers, and to consider the culinary possibilities of these "free" ingredients. I started to see the exquisite possibility in a New England forest. It was a new chapter for me as a cook, learning how the forest could feed me, both literally and figuratively.

Although the culinary bounty I found while foraging in New England forests felt to me like a discovery, there is a long New England tradition of foraging and hunting that began with the Native American tribes that first inhabited this land. Everything old is new again; seeking out ingredients in the wild connects you not only to the physical landscape but also to those who trod here before. And now that my boys are old enough, I take them to the forest with me, training them to see what I see, to appreciate the possibility of the woods, and to pass along my love of it to them.

In this chapter, you'll find recipes that use ingredients found in the woodlands of New England (though sourcing them does not require you to be a hunter or gatherer, as farmed versions of all these ingredients are readily available). Foraged mushrooms are sautéed in garlicky butter and piled on toast for a simple snack (page 279). Rabbit is confited, then shredded into silky rillettes (page 290). Duck livers are blended with butter into a silky, luxurious spread (page 289). Tiny quail are marinated in miso and grilled (page 295). Crisp-skinned roast pheasant is glazed with maple syrup (page 297); maple syrup also makes its way into a dessert cocktail, the Nor'easter (page 320).

SMOKED TROUT SALAD WITH ENDIVE, WATERCRESS, AND BLACK WALNUTS

Trout is one of the most plentiful freshwater fish in the Northeast—send a kid out with a rod to a pond or brook in New England, and they're very likely to return with a brown or rainbow trout.

Here the trout tops a light salad, which was inspired by classic British "pub greens," salads served in watering holes in more remote parts of the United Kingdom, including York, where my grandfather was from. The bitter endive, watercress, and escarole are a refreshing, crisp counterpoint to the rich fish and nuts, and the pear adds some thirst-quenching sweetness.

Black walnut trees used to be ubiquitous in New England forests, but because the wood is prized for furniture-making and gunstocks, very few of the trees remain. If you're lucky, there might be one growing near you; if not, you can purchase shelled black walnuts online (see Resources, page 331) or substitute English walnuts, which are similar in flavor, though milder. | **SERVES 6 AS A FIRST COURSE**

FOR THE DRESSING
½ cup mayonnaise
3 tablespoons half-and-half
3 tablespoons apple cider vinegar
2 tablespoons honey
1½ tablespoons poppy seeds
1 teaspoon dry mustard powder or Dijon mustard
Kosher salt and freshly ground black pepper

FOR THE SALAD
3 heads Belgian endive, cored and thinly sliced lengthwise
1 bunch watercress, stemmed and cut into 3-inch lengths
1 Anjou pear, cored and thinly sliced
15 red grapes, thinly sliced
12 ounces skinless smoked trout, broken into bite-size pieces

½ cup black walnut pieces (or substitute English walnuts), toasted
Extra-virgin olive oil, for drizzling
Flaky salt, such as Maldon, for garnish

Make the dressing: In a medium bowl, whisk together the mayonnaise, half-and-half, vinegar, honey, poppy seeds, and mustard powder. Season with kosher salt and pepper. The dressing can be made up to 3 days ahead; transfer to a jar and

CONTINUED

refrigerate until ready to use. Shake well before using.

Make the salad: Using the sliced endive as your base, begin to build six salads on individual salad plates. Place a few slices of the endive on the plates, a few pieces of watercress on top of that, a couple slices of pear, then some of the grape slices, and repeat again as necessary to create a neat layer of greens on the plate. Layering the salad is an integral part of its success, so you

should take some time with it, but don't fuss over it too much.

Top the salad with some of the trout, dividing it evenly among the plates.

With a spoon, drizzle some of the dressing over each salad. Garnish with the walnuts, a drizzle of extra-virgin olive oil, some flaky salt, and pepper. Serve immediately.

WILD MUSHROOM TOASTS
WITH TURNIP PUREE

Foraging is the simplest expression of what I love about serving wild foods: you can pluck magical fungi from the forest floor, clean them well, then simply sauté them in a little butter and pile them on toast and they'll taste delicious. Enhanced by the maple syrup and crumbled hazelnuts, this dish becomes a radical expression of autumn, my favorite season for foraging. Make this as an appetizer, for friends to eat when they're crowded around your kitchen island, glass of wine in hand. | **SERVES 6**

FOR THE TURNIP PUREE

1 tablespoon canola oil

1 pound Macomber turnips, peeled and cut into 2-inch chunks

1 garlic clove, chopped

1/2 cup chicken or vegetable stock, plus more as needed

1/2 cup heavy cream

1/2 cup cold unsalted butter

1/4 cup maple syrup

1/4 cup cream cheese

Kosher salt and freshly ground white pepper

FOR THE MUSHROOMS

2 pounds assorted wild mushrooms (preferably a combination of chicken of the woods, hen of the woods, and black trumpet mushrooms)

1/4 cup plus 2 tablespoons extra-virgin olive oil, plus more for drizzling

2 shallots, minced

2 garlic cloves, minced

1/4 cup coarsely chopped fresh thyme leaves

1/2 cup dry white wine

1 cup chicken or vegetable stock

1/4 cup cold unsalted butter

Kosher salt and freshly ground white pepper

1 baguette, cut on an angle into 1/4-inch-thick slices

Grated Parmigiano-Reggiano cheese, for serving

Make the turnip puree: In a medium saucepan over medium heat, heat the canola oil. Add the turnip chunks and sauté, stirring, until the turnip becomes tender and begins to turn slightly golden, about 5 minutes. Add the garlic and cook, stirring, 2 minutes more.

Pour in the stock and heavy cream. Bring to a boil, then reduce the heat until the liquid is simmering. Simmer until the liquid is reduced by half and the turnips are easily pierced with a fork, about 10 minutes. Remove from the heat and let cool slightly, then transfer to a blender.

Blend the mixture to a thick puree. Add the butter, maple syrup, and cream cheese and continue to process until creamy. The mixture should be the consistency of baby food; if it's too thin, return it to a pot and cook, stirring, over medium heat until it thickens. If too thick, add a splash more stock and blend. Transfer to a bowl, season to taste with salt and white pepper, and let cool.

Prepare the mushrooms: Chop the mushrooms into bite-size pieces. In a 12-inch skillet, heat 1/4 cup of the olive oil over medium heat. When the oil is hot, add the shallots and garlic and cook, stirring,

until translucent and fragrant, 4 to 5 minutes. Add the mushrooms. Don't worry if it looks like it is too much for the pan; as the mushrooms cook, they'll lose considerable volume.

Cook, stirring occasionally, until the mushrooms begin to release some of their liquid. Fold in the thyme leaves, then add the wine and continue cooking until almost all of the liquid has evaporated. Pour in the stock and reduce the heat to low.

Cook, stirring, until the stock is reduced by about half. Add the butter and continue cooking, for 5 or 6 minutes more. At this point you should have what resembles a chunky, mushroom mixture, with a small amount of liquid left in the pan; if it's still quite wet, continue cooking until most of the liquid is gone. Season to taste with salt and white pepper and set aside to cool.

Preheat the oven to 300°F. Arrange the bread slices on a baking sheet and drizzle with the remaining 2 tablespoons olive oil. Season the crostini with salt and white pepper. Bake the crostini for 10 minutes, rotating the baking sheet halfway through. The crostini should not brown, but they should be crisp. Remove from the oven and let cool to room temperature.

To serve, spread a thick layer of turnip puree on each crostini. Use a slotted spoon to spoon some of the mushrooms on top of the turnip puree. Garnish each toast with Parmigiano-Reggiano and a drizzle of olive oil. Serve warm.

FORAGING FOR MUSHROOMS

A walk in the woods means time to be alone with your thoughts, a moment to seek inspiration and gaze at beauty, and, sometimes, an opportunity to score wild food for dinner. Every forage, every hike, is successful. I don't measure success by the volume of mushrooms, wild greens, herbs, lettuces, or seaweeds that I bring back with me. A day outdoors makes me feel reflective and calm. Finding wild foods is simply a bonus. So, sometimes you'll head into the woods and come back empty-handed. That's part of foraging; it's a humbling reminder that nature is the one in control, which is an important realization for all cooks. Foraging also helps us become more attuned to the seasons and landscape and can be a tremendously satisfying hobby.

Tyler Akabane is the Townsman forager—here are his suggestions for how to get started and how to improve your haul.

• Hike smart. Begin in familiar terrain where you know foragers before you have successfully found certain wild foods. Head out early in the day and bring plenty of water with you.

• When in doubt, throw it out. Start by looking for mushrooms that are easily identifiable and have no look-alikes, including chicken of the woods, hen of the woods, and black trumpet mushrooms. Rely heavily on confirmation from field books (tailored to your region) and experts before you eat anything. Unless you are 100 percent certain of what you've got, don't eat it. Local universities and conservation or Audubon groups should be able to help if you have no other resources, and most major cities have local foraging clubs you can join.

• Learn Latin. Knowing the Latin names of mushrooms will allow you to communicate with other experts who may not be familiar with the regional "common" name of a mushroom that grows near you. For example, the mushroom that we call hen of the woods in New England is known as ram's head in the South, maitake in Japan, and *signorina* in Italy. But the mushroom's Latin name, *Grifola frondosa*, is the same wherever you go.

• Tread lightly. Mushrooms thrive in fragile habitats. It's our responsibility to protect the forests where they proliferate. Pack out what you pack in, and harvest only what you plan to eat.

• Follow the seasons. As with other vegetables, mushrooms are seasonal. In New England, mushroom season begins in late July and continues into the fall, when you'll find the largest variety (and quantity). Forage on a rainy day, or a nice clear day just after a rain.

• Protect your haul. Collect your mushrooms in a pillowcase, wooden basket, or lunch box. In summer, slip in an ice pack to keep the mushrooms cool. Field dress your mushrooms in the woods, wiping them clean of any debris and trimming the ends of the dirty stems. Once you're back home, clean the mushrooms with a damp pastry brush (do not wash them), transfer to brown paper bags—allowing them to breathe and the air to circulate around them—and store in your refrigerator. Do not store in plastic bags; the mushrooms will become slimy.

• Cook, pickle, dry. Generally speaking, mushrooms should be cooked before eating. Some, like porcini, black trumpets, and hen of the woods, are well suited to drying, while chanterelles and matsutake are best when fried in butter or pickled. Hen of the woods can also be dipped in a light batter (see page 214) and quickly fried, and meatier mushrooms, including lobster mushrooms, are sturdy enough for braising.

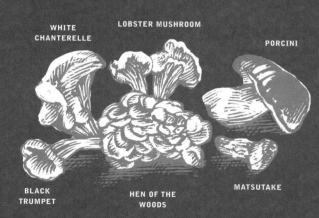

WHITE CHANTERELLE   LOBSTER MUSHROOM   PORCINI

BLACK TRUMPET   HEN OF THE WOODS   MATSUTAKE

DUCK FAT–FRIED FINGERLING POTATOES
WITH SALSA VERDE

Serve these irresistibly crispy, salty, and savory potatoes as a snack, with the salsa verde on the side for dipping, or combine with the Calabrian chile sausage (page 161) for an outstanding one-two combo meal. Duck fat can be special ordered from your butcher shop or purchased online (see Resources, page 331). | **SERVES 6 AS A FIRST COURSE OR SIDE DISH**

2 pounds fingerling potatoes, halved lengthwise 1 cup rendered duck fat	Leaves from 3 sprigs rosemary 4 garlic cloves, smashed	Kosher salt and freshly ground black pepper Salsa Verde (recipe follows), for serving

Bring a large pot of salted water to a boil over high heat, then reduce the heat so the water is vigorously simmering. Fill a large bowl with ice and water and set it near the stove. Line a baking sheet with a clean kitchen towel.

Add the potatoes to the simmering water and cook until tender but not mushy, about 10 minutes. Drain the potatoes and transfer them to the ice water bath to stop the cooking. Once cool, transfer to the prepared baking sheet to drain.

In a large cast-iron or other heavy skillet, heat the duck fat over medium heat. When the fat is hot, carefully add as many of the potatoes as will fit in a single layer, cut-side down. Reduce the heat to medium-low. Cook the potatoes until they are a deep golden brown on the cut side, about

5 minutes, then flip them and cook until browned on the second side, 3 minutes more. Remove the potatoes from the pan with a slotted spoon and transfer to a bowl. Repeat with the remaining potatoes, adding them to the bowl with the others as they're done.

When you've cooked all the potatoes, add the rosemary leaves and garlic cloves to the pan and fry, basting them with the duck fat, until the rosemary is crisp and the garlic is a light golden brown.

Drizzle some of the infused duck fat over the potatoes, season with salt and pepper, and toss to coat. Sprinkle with the fried rosemary leaves and smashed garlic cloves and serve with salsa verde alongside for dipping.

CONTINUED

SALSA VERDE

MAKES 1 CUP

1 garlic clove, minced

¾ teaspoon kosher salt, plus more as needed

½ teaspoon freshly ground black pepper, plus more as needed

½ teaspoon red pepper flakes

½ teaspoon lemon zest

3½ tablespoons fresh lemon juice

¾ cup packed chopped fresh flat-leaf parsley

1 tablespoon capers, drained and chopped

2 anchovy fillets, minced

¾ cup extra-virgin olive oil

In a medium bowl, mix the garlic, salt, black pepper, red pepper flakes, and lemon zest together. Using the back of a spoon, mash to a paste. Whisk in the lemon juice, then stir in the parsley, capers, and minced anchovy. Stir in the olive oil and season to taste with salt and black pepper. The salsa verde can be made up to a few hours in advance; stir before using.

POTTED DUCK LIVER

If you aren't sure you like liver, start with this recipe: this silky spread is a gateway drug. Duck livers are milder in flavor than chicken livers, with a faint sweetness; this mousse showcases their flavor.

Potted duck liver mousse makes a great holiday gift. If you're looking for an alternative to cookies this year, make a double batch, divide it among attractive jars, and deliver it to friends and family. | **MAKES ABOUT 1½ CUPS**

½ pound duck livers, trimmed of sinew ¾ cup (1½ sticks) unsalted butter, at room temperature 1 tablespoon extra-virgin olive oil 1 shallot, minced	1 garlic clove, minced 1 sprig sage, stems removed and leaves separated 2 tablespoons brandy ½ teaspoon ground mace	Kosher salt and freshly ground black pepper ½ teaspoon fresh thyme leaves Flaky salt, such as Maldon, for garnish Toasted baguette slices, for serving

Preheat the oven to 225°F.

Put the duck livers in a colander set in the sink to drain. Place half of the butter in an ovenproof saucepan and place it in the oven to slowly melt until it separates and the milk solids sink to the bottom of the pot, about 10 minutes. Remove the pot from the oven and carefully pour off the clarified butter into a separate bowl, leaving the milk solids behind. Discard the milk solids and let the clarified butter cool to room temperature.

In a medium skillet, heat the olive oil over medium heat. Add the shallot and garlic and cook, stirring frequently, until soft and tender, about 8 minutes. Transfer to a small plate.

Wipe out the skillet and return it to the stovetop over high heat. Add the livers to the pan, along with three-quarters of the sage leaves. Cook the livers for about 2 minutes on each side, until they are beginning to brown but are still pink inside. Do not overcook; they should be medium-rare.

Carefully pour in the brandy. It may ignite, so use caution. Allow the alcohol to cook off, then remove the pan from the heat. Transfer the livers and any liquid remaining in the pan to a food processor and add the cooked shallot and garlic. Puree while still hot until smooth. Cut the remaining butter into cubes. With the machine running, add the cubed butter and the mace and process until smooth. Season to taste with kosher salt and lots of pepper.

Transfer the mixture to a small bowl or small glass jars, and smooth the surface. Spoon the clarified butter over the top, covering the liver completely. Wipe the rim of the bowl or jars clean, then top with the thyme leaves and flaky salt.

Place the bowl or jars in the refrigerator and chill for a few hours; if storing for more than a few hours, cover the bowl or jars with plastic wrap or lids. The potted liver will keep for up to 1 week. Serve with the toasted slices of baguette.

RABBIT RILLETTES

It may require a special order from your butcher shop, but rabbit is worth seeking out. It's an underutilized yet completely versatile game meat.

Rillettes are typically made by slow-cooking meat—be it duck, pork, or rabbit—in fat until tender. My approach to rabbit rillettes is a bit different. Instead of cooking the delicate meat in fat, you'll slowly braise the meat until tender, then combine the shredded meat with some of the reduced braising liquid and duck fat. Eat the rillettes like you would a pâté—spread onto toasted slices of rye bread and topped with rosy strands of pickled shallots. | **MAKES ABOUT A QUART**

3 tablespoons extra-virgin olive oil	3 sprigs rosemary	1½ cups rendered duck fat
1 whole rabbit (2½ to 3 pounds), butchered into 6 pieces	2 star anise pods	3 tablespoons whole grain mustard
6 medium yellow onions, peeled and julienned	2 tablespoons whole black peppercorns	Maras pepper (see Note, page 148)
6 whole garlic cloves	2 tablespoons juniper berries	Toasted baguette slices or crackers, for serving
3 sprigs thyme	4 cups dry white wine	Pickled Shallots, for serving (page 241)
	Kosher salt	

In a large Dutch oven or heavy-bottomed pot, heat the olive oil over medium-high heat. Add the rabbit pieces and brown on both sides, about 3 minutes per side.

Add the onions, garlic, thyme, rosemary, star anise, peppercorns, and juniper berries. Pour in the white wine, stir, and season with salt. Bring to a boil, then reduce the heat so the liquid is simmering, cover, gently stirring occasionally, and cook until the meat pulls easily from the bone, 1½ hours.

With tongs, transfer the rabbit pieces to a plate. When cool enough to handle, shred the meat, discarding the bones, and transfer to a large bowl. Pour the braising liquid through a fine-mesh sieve

into a medium saucepan. Discard the herb stems, whole spices, and half of the onions and garlic; reserve the remaining onions and garlic. Bring the liquid to a boil over high heat and cook until reduced by three-quarters, about 10 minutes.

Pour the reduced liquid into the bowl with the shredded meat. Add the reserved onions and garlic and mix well to combine, then pour in the duck fat and mix well. Stir in the mustard until incorporated. Season to taste with salt and Maras pepper. Serve immediately, with the toasted baguette slices or crackers and pickled shallots alongside, or transfer to a lidded glass jar and refrigerate for up to 2 days; let it come to room temperature before serving.

FARRO VERDE

Farro, an ancient variety of wheat that has been cultivated for centuries, has a subtle, earthly flavor and satisfyingly toothsome bite. For this risotto-like recipe, the farro stands in for Arborio rice. If you're using whole-grain farro, you'll need to soak it in hot water to cover for at least three hours before cooking, then break up the grains in the food processor. The semi-pearled (*semiperlato*) farro cooks more quickly and doesn't require soaking, but it's less flavorful and nutty than whole-grain farro. Either will work for this recipe.

Stinging nettles, the bane of gardeners and the delight of chefs, give the risotto a bright, grassy, fresh flavor; use gloves or tongs to handle them prior to cooking; once cooked, they lose their sting. | **SERVES 6 AS A MAIN COURSE**

---

1 cup whole-grain or semipearled farro (see headnote)	½ cup fresh flat-leaf parsley leaves	2 medium shallots, peeled and minced
7 cups chicken or vegetable stock	1 tablespoon chopped fresh marjoram	2 garlic cloves, minced
3 tablespoons extra-virgin olive oil, plus more for drizzling	½ cup freshly grated Parmigiano-Reggiano cheese, plus more for garnish	½ cup dry white cooking wine
4 cups loosely packed fresh stinging nettles or spinach leaves	1 cup small cauliflower florets	Kosher salt and freshly ground black pepper
Leaves from 2 sprigs thyme		Lemon zest, for garnish

Heat a medium skillet over medium heat. Add the farro and cook, stirring, until lightly toasted, about 5 minutes. Transfer to a bowl and add 2 cups boiling water. Let stand at room temperature for 3 hours, or let cool to room temperature then refrigerate overnight. If you are using semipearled farro, this step can be skipped.

In a medium saucepan, heat the stock over medium-high heat until simmering. In a large skillet, heat 1 tablespoon of the olive oil over medium heat. Add the nettles, thyme, and parsley and cook, stirring, until the nettles begin to wilt. Add a ladleful of hot stock and cook, stirring, until

the nettles are tender and the stock has reduced, about 5 minutes. Remove from the heat and stir in the marjoram and Parmigiano-Reggiano. Transfer to the bowl of a food processor and process until smooth. Transfer the puree to a bowl and rinse out the bowl of the food processor.

Drain the farro and transfer to the bowl of a food processor (if you're using semipearled farro, you can skip this step). Pulse about 10 times. Scrape down the sides of the bowl with a rubber spatula and pulse again 5 to 10 times, until some but not all of the farro is broken. Transfer to a bowl.

CONTINUED

In a wide, heavy skillet or saucepan over medium heat, heat the remaining 2 tablespoons of olive oil. Add the cauliflower florets and cook, stirring, until lightly browned, 5 minutes. Add the shallots and cook, stirring, until just tender but not browned, 3 to 5 minutes. Add the garlic and cook, stirring, until fragrant, about 30 seconds. Add the farro and stir over medium heat until the grains dry out a bit and begin to sizzle slightly in the pot. Pour in the wine and cook, stirring, until most of the wine has evaporated and the farro is again beginning to sizzle slightly.

Add a ladleful of simmering stock to the farro, and adjust the heat so it's simmering gently. Cook, stirring often, until the farro has absorbed almost all the stock, then add another ladleful or two of the stock and continue to cook at a gentle simmer, stirring frequently and adding more stock when the farro looks dry. Continue this process until the mixture is creamy and the farro is tender, about 25 minutes.

Fold the nettle puree into the farro until incorporated. Season to taste with salt and pepper, and add additional stock as needed to maintain the creamy consistency. Divide the mixture among six warmed bowls and garnish each with a drizzle of olive oil, some grated Parmigiano-Reggiano, and some lemon zest. Serve immediately.

MISO-MARINATED GRILLED QUAIL
WITH POLE BEAN RAGOUT

Quail has more flavor per square morsel than almost any other bird. Seek out sleeve-boned quail, which are boneless save for the wings and legs; they are easier to cook and eat. Because of their diminutive size, the quail cook quickly on a hot grill, and the honey and molasses give it a sticky-sweet finger-licking quality.

Fresh pole beans are a beautiful late-summer ingredient. A good farmers' market should have a few varieties to choose from, any of which would work in this recipe. Alongside romano beans and corn kernels, this makes a perfect warm-weather ragout. | **SERVES 6 AS A MAIN COURSE**

FOR THE QUAIL

2 tablespoons extra-virgin olive oil

2 garlic cloves, smashed

1 shallot, minced

2 tablespoons fresh lemon juice

1 tablespoon honey

1 tablespoon white miso

1 tablespoon molasses
(not blackstrap)

Kosher salt and freshly ground
black pepper

6 semiboneless (sleeve-boned) quail

FOR THE BEAN RAGOUT

2 tablespoons extra-virgin olive oil

2 medium shallots, finely diced

2 garlic cloves, minced

Kosher salt and freshly ground
black pepper

1 Fresno chile, finely diced

2 cups fresh corn kernels (from
about 2 ears corn)

½ pound green beans, cut into
1-inch pieces

½ pound wax beans, cut into
1-inch pieces

¼ pound romano beans,
thinly sliced

1 cup vegetable or chicken stock

3 tablespoons unsalted butter

2 tablespoons thinly sliced
fresh chives

Marinate the quail: In a large bowl, mix together the olive oil, smashed garlic, shallot, lemon juice, honey, miso, and molasses. Add a couple pinches of salt and a few turns from the pepper mill. Add the quail and turn to coat with the marinade. Cover with plastic wrap and marinate in the refrigerator for at least 2 hours but no more than 4.

While the quail marinate, make the bean ragout: In a large saucepan, heat the olive oil over medium heat. Add the shallots and garlic and a pinch of salt and cook, stirring, until softened but not browned, about 4 minutes. Add the chile, corn, and beans and cook, stirring, for 1 minute, then add the stock and butter. Increase the heat to medium-high and cook until the liquid has reduced and the corn and beans are tender, about 6 minutes. Remove from the heat, stir in the chives, and season to taste with salt and pepper.

Remove the quail from the refrigerator and let them come to room temperature. Prepare a gas or charcoal grill for direct medium-heat grilling.

When the grill is hot, remove the quail from the marinade and lay them flat on the grill, breast-side down, and grill, turning once, until cooked through and lightly charred, 4 to 5 minutes per side. Transfer to a rimmed baking sheet and tent with aluminum foil. Serve the quail with the bean ragout alongside.

ROASTED PHEASANT
WITH SAVORY OATS, STEWED RAISINS, AND PINE NUTS

My grandfather used to take me to the western edge of southern Vermont, just along the New York border, in early fall to practice bird hunting. He and I would hide in silence, listening for a rustling in the leaves, or the sight of a wiggling fern, waiting for a bouquet of pheasants (yes, that's what a group of the birds is called) to emerge. I'd fire a shot, which rarely hit its target, though occasionally I'd get lucky and a bird would drop from the sky between two birch trees. Bring it home, dress it, and roast it for dinner—a hunter's reward.

Cooking pheasant is no more difficult than cooking a whole chicken, and you'll be rewarded for your efforts—the meat is richer, almost like a super chicken. Unless you're a hunter, you will probably need to special order it from your butcher, and it's likely to arrive frozen. Brine the pheasants, then let them air-dry in the fridge, which ensures crackling, golden skin. | **SERVES 6 AS A MAIN COURSE**

FOR THE PHEASANT
⅔ cup kosher salt
4 bay leaves
1 tablespoon crushed juniper
   berries
1½ tablespoons sugar
2 (2½- to 3-pound) whole
   pheasants
2 tablespoons unsalted butter,
   at room-temperature
1 yellow onion, quartered
1 small apple, cored and quartered
2 tablespoons unsalted butter,
   melted
2 tablespoons pure maple syrup

FOR THE OATS
1 cup steel-cut oats
1 tablespoon canola oil
2 garlic cloves, sliced paper thin
1 shallot, sliced paper thin
1 cup whole milk
¼ teaspoon kosher salt, plus more
   as needed
1 tablespoon unsalted butter
Freshly ground black pepper

FOR THE STEWED RAISINS
⅔ cup chicken stock or water
2 tablespoons honey
1 teaspoon kosher salt
½ cup golden raisins
1 tablespoon chopped fresh thyme

¼ cup pine nuts, toasted,
   for garnish

SPECIAL EQUIPMENT: Instant-read
thermometer; kitchen twine

Make the brine: In a large pot, combine the salt, bay leaves, juniper berries, sugar, and 10 cups water and bring to a boil. Cover and let cool to room temperature.

CONTINUED

Submerge the pheasants in the cooled brine (you may need to weigh them down with a plate or pot lid to keep them submerged). Transfer to the refrigerator and refrigerate for at least 4 hours or up to 8, but no longer: the longer the pheasants sit in the brine, the saltier the meat will become.

Remove the pheasants from the brine, dry well with paper towels, and set on a rimmed baking sheet or plate. Return them to the refrigerator and let the pheasants dry, uncovered, for at least 1 hour or up to 6. This step ensures the pheasants will have crispy skin.

Remove the pheasants from the fridge and let stand at room temperature for at least 30 minutes or up to 1 hour. Preheat the oven to 425°F.

Set the pheasants side by side in a roasting pan, breast-side up, and dot with butter. Stuff the cavity of each pheasant with half of the quartered onion and apple, then use kitchen twine to tie the legs together. Roast for 15 minutes. Remove the pheasants from the oven and lower the oven temperature to 350°F. (Crack the oven door to speed the cooling.)

In a small bowl, stir together the melted butter and maple syrup. Baste the pheasants all over with this mixture, then return them to the oven and roast until the skin is golden brown and an instant-read thermometer inserted into the thigh joint registers 160°F and the juices run almost clear, 30 to 40 minutes. Remove from the oven and let rest for 10 to 15 minutes.

While the pheasants are cooking at the lower temperature, make the oats: Spread the oats over a rimmed baking sheet and transfer to the oven. Toast until the oats are golden brown and smell nutty, about 7 minutes. Remove the oats from the oven.

In a large saucepan, heat the canola oil over medium heat. Add the garlic and shallot and cook, stirring, until the shallot is translucent, about

3 minutes. Add the toasted oats and stir to coat with the oil, garlic, and shallots. Pour in the milk, salt, and 3 cups water and bring to a simmer.

Simmer the oats gently, stirring occasionally, for 20 to 25 minutes, until the mixture is very thick, the majority of the liquid has been absorbed, and the oats are creamy and tender. Scrape the bottom of the pot occasionally with a wooden spoon to prevent it from scorching; reduce the heat if necessary. Remove from the heat and stir in the butter. Season with salt and pepper. Cover and keep warm.

While the oats are cooking, make the raisins: In a small saucepan, combine the stock, honey, and salt. Bring to a simmer over medium heat, then add the raisins. Cook at a vigorous simmer until the raisins are swollen with the liquid and the liquid is syrupy, about 6 minutes. Remove from the heat and stir in the thyme.

Carve each pheasant into six pieces (as you would a chicken) and transfer to a platter. To serve, put a spoonful of savory oats on each plate and top with a piece of pheasant. Garnish with a few stewed raisins and some of the toasted pine nuts and serve immediately.

PAN-ROASTED VENISON
WITH SPICED BUTTERNUT SQUASH AND BRAISED CHARD

In many parts of New England, the annual deer hunt provides much of the meat that families eat throughout the year. Happily, farmed venison is just as delicious as wild.

Venison loin is a choice cut; it's lean and flavorful, and is best cooked simply in a hot pan until medium-rare (when overcooked, it can become tough). You might want to make an extra batch of the braising paste that flavors the greens and keep it on hand. It's a way to boost the flavor of vegetables of all types, and it keeps well in the fridge. Roasted squash flavored with warming berbere, an Ethiopian chile and spice blend, completes this wintry dish. | **SERVES 6 AS A MAIN COURSE**

FOR THE SQUASH

1 large butternut squash (about 3 pounds), peeled, seeded, and cut into 1-inch cubes

3 tablespoons canola oil

1 tablespoon berbere spice blend (see Resources, page 331)

Kosher salt and freshly ground black pepper

1 tablespoon pure maple syrup

1 tablespoon fresh lemon juice

Zest of 1 lemon

FOR THE BRAISED CHARD

2 tablespoons canola oil

2 pounds Swiss chard, stemmed, leaves cut into ribbons

2 tablespoons Braising Paste (recipe follows)

Kosher salt and freshly ground black pepper

FOR THE VENISON

1 (3-pound) venison loin

1 tablespoon juniper berries

1 tablespoon whole black peppercorns

1 star anise pod

2 tablespoons canola oil

3 tablespoons unsalted butter, at room temperature

Flaky salt, such as Maldon, for garnish

SPECIAL EQUIPMENT: Instant-read thermometer

Preheat the oven to 400°F. Line a rimmed baking sheet with aluminum foil.

Make the squash: In a medium bowl, combine the squash, canola oil, and berbere and season with salt and pepper. Toss so the squash is coated, then spread over the prepared baking sheet in a single layer. Roast, stirring, until soft and caramelized, 20 to 25 minutes.

In a medium bowl, whisk together the maple syrup, lemon juice, and lemon zest. When the squash is done, remove it from the oven and let cool slightly, then add to the bowl with the syrup mixture and toss to coat. Season with salt and pepper, then return the squash to the baking sheet.

While the squash is roasting, make the braised chard: In a large saucepan, heat the canola oil over medium heat. When the oil is hot, add the Swiss chard and sauté, stirring, until it begins to wilt. Reduce the heat to medium-low and add the braising paste, stirring to evenly coat the greens. Reduce the heat to low and cook, stirring occasionally, until the chard is velvety and soft, about 15 minutes. Season to taste with salt and pepper and keep warm.

Make the venison: Remove the venison from the refrigerator and let it come to room temperature.

Using a mortar and pestle, pound the juniper berries, peppercorns, and star anise to a powder. Transfer the spice powder to a large plate and spread it into an even layer.

Rub the venison with the canola oil, then roll the meat in the spice mixture, coating the exterior evenly with a spice crust.

Heat a cast-iron or other heavy ovenproof skillet over medium-high heat. When the pan is hot, add the venison and sear, turning, until well browned on both sides, about 4 minutes total. Remove the pan from the heat and add the butter. As the butter melts and begins to brown, baste the venison with a spoon, turning the meat over once and basting the other side as well (you may need to tilt the pan so the butter pools and is easier to spoon up). Transfer the pan into the oven and cook until an instant-read thermometer inserted into the thickest part of the loin registers 130°F, about 5 minute more. Transfer to a cutting board and let rest for 5 to 6 minutes before slicing.

Return the squash to the oven to warm.

Slice the venison into 1-inch-thick slices and sprinkle with flaky salt. On each plate, arrange some of the roasted squash. Use a slotted spoon to scoop some of the braised greens onto the plate, then finish the plate with a few slices of the venison. Serve immediately.

BRAISING PASTE
MAKES ½ CUP

1 tablespoon whole-grain mustard
4 anchovy fillets
2 tablespoons grated fresh horseradish (or prepared horseradish)
2 tablespoons Worcestershire sauce
6 cloves Roasted Garlic (page 166)
2 fresh garlic cloves, thinly sliced
2 roasted shallots (page 30), peeled
Leaves from 3 sprigs oregano, chopped
½ cup water or vegetable stock, at room temperature

In a food processor, combine the mustard, anchovy fillets, horseradish, Worcestershire, roasted garlic, fresh garlic, shallots, oregano, and water and process to a smooth paste, adding more water if needed to facilitate the processing. Use immediately or store the paste in an airtight container in the refrigerator for up to 1 week.

BRAISED TURKEY THIGHS
WITH POTATO-APPLE PANCAKES

I'm a dark-meat guy. It's rich, nuanced, tender, and moist, and I'm always carving myself the leg and thigh off the Thanksgiving turkey while everyone else clamors for the breast meat. I also don't think turkey should be limited to one holiday a year plus the sandwiches that follow—this simple braise is a great year-round dinner. Serve the turkey with potato-apple cakes that are inspired by classic potato latkes. Any leftovers are great for brunch; reheat the pancakes in a hot oven, then top with a soft-boiled egg.

| SERVES 6 AS A MAIN COURSE

FOR THE TURKEY THIGHS

2 tablespoons canola oil

6 whole turkey thighs

Kosher salt and freshly ground black pepper

2 medium carrots, diced

4 celery stalks, diced

1 medium yellow or white onion, diced

10 whole black peppercorns

6 juniper berries

4 allspice berries

½ cinnamon stick

1 small bunch thyme

2 bay leaves

1 sprig rosemary

4 cups chicken or turkey stock

FOR THE POTATO-APPLE PANCAKES

4 russet potatoes (about 2 pounds), peeled

1 medium yellow onion, peeled

1 Granny Smith apple, peeled and cored

1 egg, lightly beaten

2 tablespoons all-purpose flour

2 teaspoons kosher salt

½ teaspoon freshly ground white pepper

½ cup canola oil, plus more as needed, for frying

½ cup chicken or duck fat, plus more as needed, for frying (clarified butter can be substituted)

All-purpose flour, if needed

1 tablespoon unsalted butter

SPECIAL EQUIPMENT: Cheesecloth; kitchen twine

Preheat the oven to 325°F.

Make the turkey thighs: In a large Dutch oven or heavy high-sided skillet, heat the canola oil over high heat. Season the turkey thighs on all sides with salt and black pepper. When the oil is hot, add the turkey thighs, skin-side down, and sear until golden brown on the skin side, about 6 minutes (reduce the heat if the skin begins to burn). Flip the thighs and cook until golden brown on the second side, 4 to 5 minutes more. Transfer to a rimmed plate or baking sheet and set aside.

Add the carrots, celery, and onion to the Dutch oven and cook, stirring occasionally, for 5 minutes.

Place a square of cheesecloth on a work surface. Put the peppercorns, juniper berries, allspice berries, and cinnamon stick in the center of the cheesecloth, gather up the edges to form a sachet, and tie with a piece of kitchen twine. Add the sachet to the vegetables, along with the thyme, bay leaves, and rosemary.

Return the thighs to the Dutch oven, skin-side up, and add enough stock so that the thighs are halfway submerged. Cover the pot and transfer to the oven. Braise the turkey thighs until the meat is very tender and the connective tissue has dissolved but the meat is not falling from the bone, about 1 hour.

While the legs are braising, make the potato-apple pancakes: Grate the potatoes, onion, and apple on the large holes of a box grater. Take handfuls of the grated mixture and squeeze firmly over the sink to eliminate extra moisture (the enemy of crispy pancakes!). Place in a large bowl. Add the egg, flour, salt, and white pepper and mix well to combine.

Set a wire rack over a rimmed baking sheet, line the wire rack with paper towels, and place nearby. In a large cast-iron skillet, heat the canola oil with 2 tablespoons of the chicken fat over medium heat until it is hot and shimmering. Spoon heaping tablespoons of the pancake mixture into the oil, spacing them about 2 inches apart, and flatten slightly with a fork.

Fry the pancakes until golden on the bottom, about 3 minutes, then flip and fry on the second side until golden and crisp, 2 to 3 minutes more. Transfer the pancakes to the paper towel–lined rack to drain and season with salt. Fry the remaining pancakes, adding more oil and chicken fat to the skillet as needed.

When the turkey thighs are tender, remove them from the oven, turn the oven off, and place the potato pancakes on a baking sheet in the oven to keep warm.

Carefully remove the thighs from the pot and transfer them to a large platter. Tent with aluminum foil and return to the oven to keep warm. Strain the braising liquid through a fine-mesh sieve into a medium saucepan (or back into the Dutch oven), discarding the solids and the sachet.

Bring the braising liquid in the pan to a rapid boil over high heat. Boil until the liquid has reduced by half and is thick enough to coat the back of a spoon. If it is still too thin, whisk in a tablespoon of flour and simmer until the sauce has thickened and no longer has a floury taste, 4 to 5 minutes. Whisk in the butter and remove from the heat.

Remove the turkey thighs from the oven and drizzle the sauce over the top. Serve with the potato-apple pancakes alongside.

CORNFLAKE-CRUSTED FRIED RABBIT WITH RAMP RANCH

It's the law of the universe: everyone loves fried chicken. And while I'm wary of those who describe rabbit as tasting "just like chicken," I have to admit that when coated in cornflakes and fried to a golden brown, rabbit legs are just as appealing.

This recipe is a multiday process—the first day, the rabbit legs are braised until just tender, then cooled, coated in yogurt (which helps tenderize the meat), and refrigerated overnight. This advance prep has its advantages, though: the following day, the rabbit pieces need only to be battered and quickly fried (a thirty-minute operation, tops), and they're ready to eat. It's worth noting that, like fried chicken, fried rabbit is equally good served hot or at room temperature. Serve it with a sparkling wine or hard cider or a crisp ale. | **SERVES 6 AS A MAIN COURSE**

---

4 cups pale ale or mild sparkling hard cider

1 garlic clove, smashed

Zest of 1 lemon, removed with a vegetable peeler

Zest of 1 lime, removed with a vegetable peeler

1 bay leaf

2 tablespoons coriander seeds, toasted and crushed

10 allspice berries, toasted and crushed

6 juniper berries, toasted and crushed

6 rabbit legs

1½ cups full-fat Greek yogurt

1½ tablespoons Dijon mustard

2 teaspoons chopped fresh marjoram

2 teaspoons chopped fresh thyme

2 teaspoons chopped fresh rosemary

2 teaspoons chopped fresh mint

1 tablespoon plus 1 teaspoon coarsely ground black pepper

Kosher salt

1 cup all-purpose flour

1 teaspoon red pepper flakes, ground fine

1 teaspoon onion powder

1 teaspoon sweet Spanish paprika

1 teaspoon fennel seeds, toasted and ground

1 teaspoon dry mustard powder

Canola oil, for frying

2 cups buttermilk

6 cups cornflakes, crushed by hand into medium-fine crumbs

3 tablespoons minced fresh chives, for garnish

Ramp Ranch (recipe follows), for serving

SPECIAL EQUIPMENT: Instant-read thermometer; deep-fry thermometer

---

Pour the beer and 1 cup water into a Dutch oven or high-sided pot and bring to a boil over high heat. Add the garlic, citrus zests, bay leaf, coriander, allspice, and juniper. Add the rabbit legs to the pot, making sure they are completely submerged in the liquid. Reduce the heat so the liquid is simmering and cook, turning once, until an instant-read thermometer inserted into the spot closest to the bone registers 140°F, about 25 minutes. Remove from the heat. With tongs, carefully remove the rabbit legs from the pot and transfer to a plate to cool completely. Discard the liquid.

In a bowl large enough to accommodate the rabbit legs, stir together the yogurt, mustard, marjoram, thyme, rosemary, mint, 1 teaspoon of the black pepper, and a liberal pinch of salt.

Add the rabbit legs to the yogurt mixture, turning the pieces so they're well coated on all sides. Cover the bowl with plastic wrap and refrigerate overnight.

In a large bowl, whisk together the flour, remaining 1 tablespoon black pepper, the red pepper flakes, onion powder, paprika, fennel, mustard powder, and a liberal pinch of salt.

Fill a large cast-iron skillet with canola oil to a depth of 1 inch. Heat the oil over medium heat until it registers 325°F on a deep-fry thermometer. While the oil heats, remove the rabbit legs from the yogurt mixture. Rinse them well and pat dry with paper towels.

Pour the buttermilk into a large bowl and place the crushed cornflakes in a second large bowl. Working with one piece of rabbit at a time, dip it into the seasoned flour and turn to coat, shaking off the excess. Dip into the buttermilk, coating completely, then drop into the bowl of cornflakes and coat on all sides with the cereal, pressing the cornflakes so they adhere. Repeat with the remaining pieces of rabbit until they've all been coated.

Set a wire rack over a rimmed baking sheet and place it nearby. When the oil is hot, fry the rabbit in batches, turning once, until golden brown and crispy, 4 to 5 minutes per side; an instant-read thermometer inserted close to the bone should register 165°F. Let the oil return to temperature between batches. Transfer the rabbit legs to the wire rack and season with salt.

Let cool for 5 minutes, then transfer to a platter and garnish with the chives. Serve hot or at room temperature, accompanied by the ramp ranch for dipping.

RAMP RANCH
MAKES 1 CUP

½ cup sour cream
½ cup buttermilk
¼ cup chopped Spicy Pickled Ramps (page 243) or finely chopped scallions
1½ tablespoons chopped fresh parsley
½ teaspoon kosher salt
¼ teaspoon freshly ground black pepper

In a small bowl, whisk together the sour cream, buttermilk, pickled ramps, parsley, salt, and pepper. Serve immediately, or cover with plastic wrap and refrigerate for up to 5 days.

SWEET POTATO GNOCCHI
WITH AGED CHEDDAR AND MUSHROOMS

Making great gnocchi relies on a light touch: if you overwork the dough, you'll end up with leaden gnocchi, but if you add too little flour, you risk watching your beautiful pasta disintegrate when you cook it. When it comes to making gnocchi, practice makes perfect: the more often you make this pasta, the better you'll become at judging when the dough is just right—it should be soft but not sticky, and some Italian *nonnas* will tell you that the finished dough should have the texture of an earlobe.

In this variation on the classic, I substitute sweet potatoes for russets and add some ricotta to the dough, which both lightens and enriches it. The sweetness of the potatoes is offset nicely by the addition of the mushrooms (wild, if you can get 'em) and a grating of nutty aged cheddar.

| SERVES 6 AS A MAIN COURSE

2 pounds sweet potatoes	½ teaspoon freshly grated nutmeg	1 medium shallot, thinly sliced
12 ounces whole-milk ricotta cheese, homemade (page 17) or store-bought, drained very well	2¾ cups all-purpose flour, plus more for dusting	6 tablespoons roughly chopped fresh sage
	Olive oil, for drizzling	Freshly ground black pepper
2 egg yolks	1 cup (2 sticks) unsalted butter	2 tablespoons sherry vinegar
3 ounces finely grated Parmigiano-Reggiano cheese	2 tablespoons canola oil	½ cup chicken stock
2 tablespoons packed light brown sugar	1 cup coarsely chopped hen of the woods mushrooms (or substitute cremini or oyster mushrooms)	½ pound aged cheddar cheese, preferably clothbound (see page 27), grated on the small holes of a box grater
2 teaspoons kosher salt, plus more as needed	2 garlic cloves, thinly sliced	

Preheat the oven to 400°F. Line a large baking sheet with parchment paper.

Place the sweet potatoes on the baking sheet and roast until tender and easily pierced with a skewer or the tip of a knife, about 1 hour. Remove the potatoes from the oven, cut them in half lengthwise, and let cool until you can easily handle them. Scoop the potato flesh into a large bowl (discard the skins) and mash with a fork. Add the ricotta and egg yolks and stir well with a rubber spatula. Add the Parmigiano-Reggiano, brown sugar, salt, and nutmeg and stir to combine. Mix in the flour, about ½ cup at a time, until a soft (but not sticky) dough forms.

Turn the dough out onto a lightly floured work surface. Divide the dough into six equal pieces. Roll each piece of dough into a 20-inch-long rope about 1 inch in diameter, sprinkling with additional flour as needed if sticky. With a bench scraper or knife, cut each rope into ¾-inch pieces. Roll each piece over the tines of an overturned fork or a gnocchi paddle, pressing gently to form ridges on the gnocchi, then transfer to a flour-dusted baking sheet.

Bring a large pot of salted water to a boil, then reduce the heat so the water is simmering. Working in batches, add the gnocchi to the water and simmer until tender, 5 to 6 minutes. When the gnocchi are ready, they will float to the surface of the water. Using a spider or slotted spoon, transfer the cooked gnocchi to a clean rimmed baking sheet. When all the gnocchi have been cooked, drizzle with a little olive oil and let cool completely.

In a large heavy skillet, melt the butter over medium-high heat, swirling the pan occasionally. Cook until the butter browns and has a nutty aroma, about 5 minutes. Add the canola oil, then add the mushrooms, garlic, and shallot. Sauté until the shallot is translucent and the mushrooms have begun to soften, about 3 minutes, then add the sage and season generously with salt and pepper. Add the gnocchi to the pan and cook, occasionally stirring gently with a rubber spatula, until the gnocchi are lightly browned and heated through and the mushrooms are tender, about 7 minutes.

Pour in the vinegar and stock and cook until the liquid has reduced and thickened slightly, about 5 minutes.

Divide the gnocchi among six shallow bowls. Top with the grated cheddar and serve immediately.

HOW TO MAKE GNOCCHI

1. Roll the gnocchi dough into a rope about 1 inch in diameter.

2. With a bench scraper, cut into ¾-inch pieces.

3. Roll each gnocchi over the tines of an overturned fork or on a gnocchi paddle.

4. Transfer the gnocchi to a flour-dusted baking sheet.

BIRCH BEER FLOAT

Diner culture represents a lot of what I love about cooking and food, especially the interaction between the cook and the customer seated across the counter. (Those diner memories, by the way, are part of why I wanted Townsman to have an open kitchen and counter seating, where diners could talk with the chefs.)

Like maple syrup, birch syrup is a distinctive product made by boiling the sap of birch trees—harvested in the late spring, just before the leaves emerge—until thick and sweet. Though its sugar content is similar to maple, it has a different flavor—more savory, almost molasses-y. It's highlighted in this simple float, which is a distinctly New England take on a soda jerk classic. | MAKES 1

2 large scoops Vanilla Ice Cream (page 70)	1 cup cold seltzer	2 tablespoons birch syrup (see Resources, page 331)

Scoop the ice cream into a glass. In a separate glass, stir together the seltzer and birch syrup. Slowly pour the seltzer mixture over the ice cream and serve immediately, with a straw and a spoon.

CANDY CAP MUSHROOM ICE CREAM

The signature ice cream of Townsman gets its unique flavor from candy cap mushrooms, which have a distinctive maple-y, toasted-oat flavor. Guests cringe when we tell them we're serving mushroom ice cream, but once they taste it, they're converted. | **MAKES 1 QUART**

¼ cup dried candy cap mushrooms (see Resources, page 331)	6 egg yolks	Ice cream cones, for serving (optional)
1¾ cups heavy cream	½ cup sugar	
1¼ cups whole milk	⅓ cup light corn syrup	**SPECIAL EQUIPMENT:** Cheesecloth; kitchen twine; instant-read thermometer; ice cream maker
1 vanilla bean, split lengthwise and seeds scraped	¼ teaspoon kosher salt	
	2 teaspoons pure vanilla extract	

Put the dried mushrooms in a spice grinder and pulse until they have the texture of loose-leaf tea. Divide the mushrooms into two even piles; wrap each pile in a square of cheesecloth and tie closed with kitchen twine.

In a medium saucepan, combine the cream, milk, and vanilla bean pod and seeds and one bundle of the mushrooms. Heat over medium-low heat until bubbles begin to form around the edges of the pan. Remove from the heat. Let stand for 5 minutes, then remove the mushroom bundle and carefully squeeze it over the pan to extract the liquid. Discard the bundle.

Fill a large bowl with ice and water and set it nearby.

In a large bowl, whisk together the egg yolks, sugar, corn syrup, and salt until well combined. While whisking continuously, slowly add about 1 cup of the hot cream mixture to the egg yolks, then pour the egg mixture into the saucepan with the remaining cream and add the second mushroom bundle. Heat over medium-low heat, stirring continuously, until the mixture thickens and coats the back of the spoon (if you draw your finger through it, it should leave a trail) and an instant-read thermometer registers 160°F.

Pour the custard through a fine-mesh sieve into a clean bowl; squeeze the mushroom bundle over the sieve to extract the liquid. Set the bowl with the custard in the ice water bath and let cool, stirring occasionally, until the custard is at room temperature. Stir in the vanilla extract, then remove the bowl from the ice water bath, cover with plastic wrap, and refrigerate overnight.

Transfer the chilled custard to an ice cream machine and freeze according to the manufacturer's instructions. Transfer to a freezer-proof container and freeze until solid, at least 2 hours.

S'MORES

The quintessential camping treat, there's just something about a charred marshmallow, melty chocolate, and crunchy graham crackers that is synonymous with summertime fun. Our uptown version of the campfire classic involves homemade grahams, squares of cacao nib–studded chocolate, and a generous smear of homemade marshmallow crème. The whole thing is charred under the broiler until warm and gooey. Kids love 'em, adults love 'em—who wants s'more? | MAKES 16

FOR THE GRAHAM CRACKERS
2½ cups all-purpose flour, plus more for dusting
1 cup packed light brown sugar
1 teaspoon baking soda
¾ teaspoon kosher salt
7 tablespoons cold unsalted butter, cut into cubes
⅓ cup mild honey

5 tablespoons whole milk
2 tablespoons pure vanilla extract

FOR THE CACAO NIB–CHOCOLATE SQUARES
¼ cup cacao nibs
Unsalted butter or nonstick cooking spray, for greasing
8 ounces bittersweet chocolate, chopped

4 ounces heavy cream
Pinch of flaky salt, such as Maldon

FOR THE MARSHMALLOW CRÈME
½ cup light corn syrup
1 egg white
⅛ teaspoon kosher salt
½ cup confectioners' sugar, sifted
¼ teaspoon pure vanilla extract

Make the graham crackers: In a food processor, combine the flour, brown sugar, baking soda, and salt and pulse to blend. Add the butter and pulse until the texture is similar to cornmeal. Drizzle in the honey and pulse to combine, then add the milk and vanilla and pulse until the dough comes together into a ball.

Wrap the dough tightly in plastic wrap and refrigerate for at least 4 hours or up to overnight.

Preheat the oven to 325°F.

Transfer the dough to a lightly floured work surface. Divide it into two pieces. Set half of the dough on a sheet of parchment paper and, with a lightly floured rolling pin, roll the dough into a rectangle ⅛ to ¼ inch thick. On a second sheet of parchment, repeat with the remaining dough. Set the two dough sheets (still on the parchment) on a rimmed baking sheet and refrigerate for 15 minutes. With a sharp knife, trim the edges of each dough sheet so you have a clean edge, then cut into 3-inch squares and set directly onto a rimmed baking sheet, spacing them about ½ inch apart. Using a fork, lightly prick each cookie three times. Refrigerate the cookies for 10 minutes before baking.

Bake for 10 minutes, then rotate the pan and bake for 5 to 8 minutes more, until the grahams are golden brown and crisp. Let cool on the pans for 5 minutes, then transfer to a wire rack and let cool completely.

Make the cacao nib–chocolate squares: In a small heavy skillet, toast the cacao nibs, stirring, over medium heat, until lightly toasted (because they are dark in color to begin with, the best way to determine if they are toasted enough is to taste one).

Grease a 9-inch square pan with butter or spray with nonstick cooking spray. Line the pan with parchment paper and grease the paper, too.

Put the chopped chocolate in a bowl. In a small saucepan, heat the heavy cream and toasted nibs over medium heat until bubbles begin to form around the edges of the pan. Remove from the heat and pour the warmed cream over the chocolate. Let stand for 5 minutes, then stir together until well combined. Season to taste with the flaky salt, then pour into the prepared pan and use an offset spatula to spread into an even layer. Let cool to room temperature, then transfer to the refrigerator and chill for 10 minutes. Remove the large chocolate bar from the pan and cut it into sixteen 2¼-inch squares.

Make the marshmallow crème: In the bowl of a stand mixer fitted with the whisk attachment, beat the corn syrup, egg white, and kosher salt on high speed until voluminous, 8 minutes. Reduce the mixer speed to low, add the confectioners' sugar and vanilla and mix until incorporated. Increase the speed to high and beat until fluffy and light, 2 minutes.

Preheat the broiler to high.

Arrange half the graham crackers top-side down on a rimmed baking sheet. Generously spread each graham with some of the marshmallow crème. Broil until the marshmallow is deep golden, watching carefully so it doesn't char. Remove from the oven and top with a square of chocolate and a second graham cracker to make a sandwich. Serve immediately.

THE NOR'EASTER

I call this dessert cocktail the Nor'easter because it's made from ingredients that every household should have on hand in case inclement weather strikes and you can't get to the grocery store: namely, whiskey, maple syrup, and heavy cream. Snowstorm coming? No worries. You can hunker down, pull out the provisions, and fix yourself one of these.

Kate and I enjoy packing a thermos full of this drink and hitting the street when neighbors need shoveling out after a storm. The thermos gets passed around, and this recipe should, too. | **MAKES 1 COCKTAIL**

2 ounces bourbon or rye whiskey
1 ounce pure maple syrup,
    preferably dark amber
1 ounce heavy cream
	Pinch of ground cinnamon
	1 whole nutmeg, for dusting
	1 orange
		Whipped cream, for garnish
		    (optional)
		Bittersweet chocolate,
		    for garnish (optional)

In an ice-filled cocktail shaker, combine the bourbon, maple syrup, heavy cream, and cinnamon. Shake vigorously for 2 minutes, then strain into a coupe. Grate a light dusting of nutmeg over the top. With a vegetable peeler, remove a 2-inch strip of peel from the orange and add to the glass. Top with whipped cream and a shaving of bittersweet chocolate, if you want to take the drink over the top. Drink immediately.

ON MAPLE

When I was eighteen, I was assigned to do some court-appointed community service (but that's a story for another time, as they say), and the judge sent me to the Natick Community Organic Farm, located in a suburb of Boston. Each spring, the team at the makeshift sugar shack would collect sap from maple trees growing on private land in the surrounding towns and boil it down into thick golden maple syrup, which would be distributed to supporters of the farms.

I'd never witnessed a maple boil before. Real maple syrup was always a stalwart in our kitchen cabinet (like good New Englanders, we shunned Mrs. Butterworth's), but until I saw it for myself, I didn't realize that maple syrup is produced only in a specific season, and that the season is spring, when the warm days and cold nights cause sap to begin flowing in the trees. If you've never experienced a maple syrup boil, imagine this: You're huddled inside a large wooden shed. It's frigid outside, but inside the air is moist and warm, and it smells sweet, fragranced by the aroma of sap boiling in the evaporator. When most of the water has boiled off, what's left behind is maple syrup. Watching (and smelling) the transformation is truly an intoxicating experience.

Before the Civil War, white sugar was expensive. It came from the Caribbean, and overland transportation was both difficult and costly. The upshot of this was that most people in the northeastern region of North America "grew" their own sugar in the form of maple sugar. The majority of the syrup produced was not left as syrup but boiled to a much higher temperature and poured into small tin molds where it hardened into maple sugar bricks.

A household might make hundreds of these bricks in spring and then easily store them in a pantry for the rest of the year. Every time sugar was required for cooking, a brick was taken from the shelf and the amount needed would be grated off the brick. Maple bricks were economical, easy to store, and relatively easy to make. Today, the reverse is true: white sugar is now incredibly cheap, and maple syrup and sugar are an expensive (and far more delicious) alternative.

In 2016, production of maple syrup in the northeastern states totaled 3.78 million gallons, up 27 percent from 2015's production of 2.98 million gallons. Vermont is the state that produces the most, some 47 percent of the national total.

Until recently, maple syrup was assigned letter grades: A, B, or C, which corresponded not to quality but to flavor and color (with A being the lightest in color and flavor). The grading system has been changed recently, in part to clear up consumer confusion. Now there are four A grades of syrup, each with a corresponding flavor profile.

Whether amber or deep mahogany in color, with a delicate flavor or a deeper, more robust taste, maple syrup has a million and one uses. Sure, it's good on waffles or drizzled over ice cream, but you can also use it to sweeten a brine for meat or to add a complex, nuanced flavor to a sauce or jus. At the restaurant, we whip it, burn it, smoke it, freeze it; we've even found a way to emulsify it into oil, creating maple fat. Beyond syrup, there's also maple cream, maple candy, and maple sugar, which is available in a granulated form or in a solid brick.

In the age of increased industrialization, the sugaring process can be charmingly old-fashioned. Much of the work, from emptying the buckets to stoking the hardwood fire beneath the evaporator to filling the bottles, is still done by hand, often by families who have been doing it for generations. Mapling is a way of life. It reminds me that seeking out true connections with artisans and producers is an important thing to do, and that in an increasingly homogeneous world, something with terroir—a true taste of place—is particularly special.

ROASTED STRAWBERRIES
WITH ELDERFLOWER LIQUEUR

Though it's tough to beat a fresh, sun-warmed strawberry, roasting the summer fruit is another way to coax out and concentrate the berries' sweet-tart flavor. This recipe plays on the classic combination of strawberries and cream, substituting tangy mascarpone for whipped cream.

Tiny elderflowers grow wild in New England, appearing at the start of summer (though make sure you've correctly identified the plant, as they resemble poisonous hemlock) and can be made into a floral, fragrant cordial that will last until the next year's harvest. Elderflower liqueur can be purchased, also, at a well-stocked liquor store; St-Germain is a popular brand. Only a small amount is used in this dessert, but any remaining liqueur is excellent mixed into cocktails with gin or vodka. | SERVES 4

2 quarts strawberries, hulled 2 tablespoons elderflower liqueur	¾ cup mascarpone cheese Juice of ½ lemon	2 tablespoons packed light brown sugar Pinch of kosher salt

Preheat the oven to 250°F.

Set a wire rack over a rimmed baking sheet and place the strawberries on the wire rack, stem-side down. Roast until the berries are tender to the touch but still maintain their shape, about 20 minutes. Remove from the oven. Preheat the broiler to high and then return the berries to the oven and broil just until lightly caramelized, taking care not to char them.

Let cool, then slice the strawberries and put them in a bowl. Add the elderflower liqueur and toss to coat. Pour any accumulated juices from the baking pan into a measuring cup and set aside.

In a small bowl, stir together the mascarpone, lemon juice, brown sugar, and reserved roasted strawberry juice. Season with a pinch of salt.

Divide the sliced berries among four bowls and top each with a spoonful of the mascarpone mixture.

FEAST | **MAPLE PEKING DUCK**

Let me be perfectly clear: This is the most challenging recipe in this book, and it's not something to attempt unless you're up for a (week-) long project. But if you're looking for a showstopping dish—a feast in every sense of the word—read on.

I first started playing around with my own version of the famous Chinatown classic, Peking duck, when we were getting ready to open Townsman, which is located at the corner of Boston's Chinatown. Those mahogany-colored lacquered ducks hanging in the windows of the nearby shops are so enticing, and the technique to make the crisp-skinned delicacies so exacting, I couldn't resist tackling the recipe, putting my own spin on it, one that includes glazing the duck with a sticky paste made from two beloved New England ingredients: maple syrup and molasses.

First poached, then air-dried, then smoked, roasted, and finally fried, this duck is a major undertaking. But when you take a bite of the succulent, spiced meat and the shatteringly crisp skin, I think you'll agree it's worth the effort. Serve the duck with moo shu pancakes, maple hoisin sauce, and a simple kimchi salad.

MAPLE PEKING DUCK

MOO SHU PANCAKES

MAPLE HOISIN SAUCE

**KIMCHI SALAD
WITH PEAR, FENNEL,
AND RADISH**

MAPLE PEKING DUCK

SERVES 8 TO 10

1 whole large Peking duck
(about 8 pounds)

2 tablespoons whole black
peppercorns

2 teaspoons whole pink
peppercorns

1 teaspoon fennel seeds

6 whole cloves

4 star anise pods

2 (3-inch) cinnamon sticks

½ cup plus 1 tablespoon pure
maple syrup, plus more for
drizzling

2 tablespoons hoisin sauce

1 tablespoon molasses
(not blackstrap)

1½ teaspoons gochujang
(Korean chile paste; see
Resources, page 331)

1 tablespoon kosher salt

1⅓ cup shoyu (white soy sauce)

½ cup barley syrup
(see Resources, page 331)

½ cup canola oil

SPECIAL EQUIPMENT: One pair
rubber gloves; barding needle and
butcher's twine; bicycle pump
with needle adapter; wood chips
(for smoking); propane torch;
instant-read thermometer; deep-fry
thermometer

1 Clean the duck: Position the duck
on top of a kitchen towel, breast-
side down, and look over the exterior of the duck. You will see some
remaining feathers or quills on the
skin; remove them with tweezers or
kitchen shears. Use a boning knife
to gently scrape the surface of the
bird—as though you were giving it
a shave—taking care not to punc-
ture the skin.

2 Flip the duck over and repeat
this process on the breast side. Pay
careful attention to the crevices and
joints; the areas where the legs and
wings meet the carcass may require
some extra attention. Empty the
cavity of any offal and the neck and
discard. With the boning knife or
your fingers, pull out any fat surrounding the cavity of the duck and
discard. With a clean kitchen towel,
dry the exterior of the duck well.

3 In a small skillet over medium
heat, combine 1 tablespoon of the
black peppercorns, 1 teaspoon of
the pink peppercorns, ½ teaspoon
of the fennel seeds, 3 cloves, 2 star
anise pods, and 1 cinnamon stick.
Toast until aromatic and a whiff of
smoke rises from the pan, about
1 minute. Let cool, then transfer
to a spice grinder and grind to a
fine powder. Transfer the powder
to a small mixing bowl and stir in
1 tablespoon of the maple syrup,
the hoisin sauce, molasses, gochujang, and salt until well combined.

4 Put on your rubber gloves, and
with your gloved hand, scoop up
some of the rub and smear it inside
the cavity of the duck. Make sure
you are smearing the mixture all
the way up inside the bird, and that
you are covering all exposed areas
inside the cavity with a thick layer
of the paste.

5 Thread a barding needle with a
foot of butcher's twine, tying off one
end around the needle so it doesn't
become unthreaded. Place the duck
on a cutting board, breast-side up.
Using the barding needle and twine,
sew up the opening of the cavity,
alternating between going over and
then under the skin, as if you were
lacing a shoe, pulling the thread
tight. When the cavity is sewn shut,
tie off the twine with a knot and
trim any excess.

6 Prepare the bike pump by fitting
it with the needle adapter (this is
the same adapter you would use to
blow up a ball). Alternatively, you
can use a small air compressor,
should you happen to have one.

7 At the top of the duck, where the
neck would be, carefully pull some
of the breast skin away from the
breast meat on both sides, using
only the tip of your knife. You don't
need to make huge openings, just
a small enough slit on each side in
which to insert the needle adapter.

8 Insert the tip of the needle
adapter into the slit between the
skin and meat of the breast. Pump
air into the carcass, keeping one
hand on the laced end of the cavity,
so as to not let air blow through
the bird, but into the bird. (Note:
It can be useful to have the help of
an assistant with this process; one
person to work the pump and one
to handle the duck.) You will see
the skin begin to separate from the
breast meat, inflating like a bal-
loon. As it inflates, push the needle
adapter farther in so the air reaches
the bottom of the breast and the
skin separates all the way down,
using the tip of your knife to aid the
separation. When you've pumped as
much air as possible into one side

of the breast, repeat with the other breast.

9 Carefully flip the duck over and make another slit at the top of the back and repeat, first carefully separating the skin from the carcass with the tip of your knife (the back skin is thinner and more delicate than the breast skin, so use care), then inserting the needle adapter and pumping air into the duck. As the skin on the back begins to separate from the carcass, continue to use the tip of your knife to further aid the separation.

10 Once you have pumped as much air as possible into the duck, use your barding needle and more butcher's twine to tightly sew up the neck area in the same way you did the lower cavity, this time creating a loop of twine at the end from which to hang the duck. Set the duck aside.

11 In a deep high-sided pot, bring a gallon of water to a simmer over medium heat. Add the remaining tablespoon black peppercorns, teaspoon pink peppercorns, ½ teaspoon fennel seeds, 3 cloves, 2 star anise pods, and 1 cinnamon stick.

12 Keep the water just below a simmer. Line a rimmed baking sheet with a clean kitchen towel and set nearby, along with a ladle. Hold the duck over the pot by the loop you created and, using the ladle, carefully baste the duck with the poaching liquid, starting at the top of the duck and letting the liquid drizzle down. You will see the skin contract and firm up; continue this process over and over, until you feel confident that you

have scalded every possible area of the duck's skin. It should take you 7 to 8 minutes to completely scald the duck.

13 Once scalded, carefully lay the duck on the prepared baking sheet and discard the scalding liquid.

14 Make the glaze: In a small bowl, whisk together the remaining ½ cup maple syrup and the shoyu and barley syrup.

15 Set the duck on a wire rack over a rimmed baking sheet. With a pastry brush, baste the duck with the glaze, making sure to paint the entire surface (pay attention to the nooks and crannies). Let the duck stand for 10 minutes, then brush the duck with another layer of glaze.

16 As the glaze cools, it will thicken; for the last round of glazing you may have more success pouring it over the duck rather than brushing it on. Transfer the duck, unwrapped and still on the wire rack, to the refrigerator. (If it's wintertime and the temperature is below 35°F, you can also store the duck in an uninsulated part of your home, such as the garage.)

17 Let the duck air-dry for at least 4 days or up to a week. The longer the duck air-dries, the crispier the skin will become. After the duck has dried for the proper time, remove it from the refrigerator and place on a roasting pan on top of a small wire rack, which will allow air to circulate while it roasts.

18 In a small tin can (a used, rinsed tuna fish can is the perfect size), sprinkle about ½ cup of wood

chips. Set the can in the roasting pan alongside the duck.

19 With a torch, light the wood chips until they are smoldering. Wrap the roasting pan with heavy-duty aluminum foil to seal in the smoke. Cut a small hole in the foil at the far end of the pan to encourage circulation. Let the duck smoke for about 10 minutes, then remove the foil and check the wood chips. If they are no longer smoldering, relight them with the torch, then reseal the pan and smoke for 10 minutes more. Repeat the process two more times (for a total of 40 minutes of smoking).

20 Preheat the oven to 350°F.

21 Once the duck has been smoked for 40 minutes, uncover it and remove the tin of smoldering wood chips. Extinguish the chips with water, and discard. Re-cover the roasting pan with the foil, transfer to the oven, and roast for 15 minutes. Remove the roasting pan from the oven, uncover, and gently tilt the duck to allow the fat to drain from the carcass. Re-cover and return to the oven, draining the fat as described every 10 minutes, until the duck has cooked for 45 minutes. Remove the duck from the oven and reduce the oven temperature to 300°F. When the oven has cooled, uncover the duck and return it to the oven and roast it for 8 to 9 minutes, until the skin is slightly transparent and golden brown and an instant-read thermometer inserted into the thigh registers 130°F.

22 In a large high-sided pot, heat the canola oil until it registers

350°F on a deep-fry thermometer. Set a rimmed baking sheet nearby, along with a ladle. Check the loop of butcher's twine at the neck of the duck and ensure that it is holding fast. If not, use your barding needle and more butcher's twine to add another secure loop from which to hold the bird. Place an oven mitt on your nondominant hand and use that mitted hand to hold on to the loop of twine. Suspend the duck over the pot of hot oil. Use your dominant hand to very carefully ladle hot oil over the duck, beginning at the neck and allowing the oil to pour over the sides of the duck, just as you did with the poaching liquid. The skin will begin to crisp up and become nearly translucent. Continue basting until all the skin has been treated and it's uniformly crisp, rotating the duck to reach all sides. Turn off the heat and let the oil cool completely before discarding.

23 Transfer the duck to a cutting board and, using a sharp knife, carve into sections. Transfer to a platter and serve with the moo shu pancakes and maple hoisin sauce and the kimchi salad on the side. Encourage your guests to wrap morsels of meat in the pancakes, topped with a swipe of maple hoisin.

MOO SHU PANCAKES

MAKES ABOUT 1 DOZEN PANCAKES

4 cups unbleached, all-purpose flour, plus more for dusting

4 tablespoons toasted sesame oil

1 Bring a kettle of water to boil. Put the flour in a medium bowl and add 1½ cups boiling water and mix with a fork or a pair of chopsticks until the dough begins to come together into a rough, sticky ball. Turn the dough out on a lightly floured work surface and knead it until smooth, about 3 minutes. Cover with a clean kitchen towel and let rest for at least 40 minutes or up to 1 hour.

2 With your hands, shape the dough into an even cylinder 12 inches long. With a sharp serrated knife, gently cut the cylinder into 12 even pieces. If the cutting compresses any of the pieces, stand them on end and reshape them back into rounds.

3 Lightly flour your palms and use them to flatten the pieces into 2-inch rounds. Brush the top of each round generously with sesame oil. Lay one round on top of another round, oiled sides together. Flatten the pair with the heel of your hand. Continue until you have six pairs.

4 With a lightly floured rolling pin, roll each pair into a thin pancake about 7 inches in diameter. Stack the pancakes as you finish rolling them.

5 Heat a 9-inch cast-iron skillet over medium-high heat.

6 When the pan is hot, add a pancake and cook until the bottom starts to bubble slightly and a few brown spots appear, about 2 minutes. Flip and cook on the other side until a few light brown spots appear, about 30 seconds more. Remove the pancake from the pan and, while the pancake is still hot, pick it up, look for a seam to grab, and separate it into two very thin pancakes. Stack them on a plate as you go and wrap the plate with foil to keep them warm and pliable. If not using right away, refrigerate until ready to use. To reheat, wrap in a clean, lightly moistened kitchen towel and microwave until hot and pliant, about 1 minute.

MAPLE HOISIN SAUCE

MAKES 1 CUP

½ cup maple syrup

¼ cup soy sauce

¼ cup pitted prunes

3 tablespoons rice wine vinegar

3 tablespoons sesame oil

1 tablespoon sambal

3 garlic cloves, thinly sliced

1 shallot, thinly sliced

Kosher salt and freshly ground black pepper

1 In a small saucepan, combine the maple syrup, soy sauce, prunes, vinegar, sesame oil, sambal, garlic, and shallot. Gently warm the mixture over low heat, stirring frequently, for about 5 minutes.

2 Transfer the mixture to a blender and puree until smooth. (Alternatively, puree the mixture in the pot using an immersion blender.)

3 Pass the mixture through a fine-mesh sieve into a bowl. Season to taste with salt and pepper. The sauce will keep, covered and refrigerated, for up to a week.

KIMCHI SALAD WITH PEAR, FENNEL, AND RADISH

SERVES 10

½ cup silken tofu

½ cup canola oil

½ cup plus 2 tablespoons kimchi, coarsely chopped

¼ cup white miso

1 tablespoon honey

1 tablespoon unseasoned rice vinegar

Kosher salt and freshly ground black pepper

3 small heads butter lettuce

1 large head fennel, very thinly sliced

18 French breakfast radishes, greens removed, quartered

3 Asian pears, cored, halved, and sliced into half-moons about ¼ inch thick

⅓ cup slivered almonds, lightly toasted

Leaves from 3 sprigs tarragon

1 Make the vinaigrette: In a blender, combine the tofu, canola oil, 6 tablespoons of the kimchi, miso, honey, and vinegar and blend until smooth. Transfer to a bowl and season to taste with salt and pepper. Set aside.

2 In a large salad bowl, combine the lettuce, fennel, radishes, pears, and the remaining kimchi. Drizzle in about 6 tablespoons of the vinaigrette and toss to coat; if the salad looks underdressed, add a bit more vinaigrette (any remaining vinaigrette will keep, refrigerated, for up to 3 days; let come to room temperature before using).

3 Sprinkle the almonds and tarragon over the salad and toss again, gently, to combine. Serve immediately.

NEW ENGLAND SPECIALTIES, STATE BY STATE

Maine

Blueberry pie

Fish stew

Grapenut pudding

Indian pudding

Lobster rolls

Moxie soda

Red hot dogs

Whoopie pies

Wild blueberries

New Hampshire

Fried pike

Hard cider

Maple sundaes

Steamers

Vermont

Artisan cheese, especially cheddar

Cider donuts

Craft beer

Ice cream

Maple creemees

Maple syrup

Switchel

Tourtière

Massachusetts

Baked beans

Boston cream pie

Clam chowder

Cranberries

Franks

Fried clams

Grinders

Marshmallow Fluff

Necco wafers

Connecticut

New Haven clam pie (pizza)

Pepperidge Farm cookies

PEZ

Steamed cheeseburgers

Rhode Island

Clam cakes

Coffee milk

Coffee syrup

Frozen lemonade

Hot wieners

Johnnycakes

RESOURCES

Look for these ingredients in your local specialty food markets. If you want to order online, here are some of my favorite sources.

Aleppo pepper
Oaktown Spice Shop
oaktownspiceshop.com

Bang's Island mussels
Harbor Fish Market
harborfish.com

Berbere spice blend
Penzeys Spices
penzeys.com

Black garlic
Black Garlic City
blackgarliccity.com

Black walnuts
nuts.com

Calabrian chiles
Market Hall Foods
markethallfoods.com

Candy cap mushrooms
Far West Fungi
farwestfungi.com

Clothbound cheddar and other artisan cheeses
Formaggio Kitchen
formaggiokitchen.com

Doenjang
Crazy Korean Cooking
crazykoreancooking.com

Dried orange peel
Spices Inc.
spicesinc.com

Duck fat
D'Artagnan
dartagnan.com

Gochujang and gochugaru
Crazy Korean Cooking
crazykoreancooking.com

Harissa
(I like Les Moulins Mahjoub brand)
The Spice House
thespicehouse.com

Heirloom beans
Baer's Best
baersbest.com

Rancho Gordo
ranchogordo.com

Hog casings
The Sausage Maker
sausagemaker.com

Maple jelly
Branon Family Maple Orchards
branonmaple.com

Maras pepper
Formaggio Kitchen
formaggiokitchen.com

Pheasants and quail
D'Artagnan
dartagnan.com

Sodium nitrite (Insta Cure #1)
The Sausage Maker
sausagemaker.com

Togarashi
Oaktown Spice Shop
oaktownspiceshop.com

Verjus
Terra Sonoma
terrasonoma.com

ACKNOWLEDGMENTS

I was warned by other chefs and authors prior to writing this book that it would be the undertaking of a lifetime. Boy, were they right. This project has been over two years in the making and has involved numerous cups of coffee and many late nights and early mornings and has been a beautiful sacrifice. I feel blessed. Truly. This being said, it is foolish to think that this could have all come together without the help of an incredible support system, an amazing restaurant family and professional network, and my own family. I would like to thank those who worked tirelessly in helping create a book we are all very proud of. They are:

Kate, Sawyer, and Coleman. You are literally everything. You have sacrificed so much— most notably the lack of a husband and father in your lives. I hope that the words in this book help with the realization that the personal sacrifices have not been in vain. Collectively, through your love and support, we have been able to feed a lot of people, to leave lasting impressions, and to make memories for so many guests. Kate, you are the definition of selfless. Everything you have done has been for me. Boys, Daddy promises to take you to some Red Sox games, to cook some burgers on the grill, and to chalk up a few more living room wrestling matches before the next book. Deal? I love you all so much!

My family, including my parents, sisters, and the dogs, for keeping me sane with licks and cuddles (from the latter, not the former).

The entire team at Townsman and Farmstead, without whom none of this would have been possible. You have seen my vision, contributed to my personal and professional story, and have driven me to be better every day. Know that I think of you all, often and fondly.

Huge Galdones, Catrine Kelty, Erin O'Leary Bates, and Amanda Simmons. You are the best photo crew a guy could ask for. You were dedicated to getting it right and you never settled. Thank you.

Phil Baltz, Madeline Block, Emma Rowland, and the team at Baltz & Company. It has been an absolute pleasure working with you and your talented organization. You guys just . . . get me.

Matt Leddy. My right hand. You are a soldier. A champion. A talented chef and steadfast collaborator. Your future is shining. The world of food is blessed to have you. I am always a text message away. Just keep it PG, okay?

Meghan Thompson. One of the most talented and dynamic cooks and pastry chefs I have ever met. Your influence is prominent within these pages. Thank you for being you.

I'd like to thank all dishwashers everywhere. You are the heart and soul of the kitchen. I started in the pit and part of me will never leave. It's where I learned about true hard work and camaraderie. Restaurants could not function without you. Mine have been no exception.

To my friends who have endorsed this project—Daniel Boulud, Mario Batali, Tyler Florence, David McMillan, April Bloomfield, and the inimitable Andrew Zimmern. You are inspirations, and I'm proud to call you friends and colleagues.

Judy Pray and the whole team at Artisan. You took a chance on me, embraced my reverie, and pushed me to put the best on paper. Thank you for your guidance and support.

Jessica Battilana. What can I say? We have known each other since we were dumb kids with dreams, and this project could not—and would not—have been complete without your perspective, insight, devotion, and fervent love for writing. You are a supreme talent and I can't wait to see what you do next! Mr. Moss, where are you now?!

Last, I'd like to thank my fierce faction of lifelong friends who have grown up with me in this crazy business. You know who you are. You have fielded my late-night calls. We have belly laughed and snickered and howled at the moon. We have worked doubles and triples, rubbed elbows in the dish pit, and corralled the occasional drunkard in my bar (or yours). We have wondered what the hell we are doing still cooking at middle age, and yet we know we would never do anything else. You told me to keep going and to never give up, no matter how many roadblocks stood in the way. Thank you for gathering around me and hearing the rallying cry. This book is possible because of you, as much as anyone else. ORDER, FIRE!

INDEX

Note: Page numbers in *italics* refer to photographs.

CONVERSION CHARTS

Here are rounded-off equivalents between the metric system and the traditional systems that are used in the United States to measure weight and volume.

WEIGHTS

US/UK	Metric
1 oz	30 g
2 oz	55 g
3 oz	85 g
4 oz (¼ lb)	115 g
5 oz	140 g
6 oz	170 g
7 oz	200 g
8 oz (½ lb)	225 g
9 oz	255 g
10 oz	285 g
11 oz	310 g
12 oz	340 g
13 oz	370 g
14 oz	395 g
15 oz	425 g
16 oz (1 lb)	455 g

VOLUME

American	Imperial	Metric
¼ tsp		1.25 ml
½ tsp		2.5 ml
1 tsp		5 ml
½ Tbsp (1½ tsp)		7.5 ml
1 Tbsp (3 tsp)		15 ml
¼ cup (4 Tbsp)	2 fl oz	60 ml
⅓ cup (5 Tbsp)	2½ fl oz	75 ml
½ cup (8 Tbsp)	4 fl oz	125 ml
⅔ cup (10 Tbsp)	5 fl oz	150 ml
¾ cup (12 Tbsp)	6 fl oz	175 ml
1 cup (16 Tbsp)	8 fl oz	250 ml
1¼ cups	10 fl oz	300 ml
1½ cups	12 fl oz	350 ml
2 cups (1 pint)	16 fl oz	500 ml
2½ cups	20 fl oz (1 pint)	625 ml
5 cups	40 fl oz (1 qt)	1.25 l

OVEN TEMPERATURES

	°F	°C	Gas Mark
very cool	250–275	130–140	½–1
cool	300	148	2
warm	325	163	3
moderate	350	177	4
moderately hot	375–400	190–204	5–6
hot	425	218	7
very hot	450–475	232–245	8–9

© MICHAEL PIAZZA

After a decade of success with his restaurant Farmstead in Providence, Matt Jennings returned to his native city of Boston in 2015 to open Townsman, a New England brasserie. It was named one of *Esquire*'s Best New Restaurants in America; *USA Today* named it one of the 10 Best New Restaurants in the country; and *Food & Wine* included it in their list of 10 Restaurants of the Year. Matt lives with his wife, Kate; his sons, Sawyer and Coleman; and their dog, Bert, outside of Boston. Find him on Instagram @matthewjennings and online at townsmanboston.com.

WITHDRAWN